Nancy Love
and the
WASP Ferry Pilots
of World War II

Nancy Harkness Love in WAFS flying gear, 1942.
Courtesy the Love family; electronic image courtesy the National Museum of the U.S. Air Force.

Nancy Love and the WASP Ferry Pilots of World War II

by Sarah Byrn Rickman

Number 4 in the North Texas
Military Biography and Memoir Series

University of North Texas Press

Denton, Texas

10   9   8   7   6   5   4   3   2   1

Permissions:
University of North Texas Press
P.O. Box 311336
Denton, TX 76203-1336

The paper used in this book meets the minimum requirements of the American
National Standard for Permanence of Paper for Printed Library Materials,
z39.48.1984. Binding materials have been chosen for durability.

Library of Congress Cataloging-in-Publication Data

Rickman, Sarah Byrn.
  Nancy Love and the WASP ferry pilots of World War II / by Sarah Byrn
  Rickman.
      p. cm. — (North Texas military biography and memoir series; no. 4)
  Includes bibliographical references and index.
  ISBN 978-1-57441-241-3 (cloth : alk. paper)
      1. Love, Nancy Harkness, 1914–1976. 2. Women Airforce Service Pilots
  (U.S.)—Biography. 3. United States. Army Air Forces. Air Transport Com-
  mand. Ferrying Division—Biography. 4. World War, 1939–1945—Aerial
  operations, American. 5. World War, 1939–1945—Transportation—United
  States. 6. United States. Army Air Force Transportation. 7. Air pilots—
  United States—Biography. 8. Women air pilots—United States—Biography.
  I. Title.
  D790.5.L68R53 2008
  940.54'4973092—dc22
  [B]
                                                                2007039381

Nancy Love and the WASP Ferry Pilots of World War II is Number 4 in the
North Texas Military Biography and Memoir Series

Cover photo: Nancy Harkness Love in the cockpit of a Fairchild PT-19 Army
Primary Trainer. Photo taken circa September 1942. Photo from the Nancy
Harkness Love Private Collection held by her daughters and used with their
permission. Electronic image courtesy the National Aviation Hall of Fame,
Dayton, Ohio.

Dedication

This book is dedicated to the memory of Joan Hrubec, director and later curator of the International Women's Air and Space Museum (IWASM), who planted the seed that led to its creation and whose incredible aviation memory bank I mined as I researched and wrote.

We lost Joanie February 17, 2007.

Contents

Photographs of Nancy Harkness Love

Foreword

Nancy Love is one of the most interesting figures in twentieth-century American history. I think most readers of Sarah Byrn Rickman's biography will agree with me when they reach the final pages of this fascinating book. Still, it is a very bold assertion about a young woman born in 1914 in the remote reaches of Michigan's Upper Peninsula, who made her mark during World War II and then disappeared from public view, prematurely dying from cancer in 1976.

To begin, this is a flying story. Love took her first flight in 1930 at age sixteen. A pair of barnstormers stopping in her hometown of Houghton, Michigan, offered rides for "a penny a pound." The experience was thrilling and transforming. Soon enough, she had persuaded her parents and scraped together cash to earn a pilot's license. When she earned that license in November, she was one of just 300 women in the United States who could pilot an airplane.

It is hard for us to remember just how limited aviation was at that time. Sure, the Post Office had created a new service called "air mail" and you could witness the feats of barnstormers and air racers but, even if you could have logged on to Travelocity or Orbitz, there would have been barely any flights to book. The introduction of the Boeing 247 and Douglas DC-3—those all-metal transports that defined what commercial airplanes look like to us even today and the first to make commercial aviation a viable economic proposition—was still a few years off. Nancy Love's new interest and training made her among the rarest of the rare.

In today's terms, we would call Love a "first adopter," meaning she was someone who readily acquires the skills needed to operate the newest technological device. Maybe you were among the first to buy a mobile telephone, personal computer, microwave oven, color television, automobile, or some other amazing technology that has transformed American lives in the past century. Whether or not your own temperament inclines you to experiment with new things, readers will readily recognize the qualities of curiosity, boldness, and confidence that technological pioneers often possess. As Sarah Rickman's book reveals, Nancy Love had these personal qualities, along with intelligence, grace, and incredible perseverance. If you like reading about pilots with "the right stuff," then Nancy Love's story will surely be of interest.

The author Tom Wolfe used that phrase as the title for a book about the test pilots who became America's first astronauts. Though for a short time Nancy Love was, in fact, a test pilot, her historical significance is only tangentially related to her skills as a pilot. Flying created unexpected opportunities for Nancy Love and she, in turn, helped create unprecedented ones for American women. The Women's Auxiliary Ferrying Squadron (WAFS) that she established in World War II initiated one of the American military's boldest social experiments: the training of women to fly military aircraft. The young women serving as combat pilots today owe much to Nancy Love for creating the opportunity for women to serve.

As you read this biography, it will be clear that challenging American social attitudes about the role of women was not something that Nancy Love was thinking about when she sent a note to her husband's friend Lt. Col. Robert Olds in May 1940 about using women pilots to help the Ferry Command. She knew that the group was desperate for pilots and she wanted to help. Wanting "to help" was a common sentiment after Pearl

Harbor but it was far less so before that time. Even after the fall of France to the Germans, coincidentally also in May–June 1940, the Roosevelt administration was very careful not to speed mobilization. There was still a healthy opposition to the idea of American involvement. Through her husband's military friends—Robert Love was in the reserves and would eventually be called to active duty in 1941—Nancy Love was much more aware of world events but her idea was still quite audacious.

The details of how Love's idea evolved and the establishment of the WAFS, the Women's Flying Training Detachment (WFTD), and the Women Airforce Service Pilots (WASP) are carefully presented in this book. In previous accounts, Love's important role has largely been eclipsed by the amazing story of Jacqueline Cochran. Contemporaries viewed Love and Cochran as rivals, and in one sense they were. Certainly, there was no love lost between these two leaders of women military pilots. The simplistic framing of their relationship however, has dulled historians' attention to the facts and lessened our understanding of the larger legacies of Love, Cochran, and, most importantly, the women they led.

Through years' long effort, Sarah Rickman has been able to track down new sources that will surely renew interest in the WASP. Nancy Love was not given to express many of her thoughts on paper but to the extent that documents survived, Rickman has managed to find them. This extraordinary effort made this book possible. For many years I have wished for a biography of Nancy Love because readers of my own more general history of American women in aviation have been so intrigued by Love's story. Rickman does not simply supply more words; she tells a new story.

Nancy Love's career trajectory in aviation more nearly matches that of most American women who learned to fly in the 1930s and 1940s. After the war, she stopped flying professionally to raise a family but she hardly stopped being involved in aviation. Her husband Robert was one of the founders of All American Aviation and she was an important advisor to what would become one of the significant regional commercial airlines in postwar America. Her work may have been uncompensated but her presence was invaluable to the success of that business. Rickman takes Love's supporting role seriously but she does not shy away from the sacrifices this required either.

Knowing more about Love's life after World War II changes our understanding of her role during it. For example, it has long been thought that Nancy Love did not particularly care about the militarization of the WASP. Rickman makes a convincing case that the opposite was true. It is now clear that Love was quite taken with the idea and even discussed a possible postwar military career. We see her confronting the dilemma of wanting to work and wanting a family. She loved her independence; she loved her husband. Such are the challenges faced by American women to this day.

What makes Love's story compelling is the fact that the exclusion of women from the obligations of military service has been one of the most significant barriers to the full participation of women in American society. This changed after the first Gulf War when Congress rewrote the laws that prohibited women from serving in combat. To understand how this happened, you need to go back to World War II and consider the story of the women who served in the WAFS and the WASP.

The WASP were demobilized in December 1944 (by then Love's WAFS had been folded into this larger organization). The group remained a cohesive one through the years and in the 1970s, took up the challenge of gaining official recognition for their wartime service. The early seventies were an extraordinary time for women in aviation. The commercial airlines hired their first women pilots. The military with the ending of the draft looked to women to fill new roles, including flying military aircraft again. NASA decided to bring women into the shuttle astronaut corps. As each of these occasions made news headlines, much was made of the fact that women had ferried military aircraft during World War II. Much continues to be made of that fact and it remains one of the greatest satisfactions for the women who served in the WASP that their actions have inspired their "daughters" and "granddaughters."

After reading Rickman's biography, I find I have the confidence to assert that without Nancy Love, there probably would not have been any women ferrying aircraft for the United States during World War II. Jacqueline Cochran was a visionary but it is unclear if alone she would have had success establishing a U.S. contingent of women military pilots or even if she had, whether or not *alone*, she could have sustained the operation. Love had a smaller idea but also an extraordinary dedication to making the day-to-day operations work. Together, Cochran and Love—albeit in a state of dynamic tension—created a real program with lasting impact. This is, perhaps, the book's most important contribution.

Lest readers think this is a dull account, I want to assure them that Rickman's book is accessible and engaging. Rickman tells this story in the exciting style of the journalist she once was. There are long excerpts from primary source materials but she also shares the conclusions of historians and scholars. The writing is so fresh that you often have the sense that you are discovering new things about Love right along with the author. Pathbreaking books are rarely perfect but the best leave a trail with many rewards for the scholars who choose to follow. To that end, Rickman has done her subject justice; this is a book rich in insight and opportunity.

Deborah G. Douglas
MIT Museum
author of *American Women and Flight since 1940*

Preface

Nancy Harkness Love has confounded women's aviation historians for sixty years. She was well known in aviation circles prior to 1942, made her mark on history in World War II as the founder and leader of the Women's Auxiliary Ferrying Squadron (WAFS), and then faded into relative obscurity. She died in 1976, just as the story of the women who flew for the U.S. Army during that war was emerging in the public consciousness.

As I pursued the story of the WAFS for my first book, *The Originals: The Women's Auxiliary Ferrying Squadron of World War II* (Disc-Us Books, 2001), I knew that no one had yet written Nancy Love's story. Author/editor/scholar Susan Ware asked me to write a small biographical sketch on Love for Volume V of *Notable American Women, A Biographical Dictionary Completing the Twentieth Century*, published by The Belknap Press of Harvard University Press in 2004. As I sought to verify facts in order to write that short account, I realized that the task of writing Love's biography could be mine—if I was willing to make the commitment.

Nancy Harkness Love is survived by three daughters who have talked candidly to me of the mother they remember. Graciously, they have given me unrestricted access to her papers to unearth the rest of the story. I've interviewed the surviving original WAFS who served under her.

Who WAS Nancy Harkness Love—the real person, not the myth? Not only was she the first woman to check out on and fly many Army warplanes—meaning she possessed outstanding technical skills—seasoned generals assessed her leadership capabilities and put her in charge of all the women ferrying Army airplanes. She was twenty-eight. She became a general's eyes and ears, his troubleshooter. Where did these gifts come from? And the biggest question of all, given her outstanding abilities: why did Nancy retire from public life and professional flying after the war? Why didn't she continue to build on the aviation career she began in her teens?

Love did not leave an extensive paper trail, as did her better-known rival Jacqueline Cochran. She never sought the limelight, nor was she a writer or journal keeper. Few examples of her writing survive and no taped interviews. Newspaper and magazine articles about her—circa the late 1930s and early 1940s—are mostly fluff, colored by each reporter's stereotype of who and what a woman flyer of that time should be. But buried within her responses to questions and the few writings she left are clues.

The biographer's concern, says essayist/biographer Leon Edel, "is how to ... achieve the clean mastery of the portrait painter unconcerned with archives, who reads only the lines in the face, the settled mouth, the color of the cheeks, the brush strokes and pencil marks of time."

This is the "mask of life" and, Edel continues, the biographer needs to know that mask. But that is only half of the battle, he points out. I have searched Love's story for what Edel calls "the figure under the carpet."

> The most difficult part of [the biographer's] task [is] his search for what I call the figure under the carpet, the evidence in the reverse of the tapestry, the life-myth of a given mask. In an archive, we wade simply and securely through paper and photocopies

and related concrete materials. But in our quest for the life-myth we tread on dangerous speculative and inferential ground, ground that requires all of our attention, also all of our accumulated resources. For we must read certain psychological signs that enable us to understand what people are really saying behind the faces they put on, behind the utterances they allow themselves to make before the world ... this is the "psychological evidence" a biographer must learn to read, even as he learns to read the handwriting of his personality and his slips of the pen. Armed with this kind of eyesight, a biographer reads much more in the materials than any sketcher of façades.[1]

As renowned biographer Catherine Drinker Bowen points out in *Adventures of a Biographer*:

The more I learned about Oliver Wendell Holmes, the more insupportable it became to think of him as dead, cold and motionless beneath that stone at Arlington. I found myself possessed by a witch's frenzy to ungrave this man, stand him upright, see him walk, jump, dance, tell jokes, make love, display his vanity or his courage as the case might be.[2]

That is how I felt about Nancy Love once I began to delve into her life and her personality. I hope I have portrayed *her*—not some cardboard image.

Acknowledgments

My heartfelt thanks to WAFS Barbara "B.J." Erickson London and WASP Iris Cummings Critchell who worked diligently with me to get right the story of the women's ferrying squadrons; Dawn Letson and Tracey MacGowan—the WASP Archives, Texas Woman's University; Barbara Constable and Thomas Branigar, archivists, the Jacqueline Cochran Collection—Dwight D. Eisenhower Library; the reference librarians at the Washington-Centerville Public Library who found the many books and articles I needed; to my editors Ron Chrisman and Karen DeVinney; to my family; and to many others for their support along the way.

Prologue

The Army C-54 began its takeoff roll. The lumbering giant strained to gain momentum. Finally, the wind beneath its wings lifted the aircraft from the runway into the heavy humid air of Calcutta. Fully loaded, the four-engine beast of wartime burden climbed out and away from the airfield. Inside the cockpit, the pilot executed the prescribed turnout, took an east-by-northeast heading and flew out over the jungles of east India bound for Kunming, China.

The date was January 8, 1945. A woman's hands held the controls of the big U.S. cargo/transport plane flying "the Hump"— that fabled World War II highway in the sky over the remote heights of the Himalayan Mountains and the impenetrable jungles of Burma, the all-important wartime supply route to China. The woman's name was Nancy Harkness Love.

Flying the C-54, by now, was second nature to Love. She flew her first one as copilot on November 28, 1944, checked out satisfactorily in the aircraft two days later in Long Beach, California, and began ferrying the military version of the DC-4 airliner across the U.S. on December 2. After ten cross-country flights in just thirteen days, she had 46 hours and 15 minutes in that aircraft—ultimately the biggest bird she flew in her aviation career.

In spite of the airplane's size, power, and heft, hydraulics assured that a woman could fly the 73,000-pound craft as readily as a man. The yoke—the half steering wheel that controlled the ailerons and the elevators, therefore the aircraft's roll and pitch—was not unwieldy. Surprisingly, the four throttles, configured to take up a minimum of space, nested neatly under her hand. On takeoff and landing, her copilot's hand would hover over hers, ready to assist if an unexpected problem surfaced. At five-feet-six and blessed with long legs, Love was tall enough for her feet to comfortably reach the rudders.

The familiar throb of the four 1,350-horsepower Pratt & Whitney engines soon would calm any adrenalin high spawned by her first trip over the rooftop of the world. And though Love flew the airplane, the C-54's regular captain was present and in command, and she had at her beck and call his full crew. Flying this airplane, she already had discovered, was not so different from flying the B-17, C-47, B-25, or A-20—all multi-engine aircraft she had flown many times in the last two years.

Who was Nancy Harkness Love and how did she happen to be flying an Army C-54 over the mountains and jungles of southern Asia in January 1945?

In the fall of 1942, several months into the United States' involvement in World War II, Love, a veteran pilot, had been chosen to form and lead a squadron of twenty-eight civilian women pilots who went to work ferrying airplanes for the Ferrying Division of the Army's Air Transport Command (ATC). The Army was desperate for pilots to fly small single-engine trainer planes from the factory assembly lines to the flight training fields in the South and these twenty-eight women—most of them professional pilots—fit the bill. They were known initially as the WAFS, the Women's Auxiliary Ferrying Squadron.

As the war progressed, the number of women ferry pilots grew and Love eventually had several squadrons under her leadership. The women were not militarized. They flew under the auspices of the Civil Service. One hundred thirty-four of those women qualified to ferry the Army's high-performance pursuit airplanes.

Then in 1944, male pilots—released from other duties—wanted to take over the ferrying chores. The Army felt it no longer needed the women pilots. The group was deactivated on December 20, 1944, and the women sent home.

But Love, still a Ferrying Division/ATC employee, was handed one more assignment—a fact-finding trip to India and China under orders from her friend Gen. C.R. Smith, Deputy Director of the ATC. It was on his authority—in his plane—that she flew the Hump that day. Her flight was strictly off the record. She wasn't supposed to be in the cockpit of an Army aircraft in January 1945. As of December 20, 1944, women were officially banned from Army cockpits. The ban lasted for thirty years.

Nevertheless, Love's logbook indicates that she flew the four-and-a-half-hour trip from Calcutta to Kunming.

After landing, parking the airplane, cutting the switches, and cleaning up the cockpit, she rose, dropped her headset and oxygen mask on the seat, and followed her passengers and crew out of the airplane into the pale winter sunshine. She wore an Army-issue flight suit. Had it not been for her softly curled, chin-length hair—caught behind her ears in deference to the earphones she had worn and definitely out of place in the crew-cut male world of 1945—she might have passed for a young crewman.

As she walked toward the group of officers clustered on the ground, she did not stride purposefully nor did she walk like many women would have, to call attention to herself. She was, in fact, slightly pigeon-toed and had a hint of a glide to her step. She moved with a poise that bespoke more self-assurance than she actually possessed. When she smiled, her luminous, gold-flecked hazel eyes took in each man, graciously making him feel as if he, personally, was the object of that smile. Her firm pilot's handshake, offered in greeting, belied the small, slender, feminine hand beneath.

Thirty-year-old Nancy Love was a strikingly beautiful woman with high cheekbones and delicate features. She had begun to go gray at nineteen, beginning with a streak that swept back from the right side of her forehead. By 1945, her light brown hair had turned mostly silver, casting an aura of maturity about her.

Her reserve, carefully honed over those thirty years, masked her drive. Love greeted challenges with cool assessment, never allowing the passion that lurked just beneath the surface to show in her cultured, contralto voice. That she had been asked to take part in this flight, to fly this airplane, was a coup—the high point in a distinguished aviation career that, by 1945, had covered fifteen years.

Dutifully, she recorded the Hump flight in her logbook—bible and sworn gospel to a pilot. All flights are noted. She wrote nothing else of the flight. She didn't need to. For her, having done it was what mattered. Years later she did allude to the flight in interviews. (The sources are noted in the chapter "Flying the Hump.")

And she *did* relate the story to her three daughters Hannah, Marky, and Allie. In turn, the girls have passed on what they heard.

✈ 1 ✈
Learning to Fly

H annah Lincoln (Nancy) Harkness was born on February 14, 1914, in Houghton, Michigan, the daughter of Dr. Robert Bruce and Alice (Chadbourne) Harkness. Alice wanted to name their daughter for her sister, Hannah Lincoln Chadbourne Denton. Mrs. Denton's first daughter, also named Hannah, had died in childhood. The name Hannah Lincoln was a family tradition and Alice wanted the tradition to carry forward. Precedent carried some weight with Dr. Harkness; however, he disliked his sister-in-law. Finally, he relented sufficiently for "Hannah Lincoln" to go on his daughter's birth certificate. But the name he chose to call her—Nancy—is the name that stuck.

Alice Graham Chadbourne's family originally came to North America from Norfolk, England, in the 1630s, settling first in Hingham, Massachusetts. In the 1870s, Alice's parents, Thomas L. and Georgina Kay Chadbourne, moved to the town of Houghton in Michigan's Upper Peninsula. Houghton lies in the northern-most part of the state, the scenic Keweenaw Peninsula that juts out into Lake Superior. Their move to this western outpost coincided with the growth of copper mining in that region and the attendant economic boom that began in 1865.[1]

Alice was born May 16, 1879. In addition to her sister, Hannah Lincoln, Alice also had a brother, Thomas Lincoln Chadbourne, a well to do man-about-town in New York and Palm Beach, Florida, who became a benefactor to both Alice and Nancy during the hard times of the Depression. Alice died in April 1958 and her ashes are buried in Vineyard Haven, Massachusetts.

Robert Bruce Harkness's family emigrated from Paisley, Scotland, to Wilkes-Barre, Luzerne County, Pennsylvania, in the mid-nineteenth century. He was the youngest of ten children and said to be the only one born in the United States, on October 1, 1875, in Wilkes-Barre. Their granddaughters, to this day, aren't sure how these two met. However, Alice was from a prominent Boston-based family and did spend time there as a young woman. Possibly young Bruce, with the intention of studying medicine, made his way to the country's intellectual and educational center sometime after the Spanish-American War in which the Love daughters believe he served.

Bruce and Alice were married August 3, 1905, after which they went to Germany where he continued his medical training. Sometime after 1907, they too settled in Houghton, where Dr. Harkness was named Public Health Officer for Houghton County. A son Robert Bruce Harkness Jr.—known as Bob, but called "Bobbin" by his mother—was born May 5, 1908. The Harkness family was severely rocked when Bob died as the result of a skiing accident at Wildcat Mountain in New Hampshire, on December 18, 1933. He was racing, hit a tree, and died of internal injuries.

Dr. Harkness died in 1955 and is buried in Wilkes-Barre.[2]

Nancy's earliest days coincided with those of World War I, which began in Europe in August 1914, just months after she was born. While Nancy was a young girl growing up in the deep green forests and snow-covered northern Michigan landscape, several women—intent on learning to fly in those fledgling years of aviation—already were paving the way for Nancy and the women flyers of the next couple of generations.

On May 21, 1927, Nancy was present at Le Bourget Field in Paris to witness Charles Lindbergh's landing in the *Spirit of*

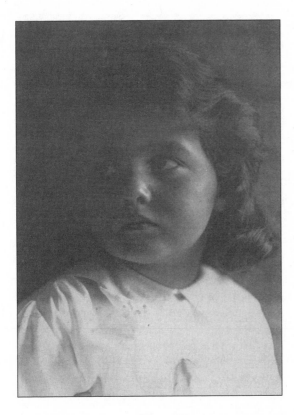

Hannah Lincoln (Nancy) Harkness at age three, Houghton, Michigan—probably taken by her father, Dr. Robert B. Harkness.

Courtesy Love family; electronic image National Aviation Hall of Fame (NAHF).

St. Louis. "You can't make an interesting story out of that," she later told a public relations person who hoped to do just that. "It didn't inspire me with an overwhelming desire to fly, as it probably should have!" Nancy, her aunt Hannah Denton and her cousin Georgina Kay Denton were on a tour of Europe that spring—a trip Nancy's mother thought would broaden her education.

It did, in ways Mrs. Harkness didn't intended. The already engaging, rapidly maturing Nancy, though only thirteen, attracted the amorous attentions of an Italian count on the beach at the Riviera—much to her aunt's dismay. It was with great delight that Nancy, whose dry sense of humor became legendary, told her own daughters the story years later.

On June 17, 1928—when Nancy was fourteen—Amelia Earhart became the first woman to cross the Atlantic in an aircraft as a passenger in a plane flown by two male pilots. Four years later, Earhart would fly the Atlantic solo. And on November 2, 1929, when Nancy was fifteen, twenty-six licensed women pilots, including Earhart, met at Curtiss Field in Valley Stream on Long Island to discuss forming a woman pilot's organization. At the time, the United States had 117 licensed women pilots. Ninety-nine of them responded either by attending the meeting or by letter indicating interest. In recognition of their charter membership, they became the Ninety-Nines, the International Organization of Women Pilots. Earhart was elected the first president.

Erroneous reports have listed Nancy Harkness Love among the founders of that organization. At that time, she had yet to make her first flight. But before the next year, 1930, was out, sixteen-year-old Nancy Harkness would spot a biplane flying near her home in Houghton and her life would be forever changed.

Nancy was out riding her horse Daisy one August day in 1930 when she saw a biplane taking off and landing. She watched, fascinated. The aircraft seemed to dance in the sun, catching and reflecting golden rays on its silver wings.

The barnstormer pilot was looking for passengers, giving five-dollar stunt rides or a less adventurous circle of the airfield for a "penny a pound." Along came Nancy. She must have been a refreshing change—a lot prettier than the civic leaders and other residents of Houghton he had been flying around that day. She paid her penny a pound and went up. Then she came up with five dollars and up they went again, this time for a stunt ride.[3]

With a chance to show off for a pretty girl, the pilot's best option was to fly her out over Lake Portage, head west to Hancock, Houghton's twin city across the shipping canal, cross the swing bridge back to Houghton, and buzz the sturdy sandstone and brick buildings along Shelden Avenue, including the Houghton National Bank and the Masonic Temple. As a child, Nancy had stood on the sidewalk and looked up at Houghton's four-story-high downtown buildings. To impress her, the pilot surely

Teenage Nancy and her horse, Daisy.

Courtesy Love family; electronic image NAHF.

asked her to point out her house and then promptly buzzed the rambling Victorian home at 253 College Avenue.

A couple of rolls—one to the left and one to the right—followed by some over-and-under loops were stock thrills barnstormers executed for first-timers. If the pilot thought these would turn her green, he was wrong. When they landed, Nancy had stars in her eyes. She was hooked. Another five dollars took her up for a second spin. When she was out of money, reluctantly she climbed out of the airplane. She wanted more. At dinner that evening, she informed her parents that she wanted to learn to fly. Flying, she said, was a lot more interesting and worthwhile than going to school.

This statement did not sit well with her mother, according to Nancy's daughters, but her father saved the day. Why should one preclude the other? he wisely asked. Why couldn't she learn to fly *and* go to school?

Nancy had an adventuresome streak that led her, on occasion, to defy her mother's admonition that "nice young ladies don't do such things." Nancy and her father struck a bargain. He would allow the flying lessons she so desperately wanted, but she must return to boarding school in September.

What must Dr. Harkness have seen in his daughter's eyes that made him give in so easily? Had he seen or suspected the mettle, the fire inside this lovely girl child of his? Certainly most fathers of that period didn't "look" for attributes of willfulness in their children—attitudes that would make them stand out in a crowd, particularly their daughters. Could he possibly have envisioned the alteration in the status of women his daughter would help bring about through her simple idea that became so practical in wartime when the need was so great?

Was he being contrary because Nancy's mother tried to keep too tight a rein on her?

Most likely, Dr. Harkness simply was being an indulgent father. Beautiful and charming, Nancy was the apple of his eye. "Grandfather indulged Mum's enthusiasms. Grinny (Nancy's mother) did not," says daughter Marky.

What he told her when she left for her first lesson simply was "do it well or not at all." Throughout the rest of his life, he kept a scrapbook of his precocious daughter's aviation exploits. Throughout the rest of her life, Nancy followed those seven words of advice from her father.[4]

Reporters frequently asked Nancy to tell them why and how she learned to fly. "I have no idea what made me catch the flying bug. A ride in a barnstorming Fleet was my undoing and from then on I knew what I wanted. Fortunately, my parents were indulgent," she wrote about her first flight. "I persuaded my family to let me take lessons in a rather broken down [biplane] that one of the barnstormers imported from parts unknown to teach me in."

On August 26, 1930, Nancy climbed into the tandem two-seater, single-engine Kinner Fleet biplane to take her first lesson. Her instructor was Jimmy Hansen of Upper Peninsula Airways. He was all of two years older than Nancy.

Surely Dr. Harkness had a long talk with Jimmy about his flying training and experience—and possibly his intentions—and then they agreed on the terms of Nancy's flight instruction, provided Jimmy found a suitable airplane. The eighteen-year-old instructor, like most men who met Nancy Harkness, was captivated when she climbed into his airplane and most likely fell head-over-heels in love the minute she exhibited a fascination with *him* and what *he* could do with an airplane.

"I wanted to fly right off, and I just about did," Nancy later told a reporter. "I'm no supergenius, you understand, but I concentrated hard and I learned fast. It was a darn nice plane I started with—a Fleet. I soloed after only five hours training. That kind of thing is not legal now." Nancy actually soloed on August 31 with only four hours and thirty minutes of flying time in her logbook.

"It was a classic example of the blind leading the blind when I soloed. He [Jimmy] had a brand new license and I was his first student ... but we made it. It was wonderful fun and quite routine at the time. I don't think he knew what made the plane stay in the air. At least he never told me. My instructions were just to 'keep up the flying speed.'"

On September 4, Nancy and Jimmy flew to Escanaba, another city in Michigan's Upper Peninsula—an hour and forty-minute flight over and an hour and thirty minutes back. It was her first dual cross-country. By September 10, 1930, she had

Girl pilot: Nancy Harkness, sixteen, earns private pilot's license # 17,797 in November 1930.

Courtesy Love family; electronic image NAHF.

earned the hours necessary for her private pilot's license. James S. Hansen signed her logbook noting "13 hours 25 minutes dual instruction and 9 hours 40 minutes solo time" by his student. He also wrote on the front of her Pilots Log:

> To Nancy
> With best wishes for Happy Landings
> Jimmy

"Our paths were to cross again during the war. He was ferrying planes and was later killed because of a malfunction."[5]

Early in November 1930, accompanied by her mother, Nancy went to Chicago to take her examination for her private pilots license and Milwaukee for her flight test.[6] She received a letter from the Department of Commerce, Aeronautics Branch, Washington, D.C., dated November 7, 1930. It said: "Dear Madam:

You have completed the tests and examinations required by the Air Commerce Regulations for a Private Pilots License."[7]

Nancy was a boarding student at Milton Academy, a girls' prep school in Milton, Massachusetts, outside Boston, but by the time she returned mid-September 1930, she mainly had flying on her mind. Her "book learning" that academic year was to be overshadowed by the realities of flight that she learned in two close calls.

She didn't waste any time getting in the air once she had returned to Milton. "I was still just sixteen when I took off on my first cross-country—from Boston to Poughkeepsie. I had two friends along and all our luggage. We were on our way from Milton to Vassar College to visit friends. In the first place, the ship was far too large and complicated for my fifteen solo hours. Once in the air, I realized I had never used an aircraft compass before. I couldn't read it! Our luggage was in the right seat beside me. My two passengers were sitting in the back. They had no idea how inadequate and frightened I suddenly felt.

"I noticed ugly clouds coming from the west and they were moving fast. I couldn't really see that well. I flew lower and lower in an effort to see out. With that, the oil gauge broke and smeared black stuff all over the windscreen. That meant I had no visibility at all to the front. I had to hang my head out the open side window. My inflamed imagination convinced me the motor was about to stop. I picked out a field that looked smooth—it was winter, so not much vegetation—and I landed. Lucky for me and my passengers, we and the ship were still intact.

"It taught me a great deal in a short time, and ended happily, but due to age and inexperience seemed tenser than any later experience."[8]

Her second close call wasn't long in coming.

One Sunday afternoon, she was flying with her brother, Bob, and he dared her to buzz the neighboring boys' prep school. She flew low down the quadrangle and tried to pull up at the far end to avoid hitting the chapel. Nancy still hadn't learned the laws of physics. She didn't realize that though you pull up, the plane doesn't immediately go up. She nearly hit the bell tower and did rattle some slates loose so they fell off the roof.

Someone got the tail number of the airplane and called the airport. Two local boys, the Fuller brothers, were known for such stunts. The irate headmaster of the boys' academy rang the airport manager. "Which one of those Fuller boys just buzzed the school?" The manager dutifully answered that the pilot of the single-engine Kinner Kitty Hawk that afternoon was Miss Nancy Harkness.

Bob drove her back to school. When she walked in the door at her residence hall, the headmistress, the housemistress, and two members of the board of trustees were waiting for her. Her brother took one look and bolted, leaving her to make the explanations by herself.

But the school had no rules about flying. Students couldn't drive cars, but nothing said they couldn't fly. Nancy wasn't suspended; rather she was severely reprimanded and told to stay out of airplanes for the remainder of the semester.

"I attended Milton in the late '60s," Nancy's youngest daughter, Allie, relates. "Nancy Harkness was still a legend at Milton. And I ended up rooming with Emily Fuller, daughter of one of the Fuller boys!"[9]

That same spring, Bob Harkness took his sister by East Boston Airport to meet Crocker Snow, a well-known Boston pilot who would be one of the men responsible for the B-29's prowess in the last year of World War II.

"She was a rosy-cheeked teenager, appropriately attired in riding breeches and boots," Snow writes in his autobiography. Her brother "explained that she was a student at Milton Academy and had already taken flying lessons in Houghton, Michigan. He asked if I would give her a check ride and see what I thought.

"The note in my logbook said: 'Check-out with 300 foot ceiling. Awful job keeping her from climbing into the soup. She ought to make a good pilot if the conditions under which she learned have any bearing. All dual and 14 hours solo in 10 days. Warner Fleet with prop held together with tacks.'" Then he adds: "She became an accomplished, skillful pilot, with a real sense of the air."[10]

Other than her penchant for flying, Nancy was a typical, if imaginative, teenager while attending Milton. One Sunday afternoon, while a white glove tea was in progress for the seniors, Nancy and a fellow student conspired to play a trick aimed at disrupting the very proper affair. The two of them moved some street signs and managed to reroute campus traffic through the circle in front of the headmistress's house where the tea was being held.

"Mum is a descendant of Benjamin Lincoln, who took Cornwallis's sword at Yorktown," the girls relate. "Her great aunts in Boston were very proud of this heritage, and of belonging to the DAR. Mum tried to burst their bubble. She had studied history at Milton and proceeded to tell them he was a bumbling drunk who couldn't get anything right. Grinny, Mum's mother, was mortified!"[11]

Discovering flight that summer of her sixteenth year gave Nancy direction that would last a lifetime and set her feet on a path utterly different from the one her strait-laced mother would have chosen for her. However eldest daughter, Hannah, believes Nancy's mother vicariously enjoyed and secretly envied her daughter's adventurous spirit.

One of Nancy's school notebooks survives from her senior year at Milton. Doodled on the front are pictures of airplanes and the words "Stearman" and "Aviation." She penciled in the initials of her friends—and likely a boyfriend or two—as well as teenage expressions like Hyper! Super! Ultra! Positively bleak! Fed Up! Be careful with those eyes! The words "Squantum" and "Forced Landing" are explained by an April 16, 1931, entry found in her logbook and in a two-inch newspaper article. Squantum was a local naval base.

> When the motor of her plane failed several hundred feet above the Squantum airport, Miss Nancy Hark-

ness was sent to earth in a forced landing. Neither she
nor her companion, Joseph H. Choate, 3rd, Harvard
freshman, was injured. The pair had taken off from
East Boston airport with Miss Harkness as pilot.
Young Choate learned to fly last summer.[12]

During 1930–1931, Nancy's senior year at Milton, her English teacher wrote the following observations on her report card. After the first marking period: "She is beginning to do her best work." The comment for the second period was: "Her work is showing increasingly a deeper, more mature interest and grasp. She must work now for more variety in composition subjects." Flight now dominated everything she wrote.

"Her work is very good. She must avoid sweeping statements, which because they are true only in part convey a false impression." The teacher's comments following the third marking period show the budding iconoclast at work. At this point, Nancy was very much her father's daughter. And finally, the observation: "Her [Nancy's] incisive thinking, keen appreciation and critical ability have made her work very commendable."

Comments from her French, history, and zoology teachers are similar. They suggest that Nancy did better in daily work than on exams and, for this reason, indicate mild concern as she approached the dreaded College Boards, required for admission to the northeast's renowned women's colleges. She passed and was accepted at Vassar.

Comments by her physical education teacher indicate a lack of interest in team sports. She played neither soccer nor field hockey. Nancy was not competitive. She liked dancing better. Under posture, the teacher noted that she carried her shoulders high—as if braced to meet whatever the world threw at her.[13] Nancy was a perfectionist, says Marky. She also suffered from bouts with depression, a tendency that resurfaced periodically throughout her life.

Nancy and a Milton classmate from Chicago were known for their prickly pride in being the lone westerners amid New Englanders. At Christmastime, when they sang "We Three Kings of

Orient Are," she and the other girl would accentuate the word "west" on the line "WESTward leading, still proceeding," so that all around knew exactly in which direction their loyalties lay.

In the fall of 1931, Nancy entered Vassar College in Poughkeepsie, New York, as a freshman. She had her eye on a career in education and declared French and French history as her majors. But she also had her eyes on the skies and, with parental permission in spite of the school's concern over the precedent, continued her flying—on weekends. With the help of Jack Ray, the assistant manager of the Poughkeepsie Airport and the chief instructor for Gyro Flyers Ltd., she worked toward her limited commercial license. She also hopped passengers to earn money to pay for her flying lessons.

Then in April 1932, Nancy had one more encounter with fate in an airplane. A superstitious person would say it was the magic number three. This time she was not the pilot-in-command, but a flight student working toward her commercial license. John Miller, a well-known flyer and a friend of Jack's, was her instructor that day. They were flying Jack's Great Lakes two-seater, single-engine trainer airplane.

An article in the April 5, 1932, Poughkeepsie newspaper says that Miller cut his motor, prepared to give it the gun before landing, but the motor failed to respond and they hit a tree about fifteen feet below the tops of the branches. The plane tipped backward and fell about thirty feet, crashing upside down across the stone wall at the edge of the field. The motor was torn loose from the craft and landed in the field east of the Vassar Road.

Miss Nancy Harkness "narrowly escaped death when their plane crashed into a tree." Miller's head struck the instrument panel. He was generally bruised and shaken and lost a tooth.[14] In truth, Nancy later told her daughters, he was badly cut about the face and lost his left eye.

Nancy, apparently uninjured, got out first. Stunned and just not thinking, she unfastened her seatbelt and, since they were upside down, fell from the airplane hitting her head on the stone wall below. Miller then extricated himself and followed her down a few seconds later. He was taken to the local hospital. In light of his serious injuries, no one realized Nancy, too, was hurt and she was simply taken back to Vassar. After that, she was plagued with serious headaches, which everyone, including her physician father, thought were brought on by a concussion. Not long after that incident, the gray streak began to creep into her hair.

"John cracked Great Lakes-303Y," Nancy wrote in her logbook. Jack and his chief mechanic told reporters at the scene that the airplane could be repaired, and it was, because Nancy was back flying it the following fall.

Nancy and Jack Ray remained lifelong friends and correspondents. In a letter dated October 16, 1971, Nancy wrote:

> Dear Jack: I'm awfully sorry about your mother's death—she was a dear person and I know you'll miss her very much. I was touched that she kept my picture on her dresser all those years. 1931 was a long time ago, wasn't it?

On March 14, 1974, she wrote:

> John Miller's letter was priceless—I could almost hear him talking. No lack of confidence there, and never was. Remember what he said just before flying me in your dear Great Lakes that grim day? "Come on, let me show you how we fly in the Marine Corps." It took me a long time to have faith in Marine pilots after that one.[15]

Nancy emerged from three youthful brushes with disaster a more cautious student of flying. Throughout a flying career that lasted forty years, never again would she overestimate her flying skills. She had done it twice herself and then witnessed what could happen even to an experienced pilot, one who was a qualified instructor. Nancy trained herself to be a careful and deliberate pilot. She established her own methodical approach to flying. She made written checklists for her preflights and paid close attention to the details of flight, traits that would pay off several years later when she was ferrying new aircraft as well as

Nancy Harkness and Jack Ray's Great Lakes trainer.
Courtesy Texas Woman's University Library, WASP Archives.

shot-up candidates for the airplane graveyard cross-country for the Army.

Nancy acquired her limited commercial license on April 25, 1932, at New York's Roosevelt Field, three weeks after the Great Lakes crack up. She was eighteen. She did it in yet another of Jack Ray's Great Lakes trainers. By then, she had eighty-seven hours to her credit.

The story of her newly won license, accompanied by a winsome photo, went out on the wire services and newspapers around the country, including one in far away Honolulu, carried the story about "the Flying Freshman" of Vassar. Her father collected and carefully pasted all the clippings sent to him into a black-paged scrapbook that Nancy's daughters still have.

The clips contain a variety of tidbits about Nancy and her flying. Several papers proclaimed that she was one of but fifty-six women in the United States holding a commercial license. When she announced that, next, she was going for her transport license, reporters came up with the fact that as of April 1932, only forty-two American women pilots held a transport rating. One article quotes Jack Ray, her instructor: "Miss Harkness is one of the few women pilots in the country who is earnestly striving to make accomplishments in the air. She is sincere and hopes to make a professional flier."[16]

A longer article appeared later in *Sportsman Pilot Magazine*, and bears no byline. "What does Vassar think about flying students?" the reporter asked her.

"They require your parents' written consent, but once you have it, they are very good about it." And she laughed about her brother's recent visit when he tried to land a big six-passenger Travel Air at the Poughkeepsie Airport. He and the five friends flying with him had to make an emergency landing at another airport. Nancy then flew there and escorted the party back to the local field that *Sportsman Pilot* described as "a tiny pockethandkerchief of a place." The piece continued:

> It's no secret, however, that demonstrating aircraft is to be her career. She has no illusions about her own ability; she says she knows too many good pilots. But she thinks being a girl will help. By which she doesn't mean that she will be coquettish about the job. The idea is that a woman demonstrator is the ideal one because people have a feeling if a woman can do things with a plane, most anyone can. That's far from being the truth. But a woman demonstrator is a selling point nevertheless.[17]

After that, Nancy set her sights on her transport license and began accruing the requisite two hundred hours.

She flew that summer in Houghton, returned to Vassar for fall semester in 1932 and again flew weekends, often with Jack. But her father was now concerned about her frequent headaches. Rather than letting her return to Vassar for the spring 1933 semester, he kept her home to let her recover her equilibrium. He blamed the concussion sustained in the fall from Jack Ray's Great Lakes trainer the previous spring.

Nancy may have been recuperating, but she didn't let that slow her down. She used the time to work on her transport license and to get in a lot of flying. And some of that flying was social as well as building time. Nancy's good friend and fellow pilot Alice Hirschman lived in the Detroit suburb of Grosse Pointe Park and Nancy visited Alice on several occasions between February and August 1933. She and Alice, in fact, spent Nancy's nineteenth birthday flying two Kinner Birds from Gratiot Airport (later Detroit City Airport) to Selfridge Field in neighboring Macomb County for lunch. They repeated that pattern for several days. On occasion, Alice's future husband, Johnny Hammond, and some of his friends joined them.[18]

A photograph taken of Nancy and Alice ran in one of the Detroit papers during Nancy's visit. Alice—the daughter of eminent Grosse Pointe physician, Dr. Louis J. Hirschman—perches on the arm of an easy chair in which Nancy is seated, legs crossed. Both are dressed in stylish dark wool dresses: Alice's with a diamond-patterned scarf at the neck, Nancy's with cowl neckline. The caption reads: "Both have limited commercial licenses. They have been spending every afternoon in their airplanes and today plan to make a trip, each taking a plane, to all the airports on the surrounding countryside."[19]

Not the usual Society Section fodder!

On August 13, 1933, Nancy logged her two hundredth hour and passed the necessary written tests for her transport license. She was not yet twenty. She returned to Vassar for fall semester.

When interviewed about obtaining her transport license, she told the reporter that she was interested in starting a student flying club at the college. Before she took the spring semester off, she had found some kindred spirits and inspired at least three other students to pursue flying. All began taking instruction from Jack Ray.[20]

Nancy did succeed in starting an aviation club at Vassar. The idea sprouted wings and spread to other eastern women's colleges.

On January 3, 1934, Nancy applied for membership in the Ninety-Nines, the international organization for women pilots founded by Amelia Earhart and several other women who later became Nancy's friends. She indicated 225 hours flown in the following airplanes: Fleet, Stearman, Waco, Great Lakes,

Aeronca, Bird, and Kitty Hawk. Did she own an airplane? "No." The initiation fee is noted as $1 and the annual dues are $2.50, which included a subscription to the Ninety Nines monthly newsletter.[21]

Beyond the hallowed halls of Vassar, other things were happening that would have a dramatic impact on Nancy's life.

The stock market crash the fall of 1929 had brought about the Great Depression. By 1933 it had reached dire proportions with an estimated sixteen million people out of work: one third of the labor force. Franklin Delano Roosevelt, elected president in November 1932, took office March 4, 1933, and immediately set upon his "First Hundred Days," during which he persuaded Congress to pass legislation creating the "New Deal" to provide for the general welfare of the U.S. populace.

Eventually, Nancy would benefit from some of this social legislation, but, by late 1933, things looked bleak for the Harkness family. Nancy's father was not as astute at handling money as he was at handling his daughter or his medical career. He had not invested well. Dr. Harkness could not afford to send his daughter back for the 1934 spring semester, so she dropped out of Vassar at the end of the fall semester in January. Nancy once told a friend that she left school because "It occurred to me that the people of the world were making history not studying it, and the airplane was in the very center of it all." But as was true for so many others at that time, lack of money was the real culprit.

✈ 2 ✈

Learning to Live

Nancy had a big decision to make. "What do I do now?"
The love of her life was aviation. She wanted to fly, but
flying was expensive. How could a young woman barely
twenty parlay her growing expertise in aviation into a job? Make
flying pay her rather than her paying to fly. And this when male
flyers found jobs few and far between.

Her uncle Thomas L. Chadbourne came to the rescue. In order to help her become "employable" he offered to send her to
Katherine Gibbs Secretarial School in New York. Not thrilled
with the prospect, but out of ideas, Nancy agreed.

She prepared to enroll in the school but also developed a
plan, which she wrote to him. She proposed dropping econom-
ics, business English, and spelling, all of which she had taken at
Vassar, and concentrate on shorthand, typing, and filing. "I will
leave school early two days a week. On one of these days I plan
to go to Newark Airport to take a course in blind flying. The
other weekly lessons I would take on Saturday or Sunday. This
work, which is necessary if I am to keep up to date in flying, will
require a total of about fifteen hours out of the week.

"I feel that I should be devoting time when I am not studying to looking for a job."

Nancy lists several job prospects, including advertising cigarettes around the country—she proposed to travel by airplane rather than car—or working for one of the aircraft companies. Her letter to her uncle continues:

> The U.S. Department of Air Commerce is trying to develop a cheap popular type of plane. They should have women flyers as well as men to work in the Department and on the road to make the idea and the plane, when developed, popular. I should like to meet Mr. Eugene Vidal, through Secretary Roper, to talk this over with him. Mr. Vidal is in charge of this work in the Department.
>
> I must be in a position to make my own way as soon as possible and to do this I must have a job.[1]

The Air Commerce contact would, eventually, pay off, but for the present, secretarial school was Nancy's only real option. To attend Katherine Gibbs, she had to move to New York.

Uncle Tom had an apartment in New York that he offered to sublease to Nancy rent-free. Nancy invited Suzanne Humphreys, a young woman who also had learned to fly in 1930 but at Roosevelt Field on Long Island, to move in with her. Margaret Thomas, called "Tommy" by her friends, was the third roommate that winter of 1934. Tommy reminisced about those days in her book, *Taking Off*, and in an article called "The Early Years," written for the Ninety-Nines newsletter. Suzanne, Tommy, and Nancy, for a time, made up a notable triumvirate of young women aviators all living together under one roof during the depths of the Depression and making the most of it. However, Tommy thought the apartment belonged to Suzanne's cousin.

"We were three young fliers. Good-looking, penniless and out to seek our fortunes," Tommy writes. "We were about the same age and our common burning interest, no, our passion, was flying."

Tommy describes Suzanne Humphreys as "a social aviatrix ... a flying debutante ... a native New Yorker ... brought up in private schools and riding-to-hounds. Her family could no longer support her, so she (in theory anyway) had a job in a fancy dress shop selling clothes to her friends." Blond, blue-eyed Susie "was like a nervous, skittish, highly-bred filly, never still, full of suppressed energy." Conversely, Tommy describes the twenty-year-old Nancy Harkness as a more "phlegmatic personality" with "some premature gray in her hair, large gray eyes and thick black lashes. Her movements were deliberate, and her voice low."

The three lived, of all places, in what had been Mark Twain's residence at 21 Fifth Avenue at the corner of Ninth Street, just down from Washington Square and on the edge of Greenwich Village. Twain had taken up residence in the newly built house in the fall of 1904. By the time the three girls arrived thirty years later, the three-story brick house had been divided into apartments. Tommy was quite taken with living "in the same rooms that one of my favorite authors had lived in." The house, she relates, was "next door to the Brevoort Hotel with its sidewalk cafe that made us think we were in Paris. We had the ground floor. Our living room had two pairs of French doors that opened onto balconies bordered with iron railings. A leap over the railings would bring you onto the sidewalk. How safe the world was in those days. On hot nights, we wouldn't even bother to close the doors, much less lock them."[2]

Nancy later delighted in telling her daughters about her New York days when "I was so poor, I lived on tomato soup."

Tommy echoes that. "Sometimes we actually missed a meal or so, but we did have a steady supply of beer because somebody whose father owned a brewery sent it—like a standing order for roses to a chorus girl. We also had a constant supply of male friends and never lacked invitations out to meals. There were plenty [of men], but pilots mostly, not a rich lot."

Since all three were young women pilots, flying was the common denominator of most conversations. One night, Tommy relates, "we all got in about the same time, very late, from our dates and nightclub visits. We talked awhile and then decided to go to Roosevelt Field and fly as soon as the sun was up. Flying made women comrades in the same way that men can be comrades, but women seldom are. There are many ties women share, woman-to-woman, to men's exclusion, but we are rarely companions in the 'Three Musketeers' sense."[3]

Observations like this would also come out of the WASP experience ten years later.

The girls' sojourn in Mark Twain's house ended as summer approached. Suzanne left to live in her parents' home in Far Hills, New Jersey, while her parents went to Martha's Vineyard for the summer. Tommy went to Springfield, Massachusetts, to work for Jacqueline Cochran overseeing the building of an airplane. Tommy had met Cochran the first week in January of 1934 when she was recruited to fly copilot for Cochran in her Waco. Cochran, at that point, was on her way to Florida for the All American Air Races, January 11–13.[4]

Nancy moved on as well. Her logbook does show several entries at Newark Airport between March 23 and April 22, 1934, as promised in her letter to her uncle. After April 22, however, flights out of Boston begin to show up regularly.

When Nancy Harkness and Robert MacLure Love met in April 1934, it wasn't love at first sight. Their daughters have related that delightful story—as they heard it told and retold over the years. It goes like this:

Nancy, not happy in secretarial school, was in Boston job hunting. Old friend and fellow pilot Henry Wilder, who was squiring her around, suggested that they go see Bob Love at East Boston Airport. He might just know of something.

Nancy didn't know Bob Love.

Bob—five feet eleven inches with sandy red hair, a broad nose that turned up slightly at the end, and in possession of a wry sense of humor—owned Inter City Aviation, a flight service out of East Boston Airport, which is better known today as Logan International Airport. He had attended Princeton and then the Massachusetts Institute of Technology (MIT), but aviation both fascinated and distracted him and he never finished college. In 1932, with financial help from his sister Margaret, he founded Inter City and proceeded to establish a flight service that offered everything from flight instruction to charter flights, aerial surveying, and an unscheduled passenger service. He also brokered airplanes.

When Nancy and Henry arrived at the Inter City Aviation office, Bob was away picking up an airplane. The mechanic said he should be back momentarily. Henry decided it was worthwhile waiting and, not in the least daunted by the fact that his friend was out, ushered Nancy into Bob's office, deposited himself in Bob's chair and put his feet up on Bob's desk. Nancy boosted herself onto the desk, crossed her legs, and picked up her conversation with Henry.

After a time, the door banged open and a man in grease-stained flight coveralls strode in. In his left hand, his leather flight helmet and goggles dangled by their straps. His red hair was mashed flat with a spike sticking up here and there—the byproduct of wearing the leather helmet. His cheeks were wind-burned and his blue eyes looked out from telltale raccoon-like white circles, the result of wearing his goggles and flying in an open cockpit airplane.

He took in the scene in one glance: Perched on *his* desk in *his* office, obviously in deep conversation with *his* friend Henry Wilder, was a very attractive young woman.

She glanced up and smiled when he walked in, but she made no move to get off the desk.

He was not happy to find either of them there. He ordered the woman off his desk and his friend out of his chair. Already Nancy was jealous of the fact that this man owned airplanes that he could fly at will. Being around airplanes, being part of this fascinating industry was what secretarial school and all those meals of tomato soup had been about. Now, he had the nerve to treat her like some apprentice from the stenographic pool. She slid gracefully from the desk, shot him a withering look, and, mustering all her presence, walked from the room. She slammed the door on her way out, leaving Henry—who was scrambling to get out of the chair—behind to do the explaining. Eventually, Henry came out, looking sheepish, and asked her to come back in the office. Bob Love, disagreeable as he had sounded, really did want to meet her.

Nancy desperately wanted a job in aviation. She had come here to meet this Bob Love person. Why pass up the opportunity? Just because he was testy didn't mean she had to be. She nodded at the apologetic Henry and deigned to re-enter the ogre's office.[5]

Crocker Snow also claims to have introduced Bob and Nancy.[6]

An article and photo in a Boston newspaper dated April 28, 1934, tells of a "first" at East Boston Airport. "A woman transport pilot took passengers on a flight-for-hire, much to their surprise and eventual gratification." That woman was Nancy Harkness. The article goes on to say that Miss Harkness was in Boston visiting "for a few days" and that she "dropped in at the airport."

The two passengers were alarmed at first when they heard that a woman was to fly them to their destination, but "on landing, they expressed much pleasure and praised the pilot's skill." The news photo shows a smiling Nancy leaning out of the cockpit window talking to the couple.[7]

The instigator of that newsworthy event was one Robert M. Love, the owner of Inter City Aviation. In spite of his initial irritation, he hired Miss Harkness. Odds are, he was smitten the minute he laid eyes on her.

Nancy had acquired her first job in aviation. Robert C. Codman wrote an article for *N.E. Aviation* headlined "Woman Flier Given Praise ... To Demonstrate Waco Line." "She's OK. She's not just somebody that flies," Bob Love was quoted as saying. The article went on to say that:

> Miss Harkness is a transport pilot and in the future will demonstrate the Waco line of airplanes to prospective customers. She has been flying for four years.... She is quite reserved but like all pilots warms up to the topic of flying so eventually some of her past experiences come to light.... It is anticipated that

when this latest employee of the ICA becomes a little
better acquainted she is going to be more than busy
with her gray demonstrator which by the way is the
only ambulance plane in New England.[8]

The first time Bob Love's name appears in Nancy's logbook
is May 7, 1934, a Boston to New York hop. She wrote, "part
time—B. Love" in the remarks section of the flight log. He flew
her back home after her Boston visit and let her fly part way.
Her recorded flight time is fifty minutes.

Over the next few weeks, they flew together four times.[9] On
May 26, he flew down to New York in the evening, picked her
up—she was still living with Suzanne and Tommy—and took her
out on the town. The following day, he again picked her up—this
time in his father's chauffeur-driven black Packard limousine—
and the two of them flew from Roosevelt Field to Boston.[10]

Nancy made the move to Boston right after that and went
to work for Inter City fulltime. Beginning June 1, her logbook
shows frequent demonstration flights and passenger hops out of
East Boston Airport. Some are designated charter, some demonstration, some simply note "passengers."

Then on September 6, Nancy and Bob left Boston together
in the Waco cabin plane and headed for Houghton. Nancy was
taking Bob home to meet Mother and Dad.[11]

On September 10, an article appeared in the Houghton,
Michigan, newspaper stating that pilot Robert Love of Boston, Massachusetts, and well-known young local aviatrix Miss
Nancy Harkness, daughter of Dr. and Mrs. R.B. Harkness, had
flown into the local airport in a Waco cabin plane. The article
also said: "The plane, a cabin ship of the latest type, is powered
by a Continental 210 HP motor. According to Harold J. Skelly,
local aviator, the plane is unique [in that] it embodies the latest
types of equipment. Behind the cabin in the tail of the ship is a
space large enough to accommodate a man should the plane be
used as an ambulance."[12]

Nancy had her sought-after start in aviation. Now she was
paid to fly, rather than paying to fly. During the fall of 1934

and winter of 1935, she continued to demonstrate planes and fly charters at Inter City.

On April 5, 1935, Bob Love bought Inter City's first Beech-craft—a Staggerwing, #14415 with a Jacobs 225-horsepower engine. Beechcraft was a major aviation company in Wichita, Kansas, owned and run by Walter and Olive Ann Beech, a couple who rank among aviation's visionaries. The stylish, luxurious Staggerwing airplane became synonymous with many of the luminaries of 1930s aviation including two women Nancy would come to interact with over the next several years: Louise Thaden and Jacqueline Cochran. Bob Love's model was one of the first built. The alliance with Beechcraft was to be a forerunner of greater things for Nancy and Bob and Inter City.

On July 22, 1935, they flew the Staggerwing to Michigan. This was Bob's second visit to Nancy's family. However, by now Dr. Harkness had taken the position of director of the Barry County Health Department, necessitating a move from Houghton in the Upper Peninsula to Hastings, near Battle Creek, in the Lower Peninsula.

On July 24—with Mrs. Harkness as a passenger—they took off for Houghton. Mrs. Harkness was going back to the Keweenaw Peninsula to visit family. Nancy and Bob returned to Inter City on July 26.[13]

Between the September 1934 trip to Houghton and July 1935 lay eleven months of courtship and a personal relationship complicated or enhanced by a working relationship, the running of a business during hard Depression times, and the often rollercoaster pleasures and stresses of everyday living as dictated by family, friends, and a score of other outside influences. During that time Nancy continued to seek other or additional aviation-related jobs. She added significantly to her aviation contacts through Bob and through the Boston social scene and she had her sources on the lookout for job opportunities on which she might capitalize.

Robert MacLure Love was born March 5, 1909, in Brooklyn, New York, but his roots were deep in the Midwest. He was the second son and third child of John Haviland and Bertha Louise (Smith) Love. An older brother, John III born in 1896, was an invalid and died in his early twenties. Bob's sister, Margaret, was born in 1901.[14]

Both Bob and Nancy had the good fortune to be born into families with means. They were people of substance and eminently acceptable as members of the social registers of the time. Neither of their fathers was born into privilege. However, Nancy's mother certainly was and Bob's mother was from a well-to-do midwestern family. Both of their families personified the American dream of late-nineteenth/early-twentieth-century America. They were the products of capitalism, free enterprise, and prosperity, and the lack of the caste system that kept the people of Europe bound tightly in their class-consciousness. In America, a man could work hard, make something of himself, raise his station in life, and if he was very fortunate, accumulate wealth for himself and his family.

Bob's father did exactly that. John personified the self-made man. He was born May 13, 1866, in Maysville, Kentucky—on the Ohio River east of Cincinnati—the seventh of nine children, seven of them girls. John was a born salesman and an astute businessman. At sixteen, he went to work for his uncle as a traveling salesman's assistant, doing accounts and inventory. He built a business empire of his own in the textile business.

By 1895, his family had moved to Muncie, Indiana, where he met the love of his life, Bertha Louise Smith. They were married June 10, 1895. John's business soon took him to New York City. In June 1907, he and his partners took over several dry goods companies, placing him in New York's "rag trade." He retired from the textile business in the 1920s and became a bank president and the president of the merchants association. In 1928, the family moved to a very fine house in Great Neck on Long Island. John, the boy from Maysville, Kentucky—son of a railroad man—had arrived.[15]

The defining moments of young Bob Love's life occurred during World War I but had nothing at all to do with the Great War. He was stricken with polio during the epidemic of 1917. He was the lucky one, say his daughters. The day before Bob got sick, the Love family chauffeur's son had died of the disease. Bob's father convinced a doctor to try an experimental blood serum taken from polio survivors. The serum was injected into his son's spine. With one son already institutionalized, John and Bertha couldn't bear the thought of losing another child. Though he was paralyzed for a time, Bob recovered fully from his bout with polio. The girls relate that, as he grew older, he did have a slight limp—obvious only when he was very tired.

What probably impacted him the most in his young life was the fact that he was sent away to school, in the old British tradition, at age eight. "He told us he cried himself to sleep every night for a year and a half," says eldest daughter Hannah. The school was St. Paul's in New York City. He then attended the Lawrenceville preparatory school in Lawrenceville, New Jersey, graduated in 1927, and entered Princeton.[16]

Sometime between prep school and April 1929, Bob became enamored with aviation. Carefully written in Robert MacLure Love's first Pilots Log Book is the notation of his first flight: "4-10-29—1 Flight—20 minutes."

Bob soloed on April 29. "Five landings—whoopee!" He had just over seven hours of dual instruction, all taken in a 1928 OX-5 American Eagle. By July 20, he was flying out of Roosevelt Field and he had his private pilot's license, #6920.[17] Three years later, he set about making aviation his life's work.

On April 23, 1933, Bob opened a flight facility that offered ground school instruction. Also in 1933, Inter City took over the terminal at East Boston Airport and the interests of the Curtiss-Wright Company. The July 1934 issue of *Aero Digest* states that the Department of Commerce had approved the Inter City Flying and Ground School that offered Kinner-powered Fleets, Monocoupes, and Fairchilds, and a Waco cabin plane for advanced instruction.[18]

By then, Nancy Harkness had walked into Bob's life.

✈ 3 ✈

Stretching Her Wings

Romance was one thing, but Nancy Harkness wasn't ready to settle down. Just twenty, she was too busy establishing her name in the world of aviation. For now, her job with Bob entailed demonstrating and selling airplanes like the Beechcraft models on a commission basis, plus being a general airport Girl Friday. In those Depression days, sales were few and far between.

By early 1935, changes were in the air.

Nancy had made good on her desire to meet Eugene Vidal, Director of the Bureau of Air Commerce. In December 1934, he was the guest of honor at the Boston Aero Club dinner held at the Hotel Lenox. A photograph taken at the dinner, of Nancy and Vidal with Aero Club member and pilot, Mrs. Teddy Kenyon, appeared in the *Boston Herald* on December 15, 1934. On February 2, 1935, Vidal wrote to Nancy at Inter City. After some opening chitchat, "talking with Amelia and G. P." (Amelia Earhart and her husband George Palmer Putnam) about Nancy possibly working with them on a project, Vidal concluded his letter with the following: "As to a government job, you'd better

33

see J.R. and ask him to talk with his mother about you. You can say that I believe you can be fitted in some niche."[1]

"J.R." happened to be James Roosevelt and, of course, his mother was Eleanor, the president's wife, the First Lady of the United States.

Suddenly, four very *big* names were on Nancy's plate. Earhart and Putnam were at the pinnacle of their aviation fame. Nineteen thirty-five was their big year. In January, Earhart became the first pilot, male or female, to fly solo from Hawaii to the mainland—a daring and dangerous feat. In April she flew solo from Burbank, California, to Mexico City. Her return flight in May from Mexico City to Newark, New Jersey, set a solo record. Earhart and her projects were big news and big business. She also had accepted a position with Purdue University as an aviation adviser and career counselor for the young women there. Was there a place for Nancy in this exciting scheme?

Nancy wrote to James Roosevelt April 1 and received a reply from him dated April 13, 1935, in which he promises to see what he can do. Then a second letter from Vidal, undated but following Roosevelt's letter, begins:

> I had a wire from James Roosevelt—his father is very well known in Washington—about your wanting a job. There's nothing for you to do but wait until P.W.A. [Public Works Administration] funds are allotted us for some interesting projects. For instance, we have an airmarking program on which we might send out a few girls in Hammond planes touring the country.[2]

In 1935, veteran aviator Phoebe Omlie was appointed Special Assistant for Intelligence of the National Advisory Committee for Aeronautics (NACA), the forerunner of the National Aeronautics and Space Administration (NASA). What that meant was that Omlie, who had been flying since 1921 and was well thought of and well connected in the aviation world of the mid-1930s, had the ear of the men in the government. These men could do something to help pilots and private airplane owners, all the little people (women included) who didn't fly for the airlines.

Omlie was the first woman in the United States to earn a transport license as well as an airplane and engine mechanics license. Now she was the first woman appointed to a government aviation position. She also made Eleanor Roosevelt's list as one of the ten most useful women in America.[3]

What all this meant for Nancy Harkness was that she just might have the opportunity to go to work for Omlie in what was to be known as the Airmarking Program. This might be the biggest break yet in her budding aviation career.

Omlie and Earhart had convinced John S. Wynne, the chief of the Airport Marking and Mapping Section of the Bureau of Air Commerce, that there was a need for making towns and cities more identifiable from the air. Few pilots in those days flew over established airways, nor did they have radios. Getting lost was frighteningly easy, even for an experienced pilot.

Omlie's solution was that each state would be marked off in sections of twenty square miles. A marker with the name of the nearest town—at each fifteen-mile interval—would be painted on the roof of the most prominent building in the town. The most visible color combinations selected were black and international orange or black and chrome yellow. Where roof space was inadequate or towns were too far apart, ground markers were constructed out of rocks and painted white. Included was an arrow pointing to the nearest airport and the number of miles to it, as well as an arrow pointing north.

"Fifty millions of Federal dollars have been spent on airway aids chiefly of benefit to the airlines. This is the first time that the government has spent money in helping the private airplane owner," Omlie pointed out. State grants for the airmarking project were awarded through President Roosevelt's New Deal program, the Works Progress Administration (WPA). The cost was close to one million dollars. The program had an immediate two-fold benefit. Not only did it help private pilots and provide a permanent benefit to the airways in the U.S., it also provided jobs for the unemployed of the Great Depression. Men were to be put to work painting the names of towns on roofs for pay.

But how was NACA going to reach out and convince city fathers in these small towns to buy into the WPA program? Omlie convinced John Wynne that this was a job for a woman—several in fact. First, she recruited gifted, veteran pilot Louise Thaden.[4]

In her autobiography, *High, Wide and Frightened*, Thaden describes how the job came about:

> Flying jobs for women pilots have always been scarce, and 1935 was no exception to the rule.... Phoebe Omlie and Amelia Earhart had been working on the Bureau of Air Commerce for two years or more endeavoring to talk them into hiring a few women pilots. Eventually these two wore down resistance, Phoebe having evolved a program whereby women could fit into the Bureau's picture.[5]

This truly was a breakthrough. Omlie was a woman ahead of her time.

Beginning spring 1935, Omlie and Thaden built the project from scratch, determining the type and size of the markers, the cost of materials, the hours of labor required in construction, the number of markers needed, etc. When they were ready, they sought two more pilots. The Bureau of Air Commerce, at their suggestion, hired two rising young stars among the available female flyers: Nancy Harkness of Boston and Helen MacCloskey of Pittsburgh. Both held transport licenses, as, of course, did Thaden. Omlie then opted to return to her NACA job, so the work was divided among Thaden and the two new pilots.

"The three of us were excited about our job," Thaden relates. "First, airmarking is an important aid to air navigation as it is a neglected one; second, we would have a plane assigned to us; third, a pay check twice a month would be useful. Above all else we felt the responsibility of doing a good job, for upon our shoulders rested the fate of future employment of women pilots by Governmental agencies."

The first disappointment was immediate. WPA funds could not be expended on additional equipment. "We were *not* to have airplanes," Thaden writes. So, though traveling around the country to sell aviation to WPA administrators to benefit aviation, the three women would have to rely on ground transportation or, where necessary, airlines.[6]

Mid-1930s America was far different technologically from the world we now know, with cell phones and their attendant towers, radio, television, cable, and satellite transmissions that reach into the back corners of the most remote country areas. Powered flight turned one hundred years old in 2003, but in 1935, it had only been around thirty-two years, and most of what we consider standard for aviation today was yet to be learned. Much of that would occur during World War II. Most planes did not have navigational aids. Weather forecasting was in its infancy, dependent on the report of a pilot who had just flown through whatever weather was brewing.

Back then, interstate travel—whether by car, bus, plane, or train—was far less comfortable. Traveling by train or in a car on narrow, two-lane roads, meant dealing with dust, soot, and grime. Women wore dresses or blouses and skirts, hats, silk stockings (no nylons yet, let alone pantyhose) and high heels. Older women still wore corsets. Men rarely went anywhere without jackets, neckties, and hats. Women pilots in the 1930s, likewise, flew in skirts and high heels. They had to be—or at least appear to be—ladies. And ladies dressed not only in skirts and high heels, but also wore hats and white gloves.

Photos of Nancy and the others from those days show lots of print dresses with skirts to mid-calf length or an occasional skirt and blouse with suit jacket. In one photo, Nancy—wearing a short-sleeved, button-down-the-front checkered dress—leans against the low wing of an airplane studying a map. Her headgear is her signature helmet with straps hanging loose, goggles pushed up on her forehead.

In her autobiography, Louise Thaden relates a particularly harrowing winter day in Oklahoma. Though she was fortunate enough to be flying in a borrowed single-engine Stinson, mechanical problems forced a landing. There she was, "the raw December wind chilling my bones to the marrow, as silk stocking legs and numb feet in thin soled high heeled shoes took me toward the nearest farmhouse a half mile down a frozen rutted road."[7]

*Twenty-one-year-old
Nancy Harkness,
joins Airmarking
team.*

Courtesy Love family,
electronic image NAHF.

Nancy Harkness's job, like Louise Thaden's, entailed traveling around her territory convincing city fathers that the name of their town painted on the roof of a prominent building would serve as an aid to pilots. Her territory was the East Coast. She began her job, officially, on September 14, 1935. Her orders specified that she could, if necessary, "travel over regularly scheduled air lines ... at cost not to exceed cost by rail plus Pullman" and that she should use government aircraft and automobiles for transportation whenever available. She could use her personally owned automobile if it was "more economical and advantageous to the United States [not to her]" and for travel that involved points not reached by common carrier. In those instances, she would be paid five cents per mile. Her per diem was five dollars.[8]

Nancy Harkness threw herself into her work. A letter to John Wynne dated October 6, 1935, indicates that she is in the process of wrapping up her work in New Jersey.[9] Two weeks later, a

story in the *Boston Post* dated Monday, October 21, 1935, tells
of her successes in New Jersey, Maryland, and Massachusetts:

> Miss Harkness has secured approval of a programme
> [*sic*] to place airmarkers in 290 cities and towns [in
> Massachusetts]. The other 65 have already been so
> marked. Since her appointment a little over a month
> ago, Miss Harkness has also got the airmarking pro-
> gramme signed up in New Jersey and now she is
> working in Maryland.
>
> "I love it. It's really useful work in the field of avia-
> tion and I get lots of chances to fly. Two other girls
> have similar jobs.... I have from Maine to Florida."
> She also has Michigan and Ohio in her territory.

The article went on to say: "But Miss Harkness, who is barely
over 20—and very pretty—can smile wisely to herself. For now
she wears a sizable and very sparkling diamond ring on her left
hand and she is engaged to the president of Inter City Airlines,
Robert Love, son of a New York banker."[10]

Then on November 22, 1935, Nancy wrote to John Wynne to
tell him that she was resigning. In his answer, dated November
29, and which he signs "alias Jack," he wrote: "Please permit
me at this time to compliment you on your splendid work and
the spirit and enthusiasm with which you carried it out at all
times." And he added that he was delighted with her work and
regretted to see her leave the service. He also wished her well in
her upcoming marriage.[11]

On January 11, 1936, in the First Presbyterian Church of Hastings, Michigan, Hannah Lincoln (Nancy) Harkness became the
bride of Robert MacLure Love. The Rev. John Kitching offici-
ated at the ceremony, which took place at high noon. A detailed
account of the wedding can be found in an article in the Society
Sections of area newspapers, which begins:

> The church was decorated with evergreen and varie-
> gated white flowers. The Wedding March from *Lo-*

> *hengrin* and Mendelssohn's recessional were played
> on the organ. The bride, who carried a bouquet of
> white orchids and lilies of the valley, wore a white
> satin dress made along princess lines, with a high cowl
> neck, long sleeves and train. She also wore a tulle veil,
> which attached to a small off-the-face cap.... Her ma-
> tron of honor, Mrs. Robert B. Harkness Jr., of Lin-
> coln, Massachusetts, wore an ankle-length gray crepe
> dress with an aquamarine sash and a gray velvet hat.
> Her bouquet was of spring flowers.

The account is typical of the write-up most well connected brides received from their local newspapers in the 1930s. The article goes on to say that both the bride's and bridegroom's mothers wore black velvet and carried bouquets of purple orchids. Some fifty relatives and friends attended the ceremony and twenty-five attended the reception, given at the Harkness's home. There is an extensive list of out-of-town guests, among them Nancy's closest flying buddy, Alice Hirschman, from Grosse Pointe, Michigan, her fiancé, John Hammond, and Bob's sister, Margaret Love, of Tucson.[12]

The wedding was *the* Hastings social event of the winter. The marriage of two professional pilots was newsworthy enough in that small Michigan city, and the fact that they were both socially prominent made it all the better. What did not make the society pages was that this was the beginning of a most uncommon marriage, one built not only on love, but on mutual trust and respect.

When Bob and Nancy departed Hastings, dodging the traditional showering of rice, they headed for Chicago. Prior to the wedding, Bob had flown the Staggerwing to Chicago where he stashed it until he and his bride could pick it up for their flying honeymoon out West.

When they left Chicago on January 13, they were headed for Cheyenne, a seven-hour flight. Bob flew the leg to Omaha (two hours fifty-seven minutes) and Nancy, from Omaha to North Platte, Nebraska (two hours fifteen minutes). "Omaha-North Platte—NHL," Bob notes. That's the first time her name ap-

Mr. and Mrs. Robert MacLure Love and their Beechcraft Staggerwing.
Courtesy Love family; electronic image NAHF.

pears in his logbooks. He took the controls again and made the two-hour flight from North Platte to Cheyenne where he notes "6200 feet—NIGHT." Thus began the flying honeymoon.[13]

A news clipping from the Cheyenne *Wyoming Eagle* tells that Nancy and Bob were guests at an elk dinner at Frontier Park given by the Wyoming Sportsmen's Association. "Mrs. Love is one of the very few women who has been a guest at a Sportsmen's Association dinner."[14] On January 16, Bob notes in his logbook a three-hour fifty-minute flight from Cheyenne to Otto, New Mexico.

"Dad was a bit of a cowboy," says Marky. "He and Mum rarely flew together because he took chances and she didn't. Their marriage almost ended in divorce right there on their honeymoon. The story, as they told it and retold it, became legend in our family. He thought they could stretch it from Cheyenne to Albuquerque. Mum told him they couldn't make Albuquerque without stopping for fuel."

He tried.

She was right.

Out of fuel, they had to make a forced landing in remote
Otto. The flight on to Albuquerque took only thirty more minutes. Only the honeymooners themselves know whether the
flight was made in stony silence or in a heated argument.

When Bob Love hired Nancy Harkness in 1934 to demonstrate and sell airplanes for Inter City Aviation, he was using—
in women in aviation historian Deborah G. Douglas's words,
"the oldest gimmick in the book. Women pilots were used not
only to persuade reluctant buyers of new aircraft but also to sell
the idea of aviation to the nation—after all, the logic went, if a
woman can do it then it must not be so difficult."[15]

Once women began to climb into the open-air cockpits of the
early airplanes, they too got hooked on flying. In *The Winged
Gospel*, aviation historian Joseph J. Corn explores America's love
affair with aviation during the first half of the twentieth century
and characterizes its fascination for women: "The attraction of
women to aviation was a strong one, for no activity better sym-
bolized the freedom and power which was lacking in their daily
lives. As pilots women experienced feelings of strength, mastery,
and confidence which, particularly at a time when Victorian
norms still rendered all strenuous effort and most public activity
by women suspect, seemed delicious indeed."[16]

But the first generation of women pilots—for all their daring—
encountered that Victorian code that stifled further advances.
The next step was left to the second generation of women flyers.
Led by Earhart, Thaden, Omlie, Blanche Noyes, Ruth Nichols,
and Helen Richey, these women of the 1920s and 1930s were
able to take advantage of much broader opportunities in aviation. By then, barnstormers thrilled Americans with their fear-
less feats in the air and the romance of flight was in full bloom.

"The rush to the cockpits by women also reflected new opportunities, which stemmed mainly from the peculiar needs of the
aeronautical industry at a time of transition," says Corn. Aviation had to "grow up" from the "toy" stage into something useful. Lindbergh's solo flight across the Atlantic in May 1927 provided the dramatic impetus and the dawning realization that the
airplane was a viable means of transportation provided the rest.

Corn continues:

> Engineers were designing safer and more reliable air-
> craft, airlines were being created, people were flying
> for recreation.... Although poised on the brink of
> maturity and promising great profits, the aviation in-
> dustry faced a paradox. The public was enthusiastic
> about airplanes and about flying in the abstract, yet
> in great numbers they refused to fly.... Fear not fare,
> airline executives maintained, kept potential passen-
> gers out of the air.... Similar anxieties were said to
> be retarding sales of planes to private users.... The
> public still thought of fliers as "intrepid birdmen."[17]

Corn quotes Bureau of Air Commerce head Eugene Vidal,
the proponent of producing a "poor man's" airplane, as saying
that "the ordinary automobile driver, in fact, could pilot his or
her own airplane." Corn also quotes Louise Thaden: "Nothing
impresses the safety of aviation on the public quite so much as
to see a woman flying an airplane." If a woman can handle it,
she said, "the public thinks it must be duck soup for men."[18]

Many of the women flyers of the 1930s were excellent pilots.
They taught flying; they performed precision aerobatics at air
shows; they set records for speed, altitude, endurance, and distance; they served as test pilots; and they flew charter, both cargo
and passengers. Helen Richey—who later flew for Nancy during
the war—became the first woman hired by a commercial airline
and, for several months in 1934, flew copilot for Central Airlines.
The public loved to hear about these women. Stories of women
pilots had far more appeal than stories about male pilots. So the
press gave their readers what they wanted. If a woman flyer did
something, it got noticed, usually with big headlines.

Still, says Corn, "of all the jobs women pilots found in the
period, demonstrating and selling planes for the private market
was the most common." Also prevalent at that time was the
belief that the family airplane would take the place of the family
automobile. Thus, the pilot/saleswoman was the way to go.[19]

The aviation industry remained a male domain. Women were
"allowed" in when, as, and where they were needed. Neverthe-

less—because women were needed in certain areas—the 1930s became the golden age for the woman pilot. Thus, Nancy Love found her niche, her entrée into the world of general aviation. And with that came what she really wanted: simply to fly as much and as often as possible.

✈ 4 ✈
Tricycle Gear Test Pilot

Nancy Harkness Love knew and flew with many of the men who made aviation their life in the 1930s—men like Crocker Snow, Henry Wilder, Clyde Pangborn, Jack Ray, his friend Johnny Miller, and of course Bob Love. Aviation was a small close-knit community. By 1935, she was on first-name basis with Eugene Vidal and John Wynne. Men liked and respected Nancy and Nancy liked and respected men. She preferred men who shared her adventurous spirit and love of flying.

Bob Love, descended from two solid midwestern families, had a purposeful ruggedness about him that set him apart from the eligible males of the Eastern social set. Spirit of adventure aside, from the beginning he was a businessman and a good one.

"Laugh crinkles set off his glacial blue eyes," says Hannah.

"Mum called him homely-handsome," says Marky. "He was very attractive to women."

Bob was completely at home with himself. He was as open and outgoing as Nancy was guarded and in control. He was like no one Nancy had ever known. Likewise, she was completely unlike any woman he had ever met. After that first shaky encounter in his office, things obviously smoothed out, but the girls never did find out how long it took before the air between them thawed. But thaw it did.

The honeymoon over, Nancy and Bob settled down outside of Boston at Trapelo Farm, Waltham, Massachusetts. Nancy was content to go about her business as usual—flying. Besides, like many a new bride in the mid-1930s, she expected to be pregnant before the year was out. Most of her flying was routine. She flew demos, hopped passengers, and continued to do those odd flying jobs for Inter City as needed. On March 20, 1936, she delivered newspapers to Concord, New Hampshire, at six a.m. In her logbook she wrote "floods."

September 1936, however, offered her a break in her routine. On August 26, she received the first of two telegrams:

> Suggest you contact Louise Thaden by telegraph—she will be at factory tomorrow—and ask to go as copilot in Bendix Race flying Four Twenty Beechcraft. I think you would be of great assistance and it would be fine experience for you. Hope to see you in Los Angeles.
>
> Bill Ong[1]

William A. "Pappy" Ong was general sales manager for Walter Beech's company, Beech Aircraft, from 1935 to 1938, well thought of in aviation circles, and a friend and admirer of Nancy and Bob Love.

Fate was tempting her, but this was not to be Nancy Love's turn for the brass ring. Thaden had already spoken to Blanche Noyes about going along as copilot. Love lost the opportunity of a lifetime: to be the copilot on the first woman-pilot team to win the prestigious Bendix.

Thaden and Noyes flew their Staggerwing to victory. They bested all the male pilots entered in the 2,500-mile race from New York's Floyd Bennett Field to Mines Field (now LAX) in Los Angeles, September 3–4, 1936, with an elapsed time of 14 hours, 55 minutes. In doing so, both women wrote their names in aviation's history and record books.[2] Thaden was awarded aviation's prestigious Harmon Trophy for 1936 in recognition of her winning effort.[3]

Ong was persistent on Nancy Love's behalf, because on August 27, he sent her a follow-up telegram:

> Sorry about Bendix but will enter you in Amelia Earhart Race flying Jacobs Beechcraft if you will accept.
> This event is handicapped close course race and I think you will have excellent chance. Wire me immediately.... Have beautiful ship here now which I could deliver to you folks at once and you could race this ship if you desire. Don't let us down and tell Bob we won't kidnap you even though we might like to.
> Bill Ong[4]

This marked Love's entry into a very brief career as an air racer.

On September 1, 1936, Nancy and Bob turned their Beechcraft west again and headed for California and the National Air Races. Beechcraft had, indeed, entered her in the Amelia Earhart Trophy Race—a handicapped pylon race. Nancy had never before participated in a pylon race. Still, she managed to place fifth behind the winner, Betty Browning. For this effort, flown at Mines Field, Love won $75.

Then on September 20, she took part in the Women's Air Race, part of the Michigan Air Races at Wayne County Airport in Detroit. She may have been the most surprised person there when she came in second, flying a Monocoupe. Nancy termed the race "a free-for-all." Racing didn't interest her. A thorough and deliberate pilot, she disliked the haste and confusion that were part of air racing. Consequently, those two efforts were the sum total of Love's racing career.[5]

Nancy enjoyed a good time. Not a party girl in the sense of frivolous and unrestrained behavior—far from it—but she had been raised as a social being. The lovely girl grew into a gracious woman who knew how to put others at ease with her ready smile, her firm handshake, and a friendly if restrained low-voiced greeting. "Mum epitomized the term social graces. She made others feel comfortable, she was polite and self-effacing," says Allie.

An outsized ego was never Love's problem, but insecurity was. Her outward self-confidence masked an inner anxiety. Rather than playing the role of a beautiful woman who knew instinctively that she had the upper hand because her physical beauty could open doors for her—an opportunity many women with her natural charms would have capitalized on—Love went about being her naturally attractive self, but she did it with a quiet reserve. A study in control, she worked at letting nothing destroy that façade. The reluctance to call attention to herself manifested itself in many ways: her aversion to the limelight and attendant publicity; the dislike of being photographed; and her reserved, controlled manner. Add to that, Nancy was a perfectionist, as her approach to flying revealed.

"She was physically aware of herself—and yet uninterested in clothes, makeup, the trappings of the world of beauty and fashion," says Allie. "She wanted to be physically attractive to men, but she was not a flirt. Dignity was very important to her."

Photos of twenty-year-old Nancy Harkness taking part in a Junior League fashion show and the Aero Club dinner in Boston in 1934 depict a slender, lovely, beautifully dressed young woman with regal carriage. She may not have cared about clothes, but she knew how to wear them. "She looked neat even in paint-spattered shorts and culottes—which she wore a lot of when we lived on Martha's Vineyard and ran the boatyard," says Allie.

Too circumspect to be the classic free spirit, Nancy was, nevertheless, adventuresome. Why else would she have climbed into that cockpit with Jimmy Hansen? He was only two years older than she and she was his first flight student. That she subsequently soloed with fewer than five hours instruction shows fierce determination.

Nancy's mother brought her up to observe the social graces and to play by society's rules. Nancy turned out to be an apt pupil—she always conducted herself with aplomb in polite society, was respected by men and women alike, and was widely known to be first and foremost a lady. She didn't care for society's dictates, though she observed them, and she did not let on that she felt that way except to family and close friends.

Sometimes, though, her keen wit and sense of irony got the best of her, particularly when she was younger, before she learned to quash her true feelings for the sake of appearance.[6]

For the most part, Love was not a joiner—and remained so throughout her life. But one organization in which she kept up her membership for several years was the Ninety-Nines. Not surprisingly, the social activities that Nancy enjoyed were those related to flying. By 1937—though only twenty-three—she was a member of the Ninety-Nines' nominating committee.[7]

As 1937 dawned, Love's aviation career took yet another turn. The Bureau of Air Commerce wanted her back. John Wynne had meant those complimentary things he had said about her in his November 1935 letter. Not only would she be touring the countryside of the eastern United States convincing town leaders that airmarking was a win-win situation—put men to work and aid in aviation navigation—she also would be testing a new "safety plane" for the bureau.

Enter the Hammond Y, the first tricycle gear aircraft that Nancy would fly.

Up until the late 1930s, airplanes were taildraggers; they had two large wheels under the wings and a small wheel or tailskid in the tail. Because on the ground the airplane sat canted up at an angle produced by the much larger front wheels, the pilot had trouble seeing over the engine cowling of a single-engine plane. The bigger the engine, the less forward visibility. When taxiing a tailwheel airplane, the pilot had to S—or zigzag—down the taxiway in order to see what was in front of him or her.

Much would be made in future years of Nancy Love's testing of tricycle gear aircraft. And she would, in several instances, be credited with designing the concept. She was always careful to correct that assumption when given the chance, though articles were published with erroneous statements to that effect. She did NOT design the tricycle gear. She, however, did have a lot to do with testing this new concept in aircraft landing gear in two small aircraft termed "safety planes."

Love was considered good copy by the Boston newspapers. Whatever she did drew attention from the press. And her work with the safety planes was no different. An article in the *Boston Traveler* dated March 1, 1937, tells of her coming to town with the first of these safety airplanes: "Her taxi is the 'Hammond Y,' winner of the design competition of the Department of Commerce, and fondly termed 'my gadget.'... She cruises at about 95 miles an hour and can go at 112; and she stops within 100 feet after she touches ground."

Love told the reporter, "Now I'm going South and then West to survey the marking that's been done. What's next? I suppose I'll keep doing what I'm doing now. It's such fun. And safer than automobiles, really. You can make a mistake of 1,000 feet in the air and correct the mistake, but make a mistake of a single foot on the highway and you'll smash into a telephone pole.... It's quite easy to fly this plane." The subhead on the article proclaimed "New Type Plane That Stops on Dime."[8]

By March 1, Love had flown eighteen hours in the Hammond. She began giving demo rides to reporters during which she allowed the "passenger" to fly the craft. The following appeared in the *Christian Science Monitor* on March 6. The headline: "Learner Proves Air Safety of Flivver Plane." The article was written first person with the reporter (initials A.D.H.) describing some of his experience "flying" the Hammond Y: "It's unbelievable and your correspondent is still pinching himself just to be sure it wasn't a dream.... After a practice spin, Mrs. Love turned over the controls to your somewhat flustered reporter. And it's true, we took off and after a short ride around the airport brought the little craft down, with a few corrections from Mrs. Love."[9]

The *Boston Evening American* wrote: "What's more, while performing this unique job, she's flying a unique plane. It's a tricycle affair that reverses the order of things.... You do everything wrong and it comes out right. In a plane of this sort, it's impossible to nose over. It simplifies landing no end. You just land, it takes no skill."[10]

March 9 is the date of the last Hammond flight recorded in Love's logbook. She flew the aircraft from Roosevelt Field in New York to Washington, D.C., noting uncooperative weather with the words "snow—wind!" in her logbook. On March 20 she resumed flying in conventional aircraft and picked up her airmarking duties.

"Official Praises Airmarking Program of WPA in Maine," says an article in a newspaper dated April 2, 1937. Love was in Portland to confer with Maine officials over airmarking progress and to lay plans for continuance of the program. The accompanying photograph shows Love, dressed in a suit and smart, narrow-brimmed hat, seated with two smiling men in business suits. To date, says the article, airmarkers had been painted in 110 towns in Maine. The article concludes: "Mrs. Love flew to Portland in her private plane, a 1937 five-passenger Stinson."[11]

In late April and early May, she checked out airmarking in New York State. Her letter to Col. Frederick Stuart Greene, Commissioner of Public Works in Albany, dated May 6, 1937, states that she is pleased with the progress there.

> I showed your swell letter to my boss in Washington and he was much impressed. Your help has made me the fair-haired girl down there and I am practically being cited as a wonderful example, all of which makes me feel very pleased and terribly grateful to you.
>
> I am sending to you, under separate cover, all the data on airmarking so that your engineers will know how to go about constructing the signs on the Department's roofs.[12]

Praise was something not easy to come by in the world of big business and big government, but obviously the people Love was interacting with on the airmarking trail liked what she was doing and took the time to say so.

A story in the Binghamton, New York, newspaper states that Love arrived in the city "over the D&H railroad yesterday." Her mission was to seek the "cooperation of officials in providing air markings for Binghamton, Endicott and Owego and two or three smaller communities in the vicinity."[13] After this, there are no more references to airmarking. Love returned to Boston where she resumed working with Bob at Inter City. One noteworthy recording in her logbook—on August 28, 1937, she took a Paramount News film crew on two separate trips to the yacht races near Marblehead. Her daughters remember their father telling them the story of how Nancy volunteered to take those photographers up and that they were quite dubious about flying with a woman.

She zoomed them in low and slow where they could get all the great shots they wanted and, when they returned to East Boston late that afternoon, the windblown, flush-faced men of the film crew had nothing but praise for the lady pilot. That put a very broad grin on the face of one Robert M. Love.[14]

Two days later, Nancy Love got her second crack at an aircraft sporting the revolutionary tricycle landing gear. Love's logbook lists her first flight in the Gwinn Aircar as August 30, 1937, Buffalo, New York.

The stubby-looking little aircraft was the dream of designer Joseph Marr Gwinn, Jr. He wanted to build an airplane that would replace the family automobile. Gwinn, a World War I pilot and noted aeronautical engineer, already had some fourteen years experience in designing trainer airplanes—those used to teach people to fly. Now he tackled something very different in style and concept.

"Safety plane" was its moniker. Nancy Love was the test pilot.[15]

Though Love's hours in the Hammond—along with her proven record with the Bureau of Air Commerce—paved the way for this new opportunity, having a woman test pilot was highly unusual, particularly in something as revolutionary as the Aircar. Why *was* Love hired as the test pilot for this job?

She was not, in fact, the first choice.

By a stroke of luck—or fate—the original test pilot, the well-known and highly respected king of speed and aviation daring Frank Hawks, had been called to Hollywood. Love was available and she had nearly sixty hours on the Hammond Y. And, by now, she had logged 500 overall hours flying time. So Joe Gwinn hired her and they went to work.

Between August 30 and October 13, 1937, Love logged forty-four hours flight time in the Aircar. The early flights took place out of Consolidated Field at Buffalo, New York, where the Gwinn Aircar Company was headquartered.

An article in *The Sportsman Pilot,* dated May 15, 1938, gives this descriptive account:

> In the right seat of the two-place ship could be found Joe Gwinn, nonchalantly working a slide rule or making mental engineering calculations, quite unconcerned about the potentialities of the attitudes of flight in which the plane was flown, no matter how extreme those attitudes might be.
>
> In the left seat throughout all these tests was Nancy Harkness Love of Boston. Since this was the pilot seat and since the one set of controls meant that she had to do all the flying and since the bulk of her experience had been on conventional aircraft, the checking of these unusual flight characteristics resulted in an experience that was unique as well as somewhat nerve-racking.

Love had confidence in Joe, but at times it was sorely tried. Joe wanted to land the plane from 2,000 feet with the control column full back, flaps down, and engine throttled. They were approaching the ground at 980 feet per minute, and this maneuver violated every flying instinct Love had learned.

"Hold the wheel back," Joe told her. Love—ignoring her pilot's instinct to push the nose down, which would have spoiled the test—gritted her teeth and did what he asked.

Gwinn wanted to determine the minimum speed at which the craft could maintain altitude. To do this, Love had to fly twenty feet above the ground with the nose slightly high, engine wide open and the flaps fully extended. Gwinn—the designer—was convinced this would work. Love—the test pilot—wasn't so sure. It turned out that the minimum speed fully loaded was forty-two miles per hour. The ship would maintain altitude at thirty-five miles per hour with one person aboard.[16]

Only a few days into the program, Love flew the Aircar for the National Air Races and the attendant parade in Cleveland

Nancy Love steps out of the Gwinn Aircar after a test flight.

Courtesy Love family;
electronic image NAHF.

making several landings to demonstrate the craft. That was on September 6 and marked the public debut of the Gwinn Aircar.

On September 28, she made her first long-distance flight in the Aircar from Buffalo to Washington, D.C., in three hours fifty-five minutes, and the following two days did demonstration flights around the D.C. area. Then she took the Aircar to New York on a similar mission, after which she departed from Roosevelt Field and returned to Buffalo—a three-hour and fifteen-minute flight. On October 12, it was off to Detroit for more demonstrations, returning to Buffalo on October 13. There are no more entries for the Gwinn Aircar in her logbook for 1937.[17]

Eventually, Love became enamored of the strange-looking little craft and a full-fledged supporter of its capabilities. She believed a family aircraft was the wave of the future and promoted it as such. She told a *New York Sun* reporter that she was interested in the development of a plane "in which grandma might ride to the meeting of the ladies' aid, without nervous tension."[18] She didn't realize how great an impact she'd had on its development.

While Nancy and Joe were flying the Aircar around the country in early October, the public relations firm Bruno & Associates already had gone to work on a sales campaign. Getting wind of some of Love's qualifications and of her astoundingly young age—twenty-three—Harry Bruno suggested to Gwinn that they make Love a member of the company's board of directors. Though Gwinn was thoroughly sold on her aviation qualifications, he wasn't sure this was a good idea.

Love didn't fit Gwinn's or the 1930s' image of a member of a corporate board of directors. Wrong sex. Too young. Too pretty. But she had exactly what Harry Bruno wanted—the sum total of those three, *sex appeal.*

Bruno's letter to Joe Gwinn, dated October 25, 1937, spells out how he planned to promote Love's experience and expertise—"her proven record with the Department of Commerce"—and then use her in the sales pitch of the Aircar: "Socially she is everything that we would want. On top of it all, this young lady has an exceptionally good head and lends herself to the type of dignified publicity we have in mind for the Aircar."

She's young, Bruno admits, but he thinks that "properly presented to the public," she will be an asset. Then he goes on to say: "We did not mean that she was to attend Board meetings or actively function as a director; I don't believe she would want to anyway, but adding her to the Board would be very impressive to that group of people who are socially prominent and who incidentally will be good prospects for our product."[19]

Bruno, one of the early PR experts, wrote to Love asking for information on her aviation career. She laid it out in three paragraphs. It is in this letter, dated December 14, 1937, that she mentions watching Lindbergh land at Le Bourget in Paris, but makes very little of the coincidence. "I think the only claim I have to fame is that I probably have an awful lot of time on tricycle landing gear ships; I mean comparatively lots, as there aren't yet many pilots of either sex who have flown them at all. I think I have well over a hundred hours on the Hammond and the Gwinn. I'm thinking of calling myself the 'screwy airplane specialist' but don't tell Joe Gwinn that."[20]

Whatever transpired after that, Joe Gwinn listened to Harry Bruno because Love was hired as assistant sales manager to help sell the Aircar. She was paired with Frank Hawks who, by then, had completed his contract with Hollywood. Hawks, a captain in the Army's Air Service, taught cadets to fly during World War I after which he barnstormed and raced his way into the 1920s and 1930s at breakneck speed, at one point establishing more than 200 flying records in the U.S. and abroad. In the fall of 1937, Hawks declared that he was giving up the pursuit of speed and the air racing circuit and was named vice president in charge of sales for the manufacture of the Aircar.

By spring of 1938, it was time to demonstrate and sell the Aircar to the general public. Love's last flight in it had been October 13, 1937, but on May 21, 1938, she was back in the cockpit—and she stayed there for the next month demonstrating the little craft throughout the East and making sales pitches.

The Gwinn Aircar team: Joseph Marr Gwinn, Nancy Love and Frank Hawks.
Courtesy Love family; electronic image NAHF.

The May 23, 1938, *Boston Transcript* carried the story in its "This Week in Aviation" column—"Gwinn Aircar May Be Brought to Boston by Nancy Love Soon." The hometown girl was in the news again. The story says, "That Gwinn Aircar, the second of the so-called safety planes that anyone can fly, has just received its A.T.C. rating, and there's a chance Nancy Love may bring it up to Boston in a couple of weeks. Capt. Frank Hawks, who is vice president in charge of sales for the manufacturers of the ship, flew here on Saturday and took Mrs. Love to the plant in Buffalo. She is assistant sales manager."

The Aircar was a two-place, side-by-side airplane. The front wheel of the tricycle landing gear was steerable. The article stated that: "To take off, you get going fast, step on a foot pedal that lets down flaps, and up you go. When you're fifty or more feet in the air you let off the pedal and keep climbing.... The steering wheel also operates the ailerons and there is no rudder. You have fore and aft control within 17 degrees up or down.... To land, you pick out a likely spot, push on the flaps with the foot pedal, lose fore and aft control, and come down in a level position."[21]

The last flight that Love recorded in the Aircar—New York City to Danbury, Connecticut—took place June 14, 1938. After that, she returned to her work at Inter City. That she didn't fly the Aircar again was fate working once more in her favor. On August 23, 1938, Frank Hawks and a prospective customer took off from a polo field near East Aurora, New York. *Time* magazine carried the following account in its September 5, 1938, issue:

> He [Hawks] landed neatly on the polo field in a nearby estate at about 5 p.m., climbed out, chatted awhile with [his prospect] and a cluster of friends. Presently he and Campbell [the prospect] took off smartly, cleared a fence, went a-tilt between two tall trees, and passed from sight. Then there was a rending crash, a smear of flame, silence. Half a mile the fearful group raced from the polo field. From the crackling wreck they pulled Frank Hawks; from beneath a burning wing, Prospect Campbell—both fatally hurt.[22]

The Boston Herald, on Wednesday, August 24, wrote:

> Hawks gave up the speed flying which made him fa-
> mous and took up "safety and comfort" flying. Hawks,
> who for years escaped death in daring speed exploits,
> lost his life in the crash of a small safety plane which he
> had said he would rather fly than any other.
>
> J.M. Gwinn, president of Gwinn Aircar Corpora-
> tion, said: "Wind conditions were against them. They
> had to take off the long way of the field and appar-
> ently they were up in the air before they saw the wires
> and it was too late to avoid them."

Hawks's passenger was thrown from the plane and "pinned
under the crumpled and burning wing." He died in the Buffalo
hospital as well. [23]

Shaken, but exerting her characteristic control, Love moved
forward with her life and her aviation career.

Love had begun taking seaplane instruction in July 1938 and by
the end of August, had her seaplane rating. Additional ratings
boosted her worth as an experienced, employable pilot. Among
her many duties at Inter City Aviation was the occasional ferrying of an airplane to another location. She and Bob demonstrated and sold airplanes. So, on occasion, she delivered the
airplane after the deal was finalized. She flew passengers, took
photographers up for aerial work, and, in general, was her husband's right-hand woman when he needed some flying done.

After she and Bob married, Nancy segued into his social life,
which included a lot of sport flying, seaplanes, and the whole
social whirl around flying those pontoon-equipped airplanes in
and out of the harbors of Maine, Massachusetts, Connecticut,
and the Maritime Provinces of Canada. Seaplane cruises were
big with a small group of socially connected aviation enthusi-
asts in the late 1930s.

Nancy and Bob were among those featured in the society
section of the *New York World Telegram* on Saturday, July 8,

1939. The headline across the top read: "Society Fliers Are Getting Ready for Annual Cruise."

The ninth annual flight, by invitation only, was limited to twenty planes and fifty participants. Named Commodore for the 1939 event was none other than A. Felix duPont of Wilmington, Delaware, society reporter Dorothy G. Walker related. "On Thursday, twenty planes will take off from various points on the Atlantic seaboard for New Hampshire's Lake Winnipesaukee. There the pilots and their guests will lunch before their joint departure for Moosehead Lake in Maine for a weekend of fishing, swimming and aviation gossip....Those inveterate fliers, the Robert M. Loves, will fly from Boston to the New Hampshire starting point."

Joining the Loves and other guests would be Mr. and Mrs. B. Allison Gillies—Betty and Bud—of Syosset, New York, on Long Island. Walker noted that Mrs. Gillies was an expert pilot and president of the Ninety-Nines, "the only large scale women's flying club in the country." Nancy and Betty already had begun to form a friendship. And in just a few years, Betty would become the first of Nancy's WAFS.

"The seaplane cruise comes as the yearly culmination of society's interest in flying. For well over a decade socialites have pioneered in private flying, experimenting in all the refinements and new developments of the industry," the article concluded.[24]

The mid-July 1939 rendezvous at Lake Winnipesaukee and Moosehead Lake marked the high point for aviation society. In six weeks, World War II began and aviation, high society, and the world at large would never be the same again.

✈ 5 ✈
War in Europe!

Germany invaded Poland on September 1, 1939. World War II had begun in Europe. Gen. Billy Mitchell's prophecy that the next war would be won in the air was about to be tested. Aviation had grown from its barnstorming adolescence in the 1920s, to a robust young adulthood by the late 1930s as commercial aviation caught hold. Now it was to become a powerful machine of war in its maturity. Pilots became a necessary commodity and, for all the press they had received in the 1930s, there weren't nearly enough of them for wartime needs.

Adventure-seeking U.S. male flyers—drawn by the allure of one-on-one combat in the skies over embattled England in 1940—rushed to fly with the Royal Air Force (RAF). At home, they had the Army Air Corps Reserve. Though it didn't promise combat in the near future, the Reserve did give young American flyers a place to train, hone their skills, and do their bit for their country. Bob Love already had taken that approach. On July 3, 1937, he accepted an appointment and commission as a second lieutenant in the Air Corps Reserve. He served two weeks of active duty in January 1938, 1939, and 1940, doing mostly experimental flying, which included weather observation flights on government projects at nearby M.I.T.[1]

Another early advocate of the Reserves was a young Air Corps captain named William H. Tunner, a 1928 West Point graduate who commanded the Memphis (Tennessee) Air Corps Detachment in the late 1930s. Tunner actively recruited local pilots for the Reserve and, in doing so, built a sizeable corps of flying officers who ultimately went to war with him after Pearl Harbor.[2]

As early as May of 1936, Ninety-Nines member "Teddy" (Mrs. Theodore) Kenyon suggested that women could assist in war by ferrying planes.[3] On September 28, 1939, Jacqueline Cochran— founder of Jacqueline Cochran Cosmetics and record-setting aviator—wrote to Eleanor Roosevelt that she felt a plan should be put in place to use American women pilots in a national emergency.[4] The two had met April 4, 1938, when Mrs. Roosevelt awarded Cochran her first Harmon Trophy.[5] She would receive several.[6]

"In the field of aviation the real 'bottle neck' in the long run is likely to be trained pilots," Cochran wrote to the First Lady. She suggested that women could be used "in all sorts of helpful back of the lines work" like flying ambulance planes, courier planes, and commercial and transport planes, "thereby releasing male pilots for combat duty." She continued: "This requires organization and not at the time of emergency but in advance. We have about 650 licensed women pilots in this country. Most of them would be of little use today, but most of them could be of great use a few months hence if properly trained and organized. And if they had some official standing or patriotic objective (rather than just fly around an airport occasionally for fun) there would be thousands more women pilots than there are now."[7] Cochran noted that England, France, Russia, and Germany already were using women pilots in their air forces.[8]

On January 1, 1940, England set up the first civilian ferry pilots' pool. Eight women were among those selected. Author Lettice Curtis, a woman pilot who joined the Air Transport

Auxiliary (ATA)—a branch of the RAF—in July 1940, writes in *The Forgotten Pilots*: "Women pilots who at the time were unaware that they had anything more than a faint chance of being accepted for the ATA would have been stunned with unbelief if they had known that they were being considered...."[9]

In May 1940, with the war in Europe eight months old, Nancy Love saw a way to help her country's efforts to aid the Allies even though the U.S. wasn't "in" the war. By then, Love had logged 825 flying hours. She had good instincts and wasn't afraid to act on them. She contacted her husband's friend Lt. Col. Robert Olds, Plans Division of the Office of the Chief of the Air Corps, about the possibility of women ferrying airplanes for the U.S. Army

Olds had made his name during the development of the B-17 bomber in the 1930s. He commanded the flight of six of the four-engine Boeing bombers on a goodwill flight from Miami to Buenos Aires and back in February 1938. Known as the Friendship Flight, their return trip to Langley Field in Virginia was, at that time, the longest nonstop flight in Air Corps history.[10]

Olds asked Love for a list of women pilots holding commercial ratings. Using the Aero Chamber of Commerce lists, she collected names and responded to Olds with a letter dated May 21, 1940:

> I enclose a list of all the women pilots in the country who hold Commercial Ratings. There is also a list of women who hold Privates, but whom I know to be experienced and capable of handling as much as the others. It's kind of an awful job to classify them as to relative ability, since I know only about a third of them personally, and, as you know, a Commercial means little in some cases, except that the holder has had over two hundred hours.
>
> As you see, I've been able to find forty-nine I can rate as excellent material, including the Privates. There are probably at least fifteen more of these whom I don't know about and so haven't starred. I really think this list is up to handling pretty complicated stuff. Most of them have in the neighborhood of a thousand hours or more—mostly more, and have flown a great many types of ships.[11]

Of that list of 105 women, only nine eventually made Love's original squadron of twenty-eight WAFS: Barbara Towne, Gertrude Meserve, Evelyn Sharp, Dorothy Fulton, Betty Gillies, Aline Rhonie, Teresa James, Lenore McElroy, and Love herself. The remainder of the women who joined the squadron had not acquired the necessary hours or ratings as of May 1940, or simply were not yet listed. Only nine of the 105 on Love's list are marked as having instrument ratings and Nancy Love is *not* one of them. Love's logbook indicates that she earned her instrument rating on October 16, 1940.

On June 2–4, 1940, Love ferried a plane, intended for the French, to Canada via Maine. Both the Loves' logbooks show the following entries: June 2, Boston–Bangor; June 3, Bangor–Houlton; June 4, Houlton–Moncton–Halifax. Love notes in her log in Houlton, "towed across border."

Nancy and Bob and two Inter City pilot-salesmen were among thirty-three American pilots to take part in a mass ferrying to Canada. Nancy was the lone woman to make the flight. The June 4, 1940, issue of the *Boston Record* tells the following story:

> With a Boston girl and three men pilots participating, 33 American sport planes destined for French war service yesterday were flown to the Canadian border in one of the first mass flights of its kind under U.S. neutrality laws.
>
> The planes, piloted to the border town of Houlton, Maine, by a group of private pilots, were hauled across the international boundary by trucks—because the neutrality law prohibits their flying over—and then with the same pilots took off for Moncton, New Brunswick, and Halifax, Nova Scotia.
>
> After entering the dominion via towing operation supervised by the Royal Canadian Mounted Police and Woodstock N.H. militiamen, the planes winged northward in three flights of eight ships each and one of nine. The pilots will return to New York by steamer from Halifax.[12]

The ferry pilots soon learned that fate had toyed with them. On June 4, the same day they delivered their airplanes to Halifax, the mass evacuation of 338,226 British soldiers from Dunkirk was completed. Ten days later, Paris fell to the Germans and on June 22, France surrendered. After that one ferrying flight to Canada, Nancy returned to her Girl Friday chores, flying for Inter City Aviation.

In June 1940, Bob Olds's Plans Division did consider using "approximately 100 women pilots as co-pilots in transport squadrons and for ferrying single engine aircraft thereby releasing a number of pilots" for other duty. The Air Corps proposed a short refresher course and to commission the women as second lieutenants in the Air Corps Reserve—once the necessary legislation had been obtained. Army Air Corps commander Gen. H.H. "Hap" Arnold turned down the proposal, but did suggest that women could be used as copilots on commercial airliners.[13]

Nothing happened for several months, then in December 1940, Jackie Cochran had lunch with Hap Arnold and Clayton Knight, acting head of the American recruiting committee for the British Ferry Command. They discussed Britain's need for airplanes and pilots. The Battle of Britain and the Blitz had left the island nation battered and reeling.[14] Cochran was anxious to do something for the war effort. Arnold suggested she might ferry a bomber over the North Atlantic to England as a publicity ploy.[15]

Knight was looking for male ferry pilots to volunteer for such flights then considered hazardous duty. This was the opportunity Cochran was looking for. Here was her chance to become the first woman to fly a bomber across the Atlantic and, while in England, she would have the opportunity to study the British ATA women's training program, with an eye to founding and leading an American women's flying auxiliary.[16] Cochran went to Montreal to check out in a twin-engine Lockheed Hudson bomber. However, she wrote in her autobiography, the male pilots responsible for checking her out "didn't want a woman in their midst." She qualified conditionally to ferry a Lockheed Hudson to England along with a male pilot who did the takeoff and landing.[17]

The male pilots of the Atlantic Ferry Organization (ATFERO) who ferried Lend Lease planes from Canada to England threatened to strike when they heard Cochran might ferry a bomber across the Atlantic. Helena Page Schrader writes, "this threat had nothing to do with Cochran's sex—much as she liked to interpret it that way and portray herself as a feminist heroine." Rather, says Schrader, most of these men were former airline pilots who had worked for years to accrue tens of thousands of flying hours. "They had no intention of letting a pilot (male or female) with twenty-five hours on twins be put in command."[18]

Historian Deborah G. Douglas writes that when Cochran qualified, the male check pilots protested. They were afraid the Germans would shoot her down and they would be blamed. It appears they also felt demeaned by the fact that a woman was going to fly a military aircraft across the Atlantic. Douglas thinks that a compromise was reached to placate the male pilots and that is why Cochran flew the flight but a male pilot did the takeoff and landing.[19]

Cochran and the crew took off from Gander, Newfoundland, on June 17, 1941, and successfully delivered the twin-engine bomber to Prestwick, Scotland. While in England, Cochran met with Pauline Gower, commander of the ATA women pilots, and checked out the British operation. By then, Gower's pilots had been ferrying airplanes for a year and a half. In return, Gower asked Cochran if she thought American women pilots might be willing to come fly for the ATA in Britain.

Bob Love entered active duty with the Air Corps on May 6, 1941, a move that ultimately would change his and Nancy's lives significantly, even though his initial job, that of enlisting officer for New England, was routine. Then on June 20, 1941, the Army Air Corps ceased to exist and the U.S. Army Air Forces and the Ferrying Command were established.

Bob Olds, now a full colonel and assigned to set up the Ferrying Command, asked Bob Love to join his Lend Lease airplane ferrying operation across the North Atlantic.[20] Bob was assigned as control officer at the Canadian border town of Houlton, Maine. Years later, he told a reporter that direction for this operation came from the White House via Roosevelt's adviser Harry Hopkins.[21]

Upon her return to the U.S., Cochran immediately met with President and Mrs. Roosevelt. Eleanor reported in her *Washington Daily News* column, "My Day," on July 3: "Miss Jacqueline Cochran is lunching with us today and I am most anxious to hear the report of her trip, about which I shall tell you more in a future column." After hearing Cochran out, President Roosevelt sent her to Secretary of War Henry Stimson to discuss having American women pilots perform a service similar to that performed by the ATA women.[22]

A few days later, Cochran, General Arnold, Colonel Olds, and Robert A. Lovett, Assistant Secretary of War for Air, met in Lovett's office. They were, in Olds's words, "to consider the possibilities of utilizing women pilots to ferry primary, basic and advanced trainers from factories to Air Corps stations thus releasing male pilots for more important combat duty." (Even though the term Air Corps was no longer correct, the general populace as well as many in the military continued to use it indiscriminately—and still do.)

Lovett arranged for Cochran to work on the proposal. In July 1941, she and members of her personal and business staff at Jacqueline Cochran Cosmetics examined the Civil Aeronautics Administration (CAA) files for names of women pilots who might qualify. They found 2,733 licensed women pilots in the United States. Of these, 154 held commercial licenses. Fifty women had more than 500 flying hours and thirty of those had more than 1,000 hours. Eighty-three women had more than 200 hours, and about 2,000 had some experience but generally less than 200 hours.[23] Cochran sent a survey to approximately 150 of the women pilots, of whom 130 responded—enthusiastically.[24]

Cochran worked up a plan that involved not only the utilization of experienced women pilots, but also the training of a far larger group to undertake a variety of aviation related duties. Olds, who considered Cochran to be simply a "tactical consultant," refused to pass her proposal on to Arnold, thinking it on a far larger scale than was called for.[25]

"Olds invited Nancy Love to come to Washington when Miss Cochran was working in his office, which she did in July 1941," military historian Lt. Col. Oliver La Farge writes in his notes from his interview with Nancy Love, October 3, 1945. "That was her [Nancy Love's] first disagreement with Miss Cochran. [Cochran] did not believe that a woman could fly a plane more than a short distance, hence she was working out an elaborate system of relays, which Mrs. Love thought quite unnecessary."[26]

Cochran, in her report to Olds, made a case for "a system of zones" across the country. The ships, she says, "are slow and a woman pilot could generally return by train in one night from the distance she could ferry a plane during the preceding day."[27]

Olds was satisfied that using women pilots was a good idea and said so to General Arnold in his report on August 1: "There appears to be no valid reason why American women pilots cannot be employed successfully by the Air Corps Ferrying Command to deliver training type aircraft from the factory to destination, thus relieving Air Corps combat pilots from such duties."

Olds then proposed a ninety-day service test in which approximately fifty women pilots with more than 500 hours flying time would "be employed as civilians by the Air Corps Ferrying Command to determine the capabilities of these pilots on this type of work." If successful, the women would be commissioned in the Air Corps Specialist Reserve. Olds recommended that during the service test period and possibly thereafter Jacqueline Cochran "be retained as Chief of the Women Pilots Section of the Air Corps Ferrying Command and that all women pilots operate under her direct administrative jurisdiction subject to policies initiated by the Commander, Air Corps Ferrying Command."[28]

Olds and Cochran never were on the same page. He was working on a solution to the Army's immediate need for ferry pilots and she was laying the groundwork for a large women pilot organization "for future usefulness in time of war with present ferrying as an initial incident."[29]

On August 25, 1941, General Arnold turned down Olds's proposal but left the door ajar pending developments. He had plenty of men, he said, and no need to involve women in flying duties. Circumstances might be altered, he pointed out, and the use of women pilots might become necessary.[30] Arnold wasn't sure that women could handle the Army's airplanes, even the small single-engine ones.

The British Air Commission officials did contact Cochran about recruiting some of the American women pilots to go to England. Her plan for an American women's air corps was stalled. By December, she was immersed in recruiting twenty-five American women pilots to go to England and fly for the ATA.

After Pearl Harbor, Olds—now a brigadier general and still the head of the Ferrying Command—needed all the pilots he could lay his hands on, and he needed them immediately! He had a number of new aircraft to deliver and not enough pilots to ferry them. Most of his pilots had been reassigned from ferrying duty to combat duty. He decided to resurrect Nancy Love's idea. He was ready to hire women pilots, right then, as civilians, the same way he was hiring male pilots where he could find them. But Cochran got wind of the plan.

Byrd Howell Granger, a woman pilot who in 1943 would graduate with the first class of women pilots trained by the Army in Texas and who eventually served under Nancy Love, writes that one of Cochran's Britain-bound pilots called her on Sunday, January 18, to cancel her commitment. She had heard the U.S. would now use women ferry pilots. Cochran asked, "Who says?" The answer: it was "being worked out through the wife of a high official in the Ferry Command"—Nancy Love, wife of Bob Love, Granger points out in the accompanying footnote.[31] Likely, the caller was Granger herself.

Cochran contacted Olds, who told her of his intentions. Cochran now had an unbreakable commitment to the British. She immediately wrote the following note to Hap Arnold dated January 18, 1942: "General Olds has informed me that he is planning on hiring women pilots for his Ferrying Command almost at once. His plan, as outlined to me, is not only bad in my opinion from the organizational standpoint, and contrary to what you told me yesterday but is in direct conflict, in fact, with the plans of a women's unit for England. In addition, it would wash me out of the supervision of the women flyers here rather than the contrary as we contemplated."[32]

Arnold, aware of Cochran's political clout with the Roosevelts, in turn wrote to Olds and told him: "You will make no plans or re-open negotiations for hiring women pilots until Miss Jacqueline Cochran has completed her present agreement with the British authorities and has returned to the United States."[33]

Olds put his idea on the back burner.

Cochran didn't leave for England as quickly as anticipated; in fact, she didn't get her future ATA pilots organized until spring 1942. At that point, she set sail for England with commitments from twenty-three of the United States' best women pilots to join the ATA.

✈ 6 ✈
Wanted: Ferry Pilots

After the attack on Pearl Harbor, all airfields within fifty miles of the U.S. coastline were shut down. That included East Boston Airport and, consequently, Inter City Aviation. Bob Love was ordered to Washington, D.C., as part of General Olds's Ferrying Command. The Loves prepared to move to the D.C. area to accommodate his new job.

Maj. Robert H. Baker arrived at Logan Field, Dundalk, Maryland, near Baltimore, January 5, 1942. His orders were to set up the Northeast Sector, Domestic Wing of the Ferrying Command. Baker had been a flying officer in World War I and prior to assignment to the Ferrying Command was with the 154th Observation Squadron of the Arkansas National Guard.[1]

On March 11, 1942, with General Olds's recommendation, Nancy Love went to work for Baker in the Operations Office of the Northeast Sector, located in the Martin Plant (where the B-26 bomber was built) in Baltimore.[2] Her job included mapping ferry flights and routes, learning military procedures, and helping find sources for pilots. Since gas for the family automobile was hard to get, Nancy commuted to work in the Loves' high-winged, single-engine, four-seater Fairchild 24. She flew the sixty-mile Washington-to-Baltimore round trip daily.

The Domestic Wing had a monumental task ahead of it: moving what promised to be an ever-increasing supply of airplanes with a minimal number of pilots. Seeing first-hand the urgent need for more ferry pilots, Love again proposed that qualified women pilots could be used in that capacity. Staff of the Domestic Wing opposed the idea, but shortly afterward, headquarters of the Ferrying Command supported it.[3]

When Bob Olds collapsed at his desk from overwork in March 1942, Hap Arnold brought Col. Harold L. George to the Ferrying Command as his temporary replacement. When Arnold learned that Olds's recovery would not be immediate, he relieved Olds of his command and asked George, a strategic bombardment specialist, to take over.

Expecting an overseas command, George was surprised. He told Arnold he knew nothing about moving men and supplies by air nor did he know anyone in the Ferrying Command who had the expertise to create the worldwide air transport system the Army would need to accomplish the daunting task. Arnold had his ace in the hole. He knew someone who did.

"Do you know C.R. Smith?" he asked George.

George knew of him—the president of American Airlines—but didn't know him personally.

"Well, I do," Arnold said. He called Smith and immediately set up a meeting of the two men in Washington. The two hit it off. They could work together. Arnold made George a brigadier general and put him in charge of the Ferrying Command. He offered to make Smith a colonel and name him George's chief of staff.[4]

Smith agreed.[5]

What about staff? Smith gave George the names of several airline executives to recruit to do the job they needed done and George went to work assembling his team.[6]

After George replaced Olds as commanding officer of the Ferrying Command in April 1942, Olds, now on the mend, was sent to head up the Second Air Force. General George reorganized the command and renamed it the Air Transport Command (ATC). In addition to Smith on his staff, he named (now) Maj. Robert M. Love, Deputy Chief of Staff for Operations. The Domestic Wing became the Ferrying Division—the main arm of the ATC that was charged with all ferrying operations, domestic and foreign.

The Northeast Sector became the 2nd Ferrying Group and, on May 29, was moved to New Castle Army Air Base (NCAAB) near Wilmington, Delaware, with (now) Colonel Baker in command.[7] Col. William H. Tunner, the man who had been recruiting Reserve pilots in Tennessee in the late 1930s and who had been the second man to join Bob Olds when the Ferrying Command was created a year earlier, was named commanding officer of the Ferrying Division.[8]

During Bill Tunner's senior year at West Point, the cadets were given a week at Mitchel Field on Long Island to learn about the Air Corps. He chose the Air Corps on the basis of five flights in five different airplanes within the space of that week. Later, he wrote in his memoir *Over the Hump*, "Though I was never permitted to touch the controls, I still remember each flight as a thrilling experience. No tricks, no stunts, nothing but just straight flying, but that was enough for me. *Man could fly.* [Tunner's emphasis] I was subjective proof of that electrifying statement. From there on, there was no question in my mind. Sure, the Air Corps was considered the lunatic fringe, but the extra pay and additional opportunities for travel more than made up for that."

Tunner's parents thought he had taken leave of his senses. With his wings pinned to his khaki shirt and wearing cavalry breeches and riding boots, and feeling, he admits in his memoir, a little bit cocky, he reported to his first Army station, Rockwell Field near San Diego, California. "We didn't fly planes in those days, we rode them. We were supposed to get the feeling of the plane through the seat of our pants."[9]

Tunner was part of the new breed in the Air Corps: *not* a veteran of WWI, younger, a man born in the twentieth, not the nineteenth century.

Now it was Tunner who desperately needed ferry pilots.

It so happened that Major Bob Love and Colonel Tunner's offices were in close proximity in a dingy basement in the old munitions building in Washington where the ATC was then housed. In *Over the Hump,* Tunner writes of a chance meeting over the water cooler one stormy spring morning. Bob was wondering aloud if his wife had managed to land the family plane safely in Baltimore and report for work.

Tunner recalls saying to Bob: "Good Lord, I'm combing the woods for pilots, and here's one right under my nose. Are there many more women like your wife?"

Bob Love, according to Tunner, replied, "Why don't you ask her?"[10]

Neither Colonel Tunner nor General George had been around for the previous discussions concerning the use of women pilots. Yes, Love told Tunner, she knew of nearly a hundred experienced women pilots. The colonel saw a partial solution to his problem.

On June 11, 1942, Tunner suggested commissioning women pilots as officers in the recently formed (May 1942) Women's Army Auxiliary Corps (WAAC). However, technical difficulties in the WAAC legislation currently before Congress stood in the way. Waiting for an amendment would take time. So, the ATC decided to pursue hiring women pilots as Civil Service employees, which would keep them civilians.[11]

Nancy Love and Colonel Tunner went to work. Love drafted the plan—the original was in her handwriting—and on June 18, Tunner sent General George their proposal for utilizing women pilots.[12] General George forwarded it to General Arnold.

The proposed qualifications for women pilots were: 500 hours, commercial license, between the ages of twenty-one and thirty-five, and a high school diploma. Added later, on Nancy Love's suggestion: a 200-horsepower rating, two letters of recommendation, and U.S. citizenship. Suggested salary was $250 a month plus $6 per diem when out on a ferrying trip, $50 less than male civilian ferry pilots received, because the women would be ferrying light, less complicated aircraft. A basic unit of twenty-five was suggested.[13]

Tunner was so sure that their plan would be approved, the same day he sent the memo to General George with a copy to chief of staff C.R. Smith (June 18) he went to NCAAB to talk to Colonel Baker. The base was under construction. Tunner hoped to line up living quarters and mess privileges for the women pilots. Colonel Baker was most cooperative, finding living quarters for the women and offering them privileges in the new officers mess. Baker, who had been working with Nancy Love for three months, suggested in his June 20 memo to Colonel Tunner that she be commissioned a first lieutenant and assigned as Operations Officer for the women pilots. "I am confident that she can handle the assignment very efficiently; in fact, I do not know of anyone who has as good qualifications as she has for the assignment." And Baker added, "as this is more or less an experiment, I believe a more thorough trial can be made with fifty women pilots instead of twenty-five."[14]

Tunner chose NCAAB because the women could be part of the 2nd Ferrying Group, and it was close to Hagerstown, Maryland, home of the Fairchild Aviation Corporation that built the primary trainers he needed the women to ferry.

On June 22, Tunner notified General George that things at Wilmington were a go. On June 30, Colonel Baker suggested that Nancy Love "come to Wilmington immediately and be employed in her former status until commissioned and until the other arrangements were completed." In a July 5 memo, Colonel Tunner concurred.[15]

Nancy Love was on duty at the 2nd Ferrying Group, July 13. That day she approved a memorandum from Colonel Baker regarding the training course for the women pilots as well as a standardized uniform to be worn by the women while on flying duty or on Post.[16]

General Arnold noted in a July 13 letter to a member of Congress that militarization of a proposed group of women pilots through the WAAC was not looking feasible at that time.[17] Because of that apparent roadblock to militarization, on July 17, General George sent General Arnold a memo proposing that the women pilots be hired as Civil Service employees for the purpose of "determining the suitability of utilizing women pilots in the delivery of military aircraft." Still, rather than giving his approval to the George-Tunner-Baker-Love plan, General Arnold asked for more up-to-date information on women pilots through the CAA and the Civil Air Patrol. But he did add the following second paragraph to his memo dated July 20: "After exhausting that supply, then reopen this proposition. Give me an outline of the number of women pilots you expect to get and require to carry out your mission."[18] Arnold knew how badly Jackie Cochran wanted the job as head of a women pilot corps but he also knew she was tied up in England.

Part of Nancy Love's job included writing the women pilots' training syllabus, which she and Lt. Joe Tracy, one of Colonel Baker's top flight instructors, did in thirty days.[19] She also was appointed an unofficial member of the three-man board that would review the women applicants.[20] During August, no further word came from General Arnold but Love, Colonel Baker, and Colonel Tunner continued their planning.

On September 1, Mrs. Roosevelt wrote the following in her "My Day" column: "It seems to me that in the civil air patrol and in our own ferry command women, if they can pass the tests imposed upon our men, should have an equal opportunity for noncombat service.... Women pilots ... are a weapon waiting to be used."[21]

On September 3, General George again recommended to General Arnold that a group of women pilots be organized in order to determine their suitability for delivering military aircraft. Again, he outlined the standards they must meet and explained that they would be hired through Civil Service. George proposed that a woman who would serve directly under the Group commanding officer handle the administration duties. The stated requirements fit Nancy Love to a T. Activities could be begun within twenty-four hours.

On September 5, General Arnold directed that immediate action be taken and that the recruiting of women pilots begin within twenty-four hours.[22] Hap Arnold denied that Mrs. Roosevelt's recent "My Day" column had anything to do with his decision. "The development," he said, "was all part of a regular plan."[23] Nancy Harkness Love was appointed director of the woman pilot group.

General George told Love he had the go-ahead from General Arnold and to ready telegrams for her top candidates. With George's approval, she sent out eighty-three telegrams to prospective women ferry pilots on September 5, 1942.[24] The Wom-

Gen. Harold L. George congratulates his new Women's Auxiliary Ferrying Squadron commander, Nancy Love.

Courtesy Texas Woman's University Library, WASP Archives.

en's Auxiliary Ferrying Squadron (WAFS) was off the runway and climbing.

General Arnold was to make the public announcement on the morning of September 10. When Nancy Love and General George arrived at his office that morning to meet Arnold and the press, Arnold unexpectedly had been called out of Washington. The Secretary of War would make the announcement instead. General George and Mrs. Love then proceeded to Secretary Stimson's office where the swearing in and introductions took place.[25] Then Stimson introduced Mrs. Love to the press with the added endorsement, "Of the two most important ladies who have so far come in contact with the Army, one is named Love and the other is named Hobby. That will show you how respectable the Army is."[26]

Things were changing—too fast, as far as some people were concerned. Having women in the U.S. armed services was new. Now women would be flying Army airplanes. What next? Congresswoman Edith Nourse Rogers of Lowell, Massachusetts, had introduced House Resolution (H.R.) 4906 on May 28, 1941, to establish a women's corps as an auxiliary to the Army. Congresswoman Rogers had served in the hospitals in Great Britain during World War I where she had observed first-hand how English women in uniform aided the war effort. She was sufficiently impressed to borrow the idea of the WAACs from the British, including the name. She was determined that women who performed jobs for the military during wartime should receive the same benefits as the men in uniform with whom they worked. During World War I she had observed that American women working for the military "received no compensation of any kind in the event they were sick or injured—and many were." And she wanted to see them recognized as patriots, entitled to the same rewards from the state as men for the "faithful" discharge of their duties.[27]

Congresswoman Rogers was both a wise and witty woman. She told a reporter that she had "expected some of her male colleagues in Congress would smile and that some would rant— and they did." She was pleased, she added to the delight of the reporter, at Army chief of staff Gen. George C. Marshall's re-

sponse to her idea. He wrote the following memo to the House
Military Affairs Committee:

> In my opinion this proposed organization [WAAC]
> would provide a sound and practicable method for
> meeting military requirements with respect to the em-
> ployment of women. There are innumerable duties
> now being performed by soldiers that actually can be
> done better by women.
>
> Timely recognition of this situation and legislative
> action, which will enable the military establishment to
> absorb and utilize its proportionate share of the avail-
> able woman power, will contribute material to the suc-
> cessful accomplishment of the task before us.[28]

Secretary of War Stimson also wrote to the committee: "Had
it not been for the usual dilly-dallying of Congress the WAACs
would be even farther along in their training and numbers than
they are now."[29]

At least two of the military's top men saw the validity of using
women to fill noncombatant military jobs. Not so the Congress
of the United States. It took Pearl Harbor to move Congress
even to bring the WAAC resolution to the floor, eight months
after it was introduced. A full year after she introduced it, Rogers finally got her resolution passed in May 1942 and Oveta
Culp Hobby was named WAAC director.

The Women Accepted for Voluntary Emergency Service
(WAVES), the Navy branch for women, was authorized in July
1942. Both the WAAC and the WAVES were operating by the
time Nancy Love's WAFS were made official. The Coast Guard
would follow suit in November 1942 with the SPARs, which
stands for Semper Paratus—Always Prepared, the Coast Guard's
motto. The Women's Reserve of the Marine Corps would debut
in February 1943. Congress finally made the WAAC into the
Army's official women's military branch in July 1943 and the
name became Women's Army Corps or WAC.

Nancy Love's WAFS, however, were not the same thing. The
others were large organizations with thousands of women performing primarily clerical and communications tasks similar

to those they were already engaged in as civilians. They were militarized, or soon would be. Love's was a highly specialized and quite small group in Army terms—an all-woman squadron (Squadron #1) to consist of twenty-five, possibly up to fifty, proven women pilots. They would be hired by the Ferrying Division and attached to the 2nd Ferrying Group at NCAAB in Wilmington, Delaware. They were *not* militarized.

The afternoon of September 10, 1942, following the announcement by the Secretary of War, Nancy Love returned to Wilmington to continue her search for qualified women pilots.

✈ 7 ✈
Two Women Pilot Groups

T he *New York Times* printed the story on September 11, accompanied by a photograph of Secretary of War Stimson, General George, and Nancy Love—who wore a hat and gloves as women did in 1942. Love is holding up her right hand to take the oath of allegiance as the head of the newly formed Women's Auxiliary Ferrying Squadron, Ferrying Division, Air Transport Command.

Jacqueline Cochran arrived back in New York from England on September 10, took one look at the *Times* front page the next morning and left immediately for Washington, D.C. She met with Hap Arnold that same day. She brandished a copy of the *New York Times*. What was this story all about?

Arnold told her he had "given instructions to prepare and submit plans for use of women pilots but that he had not seen the plan that had apparently been activated and that the announcement had been made without his knowledge and was not in accordance with his own intentions."[1]

The following footnote in Lt. Col. LaFarge's "History of the Air Transport Command: Women Pilots in the Air Transport Command," tells it differently.

> Miss Cochran suggests strongly that the establishment of the WAFS was slipped over on General Arnold.... This is hardly possible. As indicated above, General Arnold acted on General George's memorandum of September 5th, which set forth the plan fully. The original plan was that General Arnold, himself, should make the public announcement, and General George and Mrs. Love were invited to his office on the morning of September 10th to meet the press when it was made. When they reached his office, they were advised that he had been unexpectedly called out of Washington, and that the Secretary of War would make the announcement. They proceeded to the latter's office accordingly. (Interview, Mrs. Love with Lt. Col. Oliver La Farge.)[2]

Cochran drafted a memo to Arnold dated September 11 that stated, "The use of a few of our women pilots to ferry trainer planes is just one segment of a larger job to be done." Failing to properly coordinate all the women pilot resources would be wasteful, she claimed. Besides, she reminded Arnold, "The top job is what you told me I would do and is the one I have been preparing to do during the past year.... The announcement made yesterday will throw this larger plan into confusion unless you clarify immediately."[3] Handwritten below the typed contents is the following: "It was this broader phase President Roosevelt had in mind when he sent me to you last summer [1941] on his own initiative."[4]

Cochran claimed that while Arnold was in England during the summer of 1942, he had told her "the time was approaching for the activation of a women pilot program at home and that she should close out her work in England and return home to take over this new phase."[5] Cochran says that Arnold added: "I suggested that she return and left the time to her but suggested that she not wait too long."[6] Hap Arnold had promised Cochran the leadership role in a women pilot's organization.

Arnold called General George and Col. C.R. Smith, to his office. In Cochran's presence, Arnold told them that the project should be revised and that they should work it out with her for she knew his views.

General George went to work, and by the following day (September 12), he had drafted a two-part memo to General Arnold. In that memo, he suggests that the ATC's plan to employ approximately fifty experienced women ferry pilots go forward but that no extension of training of additional women pilots be planned by the ATC. The ATC, he points out, *did not have the facilities*. However, he continues, the Flight Training Command *did have the facilities* for such training. He suggests that use be made of the same basic program of flight training being used for male cadets. "The present program in progress with the Flight Training Command (FTC) is readily adaptable to the requirement of the women's flight training program. After graduation, women pilots should be assigned to or employed by ATC for flight duty. After assignment to ATC, they would have no further tie with or responsibility to the training program." And he added that Jacqueline Cochran would direct the women's pilot training program.[7]

On September 15, Arnold announced publicly that Cochran would form and lead a second women's program, the Women's Flying Training Detachment (WFTD), to train—through the FTC—more women pilots to ferry airplanes for the ATC. Also on September 15, on General Arnold's instructions, Cochran met with representatives of the ATC, the Air Staff, and the CAA to develop a plan based on General George's memo.

Colonel Tunner, not realizing how big a storm was brewing, sent Capt. James I. Teague as the ATC's representative to that September 15 meeting. Teague, a lowly captain, was flanked on one side by a determined Jacqueline Cochran and on the other by fellow officers who held the rank of colonel or higher. They hammered out the plan for the training and use of women pilots.

From the beginning, Teague was uneasy about the proceedings. He thought Cochran had it in for the ATC and the Ferrying Division. In Teague's opinion, she still wanted to be director of *all* the women pilots flying for the Army and have them organized into a separate women's corps answerable to her. She was looking for ways to undo what had been done.

Captain Teague observed the back and forth of communications in the days following the September 15 meeting and drafted a memo to Colonel Tunner dated September 22 expressing his growing concerns: "I have a definite feeling of suspicion in regard to the actions of Miss Jacqueline Cochran. This is principally a hunch, but I am convinced that we should probably do something about it, and convey to General Arnold our attitude toward her." He goes on to describe how Cochran made it plain in the meeting that she "considered herself the only person who could efficiently be in charge of the Women Ferry Pilots," though Teague states that this was done by innuendo.[8]

Teague told Tunner that he was asked to agree to have "one of our flight officers or transition officers at Wilmington give the flight check, and not to let Mrs. Love give a flight check on a woman who had already been flight checked by Miss Cochran.... Miss Cochran, as far as the public is concerned, is coming to us and bringing us women who have been trained, and we should be appreciative. I, on the other hand, fear the Greeks bearing gifts."[9]

Cochran knew the Army couldn't publicly renege on the WAFS. "Complications unfavorable to the program would have resulted," she later wrote. Accordingly, she "recommended that the ferry squadron set up be left 'as is' but that the training program be started promptly." In a press conference, Cochran said the ATC had not made a careful check of the available pilot material.[10]

Colonel Tunner, reporting to General George to tell him what had transpired at the September 15 meeting, summarized the plan for use of the WFTD pilots in writing, and added a critical sentence. *"[Graduates] will be employed at Headquarters, 2nd Ferrying Group, Ferrying Division, ATC ... only if they meet the basic requirements for the position of women civilian pilots (including physical examination and flight test) and not because they have graduated from the course outlined above."*[11]

Tunner believed he had the right to turn down WFTD graduates if he felt they didn't meet Ferrying Division standards. General George, fearing General Arnold's wrath, continually cautioned Tunner to go easy in that direction.

Another bone of contention was a "director of women pilots." Nancy Love had been appointed director of a women's squadron. The Ferrying Division felt it had no need for a director of "all" women pilots as the women would be serving under the sector commander for whom they flew, just as the women who would be flying for the 2nd Ferrying Group would be under Colonel Baker's command. General George's memo to General Arnold clearly stated that.

> The present plan of organization for women pilot groups is that they will be organized into squadrons of fifty women each, each squadron to report directly to the Sector Commander of the sector to which they are assigned.
>
> Squadron No. 1, recently announced by AAF, will report directly to the Sector Commander, Ferrying Division, Baltimore, Maryland. Subsequent squadrons will report to other Sector Commanders. Mrs. Nancy Love will supervise the first squadron; there will be other squadron leaders as other squadrons are activated.[12]

The top man in the Air Transport Command had outlined Nancy Love's orders. Later she was referred to as senior squadron leader. And Cochran had the go-ahead to put in motion a facility to train women pilots to fly for the Ferrying Division.

If only Cochran had been satisfied.

Deborah G. Douglas summed it up in her article "WASPs of WAR": "Cochran felt wronged. She met with Arnold ... and it was not an exercise in diplomacy; it was a display of rage and raw political power. It was clear to Arnold that Cochran was not playing games and that he had to make good on his promise."[13]

Arnold had a war to fight. He had more important things to worry about than playing power games with a well-connected, determined woman. He took the easy way out and let her blame the ATC for what had happened even though he had full knowledge of George and Tunner's efforts throughout the summer of 1942 to form a women's ferrying squadron.

Cochran accepted Arnold's explanation, took it very much to heart, and never forgot it. From then on, she blamed the ATC, General George, Colonel C.R. Smith, the Ferrying Division, Colonel Tunner, and Nancy Love for what she perceived as an attempt to wrest from her the leadership of the women pilots that she felt was hers by right. WASP author Byrd Granger goes so far as to finger Smith as Cochran's main nemesis. Granger wrote: "ATC—C.R. Smith—never lost a chance to swift-kick Jackie. Too bad, that. C.R. is an able fellow. And a dangerous enemy."[14]

Hap Arnold had intentionally surrounded himself with bright young men. His instructions to them: "Think of the problems confronting us. Think of the solutions to those problems. Bring in new ideas. Don't get mixed up with the routine operations of this office. Think of the future of the Air Force! ... I turned people loose and forgot about them." The Air Transport Command, he said, was a case in point. "Once it had established its bases around the world, and General George and Gen. C.R. Smith were operating it, I was able to forget about it...."[15] Arnold had handpicked Smith, put him in to do a job and basically left him alone, as he said he would. Yet, in Smith, Cochran found her scapegoat. That C.R. Smith became one of Nancy Love's most powerful and staunch supporters—as well as her friend—may have contributed to this.

"The ATC was not interested in large numbers of women pilots, but only in securing pilots of either sex who met its standards," Lt. Col. LaFarge states in his history, based on his personal observation. What created the problem was that Cochran was determined that the ATC would accept all the women flyers that graduated from the Training Command's school. Colonel Tunner felt he had the right to employ only those who met the ATC's standards. Captain Teague, who had faced Cochran personally at the September 15 meeting, was particularly concerned and informed Colonel Tunner that he felt Cochran wished to extend her authority beyond supervision of the training program to some form of control over the WAFS within the Ferrying Division. He was afraid that "Miss Cochran will take inch by inch and try to move in on us."[16]

Douglas concurs:

> ... Cochran made it quite clear that she was holding the ATC accountable for its actions, and she would do everything possible to take control of the WAFS away from it.... The two women's pilots programs were highly visible pawns in this struggle—Cochran had recognized this fact in her first encounter with Robert Olds. Love was not ignorant of the dynamics involved, but she did not believe it was appropriate or useful to exploit the situation. Cochran had no qualms about pressing her views.[17]

On September 1, 1942, the Army had no women's flying programs. By September 15, it had two.

A news story in the September 25 issue of the *Washington Daily News* caught Colonel Tunner's attention. It quoted Cochran, "Yes, I've been called back by General Arnold to be head of a women's air corps in this country. Our goal is 1,500." Fewer hours would be required of recruits in the future, she went on to say. "I've had such success with my girls in England that I know this will work."[18]

Colonel Tunner was *not* happy. He did not like Cochran's tactics. He was *not* going to have pilots who couldn't meet Ferrying Division standards flying for him. He asked a friend in London to do some checking for him. The American women pilots with the ATA were doing just fine, the man reported. But Jacqueline Cochran had created a stir with her flamboyant behavior, causing some resentment on the part of the military. He added that Cochran had had no role in the training procedures in England. She had held a volunteer, administrative position with the ATA, coupled with an honorary commission.[19]

Tunner was not averse to having more women pilots. If they could meet his standards, he would welcome them. Again, General George cautioned Tunner that he would have to step carefully in order not to alienate General Arnold.

Nancy Love was in Wilmington, beginning to get candidates in response to her telegrams and the newspaper publicity. She went about her task, working with Colonel Baker to select from those candidates the women who could best do the job of ferrying airplanes for the Army.

Jackie Cochran soon would be on her way to Texas to set up the women's flight training facility and recruit her first WFTD trainees. However, Douglas points out, "Cochran's success in playing hardball politics came at a stiff cost. She had alienated the people and organizations who should have been her most important allies: Love, the ATC, Oveta Culp Hobby and the WAC."[20]

Hardball was not what the Army brass had expected. They were used to dealing with a different kind of woman, as was borne out by those individuals who had already been appointed to lead the various women's military corps being formed. Hobby, commander of the WAAC (to become WAC) was the wife of a former Texas governor. She also was a well-known newspaper and radio executive. Mildred McAfee, selected to head the WAVES, was a former president of Wellesley College. Dorothy Stratton left her post as Dean of Women at Purdue University in 1942 to join the WAVES. Soon after, she was appointed director and captain of the Coast Guard Women's Reserve, the SPARs, which she also officially named. Ruth Cheney Streeter was serving as the first woman president of the Morris County (New Jersey) Welfare Board when she was appointed director of the United States Marine Corps Women's Reserve in 1943. Jeanne Holm, who enlisted in the WACs and, after WWII, rose to the rank of Major General in the U.S. Air Force, writes: "The best thing [these women] had going for them were their backgrounds and personal qualities—experience with women, basic intelligence, and ability to get along with people."[21]

Nancy Love fit right into this group. Jackie Cochran did not.

"Unlike Cochran, Love recognized the need for flexibility and compromise," Douglas writes.

> Essentially, she acted on the belief that experienced
> women pilots could offer modest assistance to the

war effort, but that they could not do so as long
as the top brass squabbled over the details. In her
mind, it was far better to get the flying started and
then work out the details. This attitude reveals one of
the fundamental distinctions between Cochran and
Love. Cochran wanted to administer a training program that produced women pilots for the military;
Love knew she and others already had an exceptionally high level of flying experience and that this might
be useful to the military.[22]

The world was changing. The war was bringing about an up-
heaval that affected all walks of life and in the long run, the role
of women would be one of the most changed. The fight for the
leadership of the Army's women pilots was on.

General George had observed Love throughout the summer of
1942 and the September skirmishes and he was impressed with
her good judgment and calm, discreet manner on the job. Command was not her goal. She wanted to fly. But command is what
she got. And she proved to be good at it. She *was* ambitious. She
believed in what she was doing and was confident in her ability
to recruit like-minded women pilots to perform a specific set of
duties. Love led by example by continuing to fly on the job.

Did she have selfish reasons for doing this? Of course she
did. Love was smart, she was flexible, and she was an astute
pilot: an aviation professional. "On the surface, Nancy played
the game," says WAFS Barbara (B.J.) Erickson London. "She
was practical, sensible, reserved. But underneath was this bub-
bling cauldron, a desire to accomplish things. And she was very
strong-willed."[23] Love wanted to better herself in her chosen
field and be given the opportunity to use her skills and to perform. She had received high marks for her work with the Airmarking project. Joe Gwinn had put a lot of faith and trust in
her. She obviously had ability. She had worked hard to build
a reputation. Now she had the opportunity to capitalize on it.
Nor was Nancy Love immune to pride. She may not have been
competitive by nature, but she certainly didn't want to lose
something this important, something she had put a lot of time,

thought, effort, and heart into. She was not going to walk away from the opportunity of a lifetime.

So if she didn't actually seek the command position, what did she really want? Her rock-bottom prime motivation was pure and simple: she wanted to fly the Army's airplanes—all of them, the bigger, the faster, the better! A patriot, typical of the mindset of many Americans in WWII, she also wanted to serve her country, but preferably from the cockpit of an Army airplane rather than flying a desk.

Power did lie at the root of motivation for most of the women who flew. Mid-twentieth-century America ran on power—the power of machinery. A woman who could master a machine, a mechanical marvel like an airplane, moved to yet another dimension. Iris Cummings Critchell, WASP Class 43-2 who majored in aeronautical engineering and learned to fly in college, describes it this way: "Flying and the mastery of flight was a physical and technical challenge. I loved learning each different airplane, its systems and characteristics, and to learn to fly it well."[24]

To master the controls of an airplane meant freedom to soar above the earth unfettered. As Louise Thaden, writing about the experience of flying and the sensations of flight, put it: "Flying is the only real freedom we [women] are privileged to possess."[25] Pilot/author Margery Brown said, "Flying is a symbol of freedom from limitation."[26]

Love discovered that power and that freedom early. She had found a way to both use and enjoy it, and she was going to fight for it. But the struggle to keep the WAFS concept intact and to keep Cochran's hands off it did affect Love adversely. To General George and Colonel Tunner she may have appeared, outwardly, to be calm and collected. One did not give in to adversity, show one's feelings. One kept all agitation and anger inside. That was how a well-brought-up woman—a lady—reacted. Nancy had learned her mother's lessons well.

As the unsettling events of mid-September 1942 played out in Washington, Nancy vented her displeasure to the one person she could with impunity—her husband. This was done via long distance telephone as he was stationed in Washington and she in Wilmington. He also wrote her several letters during that time.

"My golly, don't get upset like that again when I can't do anything about it," he wrote September 12, 1942. "There is nothing certain in this shift and the General is ready to take things in hand if they try it." (Presumably he meant General George.) Bob goes on to try to lighten his message with some humor. "Such notorious *pipple* [*sic*] the Loves. I have become Mr. Nancy Love as we once joked about, but I love it."[27]

September 13, 1942, was a really bad day for Nancy because General George's memo had gone to Arnold and she had no idea how it had been received. Everything she had worked for was on the line. And while the tempest was building in Washington, she had to keep her mind on the job at hand. Women pilots were descending on Wilmington for interviews and flight checks. She had decisions to make.

Early in October, Love received a letter from Maj. Gen. Robert Olds. He was most pleased at her appointment. "I think one of the smartest things we ever did after the Jackie Cochran flare up [referring to January 1942] was to lay low, quietly, give you the opportunity to work into the system at Baltimore, keeping your eye on the situation at Hagerstown, and be in the most favorable and strategic position to take over when the higher-ups were finally forced to see the necessity for it. I know that you can handle the job and build it up far beyond the scope authorized at present."

Love and Olds had not taken Arnold's January "no" as final.

"Keep your chin up. Be firm and patient," he writes. And then adds a prescient warning, "Watch your weather like a hawk."[28]

✈ 8 ✈

The Originals Gather

First to arrive was Betty Gillies, age thirty-five, of Syosset, Long Island.

Betty and her husband Bud knew the Loves socially through the Aviation Country Club on Long Island and the annual seaplane cruises. The two women had begun to establish a solid friendship. Both were active in East Coast chapters of the Ninety-Nines. Love served on the nominating committee for the New England Section in 1937 and then as a voting delegate for the Section during Betty's two-year term (1939–1941) as international president.[1]

On receipt of Love's telegram, Betty asked her husband, Bud (B.A. Gillies), "What should I do?" And he answered, "Isn't that just what you have been preparing for and wanting to do? Go, of course."[2]

Bud Gillies was a vice president and engineering test pilot for Grumman Aircraft and Betty was listed as a utility pilot, flying a Grumman Widgeon twin-engine airplane. Her job was to fly the engineers and the Navy inspectors to their urgent wartime meetings. She also picked up needed parts from satellite manufacturers and flew them back to the factory on Long Island.

Both had been flying since the 1920s. Any other response would have been totally out of character.

Betty Gillies was one of the charter members of the Ninety-Nines and it was she who, during her term as president in the late 1930s, led an early battle against the Civil Aeronautics Authority (CAA) over pregnancy regulations. It was a personal crusade as during that decade she was in the process of becoming the mother of three children while continuing to fly. Betty's contention was, if a woman can't fly while she's pregnant or during her recovery period afterwards, she can't get in her required ten hours in six months to keep her hard-earned commercial license. If she lost her license on that kind of technicality, then she would have to take all the tests over again after the baby came. It wasn't fair, she said. And it was potentially expensive.[3] She and the Ninety-Nines were successful in having these regulations modified as well as in exposing the exaggerated views of the dangers of flying to a pregnant woman.[4]

When Bud had said, "this is what you've been preparing for," he knew his lady. Throughout her term as president of the Ninety-Nines, Betty had urged the membership to think ahead to potential service to their country and to upgrade their skills should the war widen to include the United States. She spoke at luncheons, wrote articles, and served as a reliable source for the news media in its write-ups telling of the need for pilots in the coming hostilities. When Love's telegram came, Betty Gillies was ready for the commitment.[5]

Betty and Bud Gillies had two school-age children at home. Right before Christmas 1941, the Gillies' youngest child, a daughter, had died at age four of leukemia. Friends and family thought being part of the first all-woman ferrying squadron attached to the Army was a way for Betty to get her mind off the family tragedy by using her considerable aviation skills to help the war effort. Bud's position with Grumman was critical to the war effort and made him exempt from the draft. And, to further ease the decision, "Mother Gillies," Bud's mother, agreed to help care for the two children, ages eight and nine, in Betty's absence.

*Nancy with Betty
Gillies in a PT-19.*
Courtesy Love family;
electronic image NAHF.

The day after she received Love's telegram, Betty flew to Wilmington to learn just what might be expected of her if she became a pilot for the military. "You don't have to stay for long," Love told her. "Just the first ninety days until we get started." For Betty Gillies, those ninety days turned into twenty-eight-months. In her diary she noted:

> I didn't get back to New Castle AAB until [September] tenth. I took the train down because the weather was lousy in the morning. But it cleared in time for me to get my check flight with Lt. Joe Tracy in a Fairchild trainer. Lieutenant Joe was a civilian pilot before they let him into the ATC, so his flight test didn't have any surprises. We were out about fifty minutes. Then after a bull session with Nancy Love, I caught the train for home.
>
> I guess I'm going to join the WAFS. Bud thinks it's very worthwhile trying out, and so do I. We have to sign up for three month stretches and duty begins on September 21.[6]

She was the first woman after Nancy Love to sign up for the required ninety-day commitment. She finished setting up arrangements for her children and reported for duty at 8 a.m. on September 21. By then, nine WAFS, counting Betty and Nancy, had passed their tests and moved into the newly opened BOQ 14: Cornelia Fort, Aline "Pat" Rhonie, Helen Mary Clark, Catherine Slocum, Adela Scharr, Esther Nelson, and Teresa James.

BOQ 14 had housed men up until then. Getting it ready for female inhabitants took some reorganization, including Venetian blinds to cover the windows. A ditch ran in front of BOQ 14. Love ordered wood planks installed to allow her pilots to walk across without tumbling into the mire below.

Both Love and Colonel Baker were concerned that the squadron was not growing as quickly as they hoped. But Love assured the colonel that many of the younger women who were eligible were under contract doing flight instructing for the military. In

Helen Mary Clark, the fifth woman to join the WAFS, being interviewed by Nancy Love, Colonel Baker (center) and two of his staff, mid September 1942.
Photo courtesy Texas Woman's University Library, WASP Archives.

December 1938, President Frankin D. Roosevelt had unveiled a trial program of subsidized flying instruction known as the Civilian Pilot Training (CPT) Program destined for college campuses. One woman could enroll for every ten men. Consequently, many air-minded college coeds learned to fly between 1939 and 1941. The program was the brainchild of the Civil Aeronautics Authority (to be renamed the Civil Aeronautics Administration in the 1940s and the precursor of the Federal Aviation Administration). CPT was based on similar programs tried in Europe and was expected to provide pilot training for 20,000 college students per year. The program was restructured in 1941 and renamed War Training Service (WTS). At that point, women were eliminated from the program.[7]

Before that happened, CPT turned out several of the young women who qualified for Nancy Love's WAFS in the fall of 1942. Other female CPT graduates were instructing through WTS. It would take them some time to fulfill their contracts and get away. CPT also provided a significant number of the young women who entered the Army's Flying Training Command school in Texas and who went on to earn their wings.

Eventually, in late September, the younger women began to arrive.

On October 6, Betty Gillies was named executive officer to act as Love's second in command. October 19 was graduation day for the first nine WAFS. Catherine Slocum, the wife of Richard W. Slocum, general manager of the *Philadelphia Evening Bulletin*, immediately resigned.[8] Their plans to care for their four children had gone awry and she was needed at home. By then a dozen more women had passed the flight test and the Army flight physical, had been accepted, and were in the midst of their thirty-day Army indoctrination program.

By the time the women began to arrive, Nancy had announced what kind of uniform the WAFS would wear: a tailored, gray-green wool gabardine jacket with squared shoulders, straight set-in sleeves, and a detached belt of the same material, trimmed with brass buttons. "The blouses (the Army name for the uniform jacket) will have four patch pockets and will be short—so as not

*Nancy Love
wearing the WAFS
dress uniform.*
Courtesy the Love family.

to interfere with parachute wearing," Nancy told the press gathered at New Castle AAB for the announcement. The gored skirt for street wear and the slim-cut slacks for flying were of matching material. Shirts and ties were of contrasting tan broadcloth. Brown leather low-heeled pumps, a brown leather shoulder bag, an overseas cap, overcoat, and gloves completed the outfit.

"The women will pay for their own uniforms and will be required to wear them while on ferry duty or at their station here." She added that the WAFS would wear the command insignia—the civilian pilot wings of the Air Transport Command—over the left breast pocket.

For flying, they were issued khaki flight coveralls (made to fit men, therefore far too large for most of the women), a parachute, goggles, a white silk AAF flying scarf and leather flying jackets with the ATC patch.[9]

The WAFS' first ferrying assignment took place October 22–23, 1942. Love appointed Betty Gillies to lead a flight of six L-4B Cubs, flown by six WAFS, from the Piper factory in Lockhaven, Pennsylvania, to Mitchel Field on Long Island. (The L-4B was a 65-horsepower, single-engine liaison plane, a Piper Cub.) Fort, Clark, Rhonie, Scharr, and James made up her team. The six wore their new uniforms for the first time.

Then on November 1, when the squadron stood at twenty, ferrying began in earnest. Throughout November and December, they ferried Cubs from Lockhaven and open-cockpit PT-19 Fairchild single-engine, 175-horsepower trainers to Army flight training bases in the South. "PT" stands for "primary trainers." The arrival of November also meant a change for the worse in weather. The women were frequently weathered in enroute and had to RON (remain over night). If the weather was particularly bad, it took them several days to get the planes to their destination.

Dorothy Scott, number twenty-five, arrived on November 21 and when she had passed her tests and been accepted, the squadron was considered complete. Twenty-five was the magic number toward which Love and Colonel Baker had pointed. The original WAFS in the order they joined were: Nancy Love, Betty Gillies, Cornelia Fort, Aline "Pat" Rhonie, Helen Mary Clark, Adela "Del" Scharr, Esther Nelson, Teresa James, Barbara Poole, Helen Richards, Barbara Towne, Gertrude Meserve, Florene Miller, Barbara Jane "B.J." Erickson, Delphine Bohn, Barbara "Donnie" Donahue, Evelyn Sharp, Phyllis Burchfield, Esther Manning, Nancy Batson, Katherine "Kay" Rawls Thompson, Dorothy Fulton, Opal "Betsy" Ferguson, Bernice Batten, and Dorothy Scott. Joining after January 1, 1943, were Helen "Little Mac" McGilvery, Kathryn "Sis" Bernheim, and Lenore "Mac" McElroy.

The original squadron would finally settle in at twenty-seven. Pat Rhonie left December 31 following a controversy with Colonel Baker. The story was that she spent an additional night away from base after the colonel told her to return. Some WAFS

*By early October 1942, the WAFS were hard at work in ground school,
including navigation, as shown by Gertrude Meserve, Catherine Slocum,
Nancy Love, Del Scharr and Barbara Towne.*

Courtesy of the National Museum of the U.S. Air Force.

thought she resigned after the incident. In an interview after the
war, Nancy Love told AAF historian Lt. Col. Oliver La Farge
that Rhonie was discharged. "This was done through normal
civil service procedures. She [Rhonie] was given a hearing before a board first. Male civilian pilots were discharged in this
way."[10] Rhonie later flew in England with the ATA.

On January 3, Helen McGilvery and Sis Bernheim passed
their tests. Lenore McElroy became the final member of the
original WAFS on January 23, 1943.

Catherine Slocum is not counted in the final twenty-eight because she never ferried. An early applicant and veteran Cub pilot, Alma Heflin McCormick, did not return with her 200-horse-
power rating. Pat Rhonie is counted because she ferried from
October 22 to December 31, 1942.

Love was the squadron's disciplinarian and initially had to act as housemother. She and Colonel Baker soon hired Mrs. Anderson ("Andy") to fulfill that function. "Before Mrs. Anderson came to us, she had been a housemother for wayward girls," Gertrude Meserve LeValley said. "You know, we were older. We weren't teenagers. I guess it just sounded better to our parents if we had a housemother. But several of the women were married and a couple had children."[11]

Once they had uniforms and a sufficient number of women to practice close-order drill, Colonel Baker ordered them to march in review every Saturday morning with the rest of the troops stationed on base. This was one function Nancy Love was *not* cut out for. Delphine Bohn wrote about the marching sessions in her WAFS memoir: "As our squadron commander, Nancy Love led the formation. The lovely voice with which she gave commands was painfully self-conscious and definitely untrained for such use. Her inability to develop a loud-mouthed 'hup, two, three, four' Marine drill sergeant style was legend." Then Bohn quotes Love herself, telling about her difficulties with close-order drill.

> We were obliged to learn close order drill. As Commander, I had to lead the formation and give the commands, which, because I was very self-conscious, was not one of my strong points. In fact, I so hated having to roar out orders that I occasionally drew a blank on what command to give next.
>
> One dreary morning when we were drilling on the inactive runway, the squadron was marching smartly down the paved runway toward its end, where there was a sharp drop-off of about ten feet. Panic struck me as we approached the precipice and I found myself incapable of giving the command, "To the rear—march!" So off went twenty-four girls, still in close formation and roaring with laughter. Straight down the embankment they went and into the field, leaving me standing at the top, still speechless.[12]

Nancy Batson had picked up a bad cold, but the group was going dancing one Friday night at Wilmington's posh duPont Hotel. Batson couldn't miss out on that, so she went, danced away the night, had a couple of drinks, and thoroughly enjoyed herself. Of course, when she had to get up the next morning to march in parade review at eight a.m., she could hardly drag herself out of bed.

"I got my robe on, staggered down the hall to Nancy Love's room and knocked. She was already dressed for the review. I said, 'Miz Love, I just don't think I can march this morning, I've got this *awful* cold and feel just lousy.'

"She said, 'Didn't I see you out dancing at the duPont Hotel last night, Nancy?'

"Well, I hung my head and studied my feet a minute. 'Yes, ma'am.'

"'Well then, Nancy,' Miz Love said, 'I think you can manage to march this morning.'"[13]

Nancy Love kept a close eye on her pilots' behavior. Not a hint of a scandal would be tolerated.

Teresa James remembers when she was summoned to Nancy Love's office. Someone had seen James out on the town in Wilmington dancing with another woman and had promptly reported the incident to Mrs. Love.

"I told her, yeah my sister Betty was visiting. I took her out on the town."

Teresa wondered what all the fuss was about. "Nancy told me it wasn't proper—that it was not the thing to do. I had never heard that. Back in Pittsburgh, we did it all the time. A lot of the guys won't dance. The only way the women can get out on the floor is to dance with each other."[14] The WAFS were turning into a real learning experience for Love. Still, she had to make sure her women were above reproach, custom or no. She suggested that Teresa not do it again.

Major General Jeanne Holm writes of the prevailing attitudes in 1942 when the Women's Army Corps (as well as the WAFS) was being considered: "This notion that women should be of high moral character and technical competence while no such standards were used for men set the tone for the double standards that were to characterize the women's [military] programs for the next forty years."[15]

Once the press got wind of the fact that women were being hired to fly airplanes for the Army, New Castle Army Air Base was deluged with reporters and photographers and requests for interviews. This, it seemed, was the story of the century. As was customary in the early 1940s, thanks to Hollywood's influence, Nancy Love was subjected to requests for cheesecake shots—photos showing lots of leg or bare shoulder. She heard many requests to "Give us a smile—a big one now" and "Show your teeth."[16]

"No one had anticipated the heavy, widespread publicity," Delphine Bohn writes. "The military was deeply affronted that this strange, multifaceted publicity could afflict them so. We were women looked upon as two-headed oddities. Everyone wished to examine each of us minutely. For some of us it was purely terrorizing."[17]

Many of the stories written and disseminated were blatantly incorrect, grossly exaggerated, or just plain fabricated. The Army tried to protect the women from the spotlight, but they were under not only the bright glare of publicity, but the microscope of public opinion as well. To their credit, not a word of scandal was ever connected with one of the original WAFS during the time they served Uncle Sam.[18]

Following several requests from magazines for ghostwritten accounts of WAFS on duty, Colonel Tunner put a ban on that type of publicity. "Stories of this type are not considered to be for the best interests of the Ferrying Division and will tend to over-glamorize the members of the WAFS."[19] But the word was already out.

The early arrivals established social rituals. Before dinner, Nancy, Betty, Pat, Cornelia, Helen Mary, and Catherine gathered in Nancy or Betty's room at the far end of the hall for cocktails. Rum and Coke, also known as Cuba Libra, was the odds-on favorite. Cocktail hour was a time-honored tradition in these women's homes. All but Cornelia were married and older, but Cornelia, at twenty-three, carried an elegant maturity about her despite her youth. Rhonie was divorced, which distanced her even further in life experience from the younger women who were now beginning to arrive. Betty, Helen Mary, and Catherine had children at home.

The other early arrivals—Teresa James, Del Scharr, Esther Nelson, and Barbara Poole—gravitated together. They considered the group at the far end of the hall to be a bit snobbish. Those women had come from a more social background, and—with the exception of Cornelia, from one of Nashville's prominent families—were East Coasters and members of the exclusive Aviation Country Club. Out of this arose the myth that *all* the WAFS were socially prominent women from wealthy families. Jackie Cochran once referred to them as "Nothing of importance. A bunch of society dames."[20] "Socially prominent and wealthy" applied to only a very few of the twenty-eight women who came to be known as "the Originals." Nevertheless, they were forever saddled with the "society women" label.

The twenty-eight WAFS never were all in the same place at the same time as a cohesive unit. Three didn't even join until January 1943, and, by then, Rhonie had already left. But ferrying is an individual effort, not the work of a team. Consequently, the emphasis of the unit was on independent initiative. The women training in Texas were together for several months, united as members of a class. They banded together rather like a sorority. The WAFS did not have that opportunity.

Once they began ferrying, eight to ten women would be gone on a trip, leaving eight to ten behind, some still in orientation training. They arrived at different times during the fall and tended to make friendships in twos and threes: those who arrived together, those who were the same age or from the same area, those who had similar outside interests.

Most close friendships were developed on ferrying trips where two or more WAFS would get weathered in enroute. They began—as women will do—to share their lives with each other in an attempt to ward off the boredom of being stuck on some airfield with nothing to do but wait out the weather.

In those days, the WAFS did fly in groups because they were ferrying slower airplanes that needed to refuel frequently and several were destined for the same base. But already the lonely nature of the job had been revealed to them—something that would become second nature when they began ferrying coast to coast alone.

✈ 9 ✈
Growing Pains

While Nancy Love was building her squadron that would eventually number twenty-eight, Jacqueline Cochran was in Ft. Worth working with the Army Flying Training Command (FTC) to organize and implement the Women's Flying Training Detachment (WFTD). General Arnold wanted 500 women pilots qualified for ferrying duty by the end of 1943. Training those women pilots fell to the Training Command. The ATC would employ them once they were trained.[1]

The ATC wanted recruits to have a minimum of 300 hours flying time to qualify for acceptance into the WFTD program. ATC lost that battle at the September 15 meeting. The compromise was 200, though Cochran said she didn't think there were more than 150 women pilots with 200 hours and that the ATC's demands were "ridiculous." She later denied using the word ridiculous.[2] That requirement was quickly dropped to seventy-five hours. "Limitations of hours will not be published. Individuals will be selected based upon their own qualifications," said an October 7, 1942, directive from the commander of the Training Command.[3] By April 1943, the entrance requirements had

103

changed again and the recruits needed only thirty-five hours: the time required for a private pilot's license.[4]

More than the number of hours had changed. The small number concept advocated by Nancy Love and Colonel Olds had been abandoned. The graduates of the training facility would be used for more than ferrying airplanes. Cochran's large number concept was here to stay.

General Arnold sent a directive to the training command dated November 3, 1942:

> Contemplated expansion of the armed forces will tax the nation's manpower. Women must be used wherever it is practicable to do so. It is desired that you take immediate and positive action to augment to the maximum possible extent the training of women pilots. The Air Forces objective is to provide at the earliest possible date a sufficient number of women pilots to replace men in every noncombatant flying duty in which it is feasible to employ women ... Courses of instruction should be designed to improve the ability of training pilots as well as training for women with no previous flying experience.[5]

Hap Arnold had reversed his original position. He was now firmly in the women pilots' camp.

While her ATC superiors dealt with the fallout from any attempts by Cochran to encroach on her territory, Nancy concentrated on her growing squadron and the initial ferrying trips her women pilots were to undertake.

Bob was about to embark on a six-week trip, during November and December 1942, to India and China. No longer a phone call away, he would be halfway around the world. Flying a DC-3, Bob covered the newly charted route known as Fireball: Puerto Rico, British Guiana, Brazil, across the Mid-Atlantic to Ascension Island, Nigeria, Egypt, Iraq and on into India. The ATC was pioneering its wartime supply routes to India. This would lead to establishing "the Hump" airlift over the Himalayas and the Burmese jungle to Kunming, China. Bob carried a special set of orders.

Delphine Bohn writes that Bob "was assigned to seek out over the supply line any stumbling blocks, unconscionable delays or dangers; and to learn the manner in which helpful improvements might be expressed. Along the route, [Bob] presented himself as a ferry pilot, making no fuss over his true status, thereby learning things about how these pilots were lodged and handled at different bases which he could never have discovered if he had aired his brass."[6]

While in India, Bob made two trips over the Hump to Kunming—one in a C-53 and one in a C-47—before returning to the United States. Now Nancy and Bob realized that their wartime separation was going to be over the long haul, not one of short duration. As it turned out, they would see little of each other for the next two years—not unusual in a war-torn world.

By December, change was in the air.

Nancy Love and six of her WAFS were to leave Wilmington on the train December 3, 1942, for Great Falls, Montana, to ferry 220-horsepower, bi-wing, open-cockpit Stearman PT-17s from there to Jackson, Tennessee. They were to join a group of male ferry pilots to get thirty-three trainers—recently returned by the Canadian RAF—to a training field in a warmer climate. But Love was called to Washington. When she got back she informed the others that she wasn't going, and they were leaving the next day. She named Teresa James flight leader. Something big was afoot.

Cochran now had her first class of twenty-five trainees at Houston Municipal Airport learning to fly the Army way. They had begun training November 16, and a second class of fifty women was to report in December. The Ferrying Division had to start making plans for incorporating these women into the WAFS. Colonel Tunner sent Love and several Ferrying Division officers to visit the other ferrying groups to determine if they could or would accept a woman's squadron and, if the answer was yes, the kind of arrangements needed to house and feed those women.

It so happened that Love and the officers arrived in Great Falls on December 11, the day before the flight of Stearmans was to take off for Jackson. They were there to talk to the command of the 7th Ferrying Group. The contingent had left Washington on December 8. Love flew copilot in the Lockheed C-36, twin-engine (450-horsepower each) cargo/transport.

While in Great Falls, Love met with her six WAFS and told them what was about to take place. The WAFS were being split up. A few would go to each of the Ferrying Groups who would accept women and they would form the core of the new squadrons. Some would remain in Wilmington. The women from Houston would arrive in the spring to augment the numbers of each of the squadrons.

Love and the male officers left Great Falls on December 13. They flew to Long Beach, home of the 6th Ferrying Group where Love checked out in the single-engine, 450-horsepower BT-13 basic trainer built at the nearby Vultee factory. On December 16, she flew an hour and forty-five minutes as pilot in command on the C-36 on the flight from Phoenix to Dallas, where she met with officials from the 5th Ferrying Group at Love Field.[7] Since World War II, people have made the mistake of thinking Love Field is named for Nancy or Bob Love or both. In fact, it is named for 1st Lt. Moss L. Love, of Wright County, South Carolina, the tenth Army officer to lose his life in an airplane accident on September 4, 1913.[8]

From there, Love went to Memphis to talk to the 4th Ferrying Group and to Romulus, Michigan (Wayne County Airport) where she conferred with the command of the 3rd Ferrying Group. She also flew as copilot in a twin-engine B-25.

Back in Washington, Love and the Ferrying Division officials compiled what they had learned. Women's ferrying squadrons would be formed at Love Field in Dallas under the 5th Ferrying Group; at Romulus under the 3rd Ferrying Group; and at Long

Beach under the 6th Ferrying Group—in that order. Florene Miller would command the Dallas contingent of Helen Richards, Dorothy Scott, Betsy Ferguson, and Love herself. The WAFS would be ferrying PT-17s, AT-6s, and twin-engine Cessna AT-17s.

Why did Love put Miller in charge? Because Love had bigger things in mind and would be stationed at Dallas only briefly. She planned to check out on every available aircraft in an effort to pave the way for her pilots to fly any and everything in the Army's aviation arsenal. And she would be making trips to Long Beach and Romulus to help start up the squadrons there. After that, she would travel between units to check periodically on her commanders and their charges. Now she truly was senior squadron leader.

What was Nancy Love's effect on the women under her command? Delphine Bohn sums it up: "All this took place as Nancy subtly pressured Operations for increased transition for the women. [Transition means to move up in the classification, size and power of aircraft.] Through necessity, Mrs. Love became a real artist in the promotion of progressive airplane transition for herself and for her squadrons. While at NCAAB, she had carefully researched her superiors and checked out problems of possible delayed transition plans, all of which might lead to permanent restriction to liaison and primary-trainer airplanes. Her research consolidation developed a helpful data bank."[9]

Del Scharr would command the Romulus group consisting of Barbara Donahue, Barbara Poole, Katherine Thompson, and Phyllis Burchfield. Lenore McElroy joined the group in January. There, the WAFS could ferry L-2Bs (Taylorcraft, single-engine 65-horsepower), L-5s (Vultee, single-engine, 185 horsepower), PT-23s (single-engine, 220-horsepower), PT-26s (Fairchild PT-19s with cockpits enclosed with a canopy), AT-19s (280-horsepower, single engine), and AT-6s.

Leader of the Long Beach contingent would be Barbara Jane (B.J.) Erickson and stationed with her would be Cornelia Fort, Evelyn Sharp, Barbara Towne, and Bernice Batten. The women of Long Beach initially would ferry BT-13s built at the nearby Vultee factory. The remaining ten would make up the Wilming-

The women sent to the 6th Ferrying Group in Long Beach: Barbara Towne, Cornelia Fort, Evelyn Sharp, Barbara Jane Erickson and Bernice Batten.

Courtesy the Barbara Erickson London private collection.

ton women's squadron with Betty Gillies in command. Helen Mary Clark would be her executive officer.

Life in the WAFS would never be the same.

As 1942 ended, twenty-four WAFS were engaged in ferrying Cubstuff (liaison airplanes) and PT-17s and 19s. Love did not begin ferrying until January 1943, and even then her activities were limited because of her desk job and command responsibilities.

When the six who ferried the Stearmans returned to Wilmington from Jackson on New Year's Day, Pat Rhonie was already packed and gone.

More changes were coming. The Ferrying Division had decided—considering winter weather restrictions, small gas tanks and frequent refueling stops—that the Cubs could be delivered faster by removing the wings and shipping them by rail to the bases down South. The WAFS assigned to other ferrying groups were going to come in contact with more and different airplanes, most of them bigger than the 175-horsepower PT-19s they now were ferrying.

Two classes of young women recruited by Jacqueline Cochran were now in training in Houston. They began on civilian-type airplanes, but military replacements had been ordered: PT-19s, to be followed by basic trainers and then advanced trainers.[10] Advanced training meant the AT-6, a most desirable airplane to fly. Nancy Love did not wish to see her women's flying abilities and experience eclipsed by the trainees in Houston. Keeping up, in fact staying ahead of them, was a necessity to her.

However, Colonel Baker was satisfied having his WAFS in Wilmington ferrying the Fairchilds out of Hagerstown. He didn't think they needed to advance, or possibly that they even were capable of it. They were doing the job they were hired to do. Conversely, Love's intent was to check out in all classifications, size, and power of military aircraft available. No sooner did she get her feet on Texas soil, than she focused on the 650-horsepower, single-engine AT-6. She checked out on it January 3, 1943.

Love flew an AT-6 into Romulus on January 13 to help establish her new squadron. The weather closed in and she was grounded for several days. When the low ceiling finally lifted enough to fly, if only briefly, Love flight-tested Lenore McElroy in the AT-6. Lenore was a thirty-five-year-old flight instructor with 3,500 hours. The wife of a Romulus ferry pilot and mother of three teenagers, she was accepted, and on January 23, 1943, became the final original WAFS.

On January 25, 1943, General Arnold's office sent a message to Colonel Tunner stating that, from that date, the Ferrying Division would employ only those women who had graduated from the Women's Flying Training (WFT) school in Texas. "This was a big blow to the Command," says Betty Gillies. "There were still many eligible women pilots and the first graduates from WFT would not be available until mid-May—almost four months away—and the pilot shortage continued to be a matter of great concern."[11]

One of those who just missed the deadline was Love's old friend from Airmarking days, Helen Richey. Richey had served with the ATA, flying some eighteen different single- and multi-engine British airplanes from spring through the end of 1942. When Cochran returned to the States in September, she put thirty-two-year-old Richey in charge of the ATA's American women flyers. But Helen resigned in January 1943 to return to the States. She contacted Cochran about joining the women's ferrying squadrons. In spite of Richey's experience—she had more than 2,000 hours and had flown for the airlines—and even though the Ferrying Division desperately needed experienced pilots, Cochran sent her to Texas as a member of Class 43-5.[12]

In February, Love asked for a transfer from Dallas to Long Beach where her third new squadron was to be located. Though she was going there to help with the organization of the new squadron, uppermost in her mind was advancement in aircraft in which she was qualified. Many of the airplanes flown by the Army Air Forces in World War II were built in the LA Basin. Love planned to fly them all. "She wanted to see if her stature and strength—and therefore most of her girls' stature and strength—would be a limiting factor," Barbara Erickson London says. "Were there complications? She was looking not just at her limitations, but others' as well."[13]

Love, at five-feet six-inches, 125 pounds, was close to the median of the WAFS. Cornelia Fort, Del Scharr, Helen Richards, and Esther Nelson were considerably taller and Betty Gillies, Phyllis Burchfield, and Bernice Batten, at the other end of the measuring stick, were five feet or five feet one. In this quest for advancement, Love had the tacit approval of Colonel Tunner to fly any airplane she felt she could handle.

Love had set her sights on the P-51, the fastest of the single-engine, single-seat pursuit aircraft. Pursuits, as they were called during WWII, were fighter airplanes and carried the P designation. The single-engine pursuits were the P-39, P-40, P-47, P-51, and P-63. The twin engine pursuits were the P-38 and P-61.[14] They were high-performance aircraft and tricky to fly.

The first step in transition was to fly the AT-6 from the back seat, with an instructor in the front seat. The big engine coupled with the bigger tires in the front and the small tail wheel in the rear put the pilot's view of the world at a decided angle. This, combined with the bulk of another human being in the front seat, made it difficult to see over the engine cowling. In the taildragger pursuit planes like the P-51, P-40, and P-47, forward visibility was limited. So, the fledgling pursuit pilot had to learn to look to the sides of the runway when landing and taking off and to execute a series of S-turns for visibility when negotiating the taxiway.

Delphine Bohn describes Love's P-51 checkout: "She familiarized herself with the technical specifications and one sunny morning Nancy met at the end of an isolated runway a high-ranking officer in a P-51. The officer traded places with her, gave her a cockpit check and waved her off. Both were happy with the success of her flight."[15]

Her instructor was an old friend, Maj. Samuel C. Dunlap, III, at that time the Operations Officer, 6th Ferrying Group at Long Beach.

This was a far different flight from her first solo, at age sixteen, back on August 31, 1930. This time she was wedged down in that form-fitting, one-person cockpit with Sam squatting on the wing beside her. In 1930, Jimmy Hansen had squatted on the lower wing of that old tandem Fleet Biplane they had flown together. Just as Jimmy had grilled her on the Fleet's flight characteristics, Sam grilled her on the Mustang's. The difference was, Jimmy had flown with her until he was satisfied she could handle the Fleet by herself. In the Mustang, her first flight *was* solo. Whether she got off and landed safely was completely in her hands.

The moment of truth for a fledgling pursuit pilot comes when she sits at the end of the runway and stands on the toe brakes to keep tenuous control on all that pent-up power—to keep the aircraft grounded a few more critical seconds. When Love released the brakes on that Mustang and pushed the throttle to the firewall, the airplane surged forward. When the tail lifted, she could

Nancy Love on the wing of a P-51 Mustang, Long Beach. On February 27, 1943, she became the first woman to fly the swift pursuit, paving the way for one hundred or more other pilots who would follow her.

Courtesy Love family; electronic image NAHF.

see straight down the runway. Wind under the wings, the airplane lifted and climbed swiftly into the California desert sky.

The Mustang, she discovered, flew like any other airplane, only faster. The response to the stick and rudders was immediate and sweet. For an hour, she practiced maneuvers aloft. Then she began her descent, bleeding off altitude and, finally, set up for her landing. She entered the downwind at the required forty-five-degree angle and, moments later the Mustang was down and rolling along the runway. When asked later about her historic flight, Love said, simply, that she felt "the same lonely but wonderful feeling you get on your first solo."[16]

Major Dunlap signed off in her logbook. "Qualified at Long Beach, Calif."[17]

The date was February 27, 1943. A woman had just flown one of the fastest airplanes ever built.

Evelyn Sharp, Barbara Towne and B.J. Erickson were the next three to check out in the P-51 after Nancy Love.

Photo courtesy of Diane Bartels.

"Boy what news your call brought! You've just about reached the top!" Bob wrote to her that very same night, after learning from her via telephone that she had flown the P-51. But he also wrote, "I'm so afraid you will be so famous and involved with things that you won't care for the things that we have longed for before."[18]

That concern would resurface in Bob's letters a little over a year later.

Love made her second and third P-51 flights on March 1 and 2. Those were her last. As much as she took to the swift pursuit, she never again noted that particular airplane in her logbook. The model Love flew was an A-36/P-51 with a 1325-horsepower Allison engine.[19] This was an older model than the high-altitude performance P-51 C and D, equipped with a Merlin engine that the women pursuit pilots of the Ferrying Division flew throughout 1944.

Nor did Love ever fly the other single-engine pursuits, the P-47, P-40, or P-39. She left those to the other women ferry pilots.

Getting ready to check out on the C-47: Evelyn Sharp, Nancy Love, Barbara Towne and B.J. Erickson.

Courtesy Love family; electronic image NAHF.

Instead, she concentrated on twin-engine aircraft—including the twin-engine pursuit, the P-38, and the A-20 attack bomber—and, eventually, graduated to four-engine aircraft. Methodically, over time, she worked her way up the list.

Love also took her first flight in a C-47 (twin-engine/1200-horsepower each, cargo/transport plane) on February 27. On March 5, B.J. Erickson joined her as copilot in one, the first of many times the two would fly that and other airplanes together. On the East Coast, Betty Gillies was getting ready to fly the biggest pursuit of all, the P-47. Built by Republic, it was known as the "Thunderbolt," or just "The Jug."

Between January 12 and March 7, Gillies moved through transition despite Colonel Baker's aversion to women flying heavy, high-horsepower aircraft. He finally allowed Gillies's transition in the big pursuit because Nancy Love had told him, quite frankly, that his reluctance to let women transition into high-powered aircraft was the reason she transferred out of Wilmington and went to Dallas.

In preparation, Gillies got orders to go to Farmingdale, New York, where the Republic Aviation factory on Long Island built the P-47, and meet with the control officer. "He had me play with the landing gear and other equipment. He answered every question I had."[20]

Petite Gillies had only one problem with the P-47. She couldn't reach the rudder pedals of the monster pursuit and still see out of the cockpit. So she asked a pilot she knew who worked with her husband at Grumman Aircraft—a man not much taller than her five-feet one-inch—to make her a set of blocks to go over the rudder pedals so that she could reach and control them with her feet and still see out. He had done the same thing himself in order to be able to fly some of the bigger aircraft. With the blocks in place, Gillies, with fifteen years of flying experience and some 1,500 hours in the cockpit, began her quest.

On March 8, 1943, she flew the mighty single-seat, single-engine, 2300-horsepower Thunderbolt. After her first flight, she put in fourteen hours practicing landings at New Castle and made a required cross-country with landings at two other airports. On May 4, 1943, she ferried her first P-47. It was the first pursuit delivery made by a woman pilot.

✈ 10 ✈
Killed in Service of Her Country

✈ ✈ ✈ ✈ ✈

The blackest days Nancy Love faced during World War II were March 21-27, 1943. On March 21, one of her original WAFS, Cornelia Fort, died in a mid-air collision near Merkel, Texas. Fort had been with Love from the beginning, arriving in Wilmington only a day after Betty Gillies.

✈ ✈ ✈ ✈ ✈

On Sunday, March 21, 1943, Fort and six male Long Beach ferry pilots took off to deliver BT-13s to Dallas. Stories of what happened vary. Fort's biographer, Rob Simbeck, writes in *Daughter of the Air* that Fort agreed, if somewhat reluctantly, to practice formation flying over sparsely inhabited West Texas between Midland and their destination, which was Dallas. The WAFS' instructions were to stay 500 feet away from any other airplane. But, according to Simbeck's sources, apparently Fort chose to ignore the order.[1]

The official Army accident report reads: "On March 21 at approximately 15:30 CWT (Central War Time) seven ships

116

were proceeding East in formation, in the vicinity of Merkel, Texas. Of these seven ships, one BT-13A flown by Civilian Pilot Cornelia Fort and [a] BT-13A flown by F/O Frank E. Stamme, Jr., were involved in a mid-air collision."

The report continues to say that the landing gear of Stamme's aircraft apparently struck the left wing of Fort's aircraft, causing part of it to break off. The left wingtip of Fort's airplane was wood, and the right wingtip was metal. Stamme's aircraft did not go out of control but Fort's rolled and went into an inverted dive. There was apparently no attempt to recover or to use the parachute. The emergency latch on the hatch release was found to be locked. Judging from the condition of the propeller blades, power was completely retarded after control was lost. [2]

Stories circulated that the young male flyers were horsing around and harassing Fort, who may have had more flying experience than they did but did not have the formation flying or advanced aerobatic training they had. However, Barbara Erickson, Fort's squadron commander at Long Beach, says: "They were in two or three airplanes out there in the middle of nowhere trying to fly formation. I don't think there was anything malicious about it. I think it was a plain accident."[3]

Whatever the cause, Cornelia Fort, one of Nancy Love's first recruits, was dead.

Word spread quickly through the WAFS' ranks. Cornelia was well-liked and, though she was quiet and kept to herself, all her fellow WAFS knew she was a solid flyer and an extraordinary person. From the beginning, Fort had planned to write the history of the WAFS. She had kept diaries of her entire aviation career and already was preparing to commit those jottings to a memoir about the squadron and its exploits, once the war was over. Fort had witnessed, first-hand, and already written about the bombing of Pearl Harbor. A flight instructor at Honolulu's John Rodgers Airport, she was flying with a student on the morning of December 7, 1941. They were shot at by a Zero but managed to land safely in a hail of bullets.[4]

Love, though she had faced the loss of her brother ten years earlier, had never been affected quite so deeply by death. Intellectually she knew that Cornelia, like all of her WAFS, had come of her own free will. But suddenly Love had been thrown into a new, unfamiliar role, that of a wartime commander who had just lost a trusted lieutenant.

Years later, Nancy Batson said that she thought Nancy Love never truly recovered from Cornelia's death. The WAFS, the original squadron, was her creation. She had hand-picked her pilots. Now she had lost one of them. And she would have to endure the deaths of two more. Nancy Love would not attend those two funerals. She would send another of the Originals to represent her. Nancy Batson was one of those who would later take a fellow Original home for the last time.[5] But Nancy Love did attend Cornelia's funeral. She and B.J. Erickson flew a C-47 from Long Beach to Nashville, March 25. Maj. Samuel Dunlap—the Operations Officer who had checked Love out in the P-51—accompanied them. Love and Erickson were actually on orders ferrying the C-47 to North Carolina, but with an approved stopover in Nashville.

Erickson wrote a letter home to reassure her parents that she, herself, was all right. In the letter, she described many of her feelings, and Love's, over the two-day ordeal. The letter is excerpted throughout this chapter, with Barbara Erickson London's permission.

> Wednesday night (March 24th) Major Dunlap, Nancy and I left Albuquerque about 10 p.m. and flew non-stop into Nashville and arrived there at 5:30 a.m. Thursday morning. It was fairly bad weather—rain, etc.—most of the way and Major D. did most of the flying and Nancy and I alternated flying co-pilot and trying to sleep on the floor in the navigator's place.
>
> When we arrived, it took quite a while to finally get a hotel room as nearly everything was full, but finally did. We cleaned up, ate breakfast and by that time it was 8:30—so we called Mrs. Fort for we knew she was waiting to hear we all had arrived OK. From then on, the day was one terrible one. We went out to their home about 10 and met Mrs. Fort and all the family. Naturally they wanted to know everything and we couldn't tell them anything. It gave me

the creeps talking to all these bereaved people about
something I didn't know anything about.[6]

The Army had released no information and Nancy and B.J.
were as much in the dark as the family regarding details of the
accident.

Because of the Fort family's standing in Nashville society,
and because of Cornelia's popularity with a wide assortment
of friends, the funeral in Christ Episcopal Church was very
nearly a state occasion. Love, Erickson, and Major Dunlap—
all in uniform—led the processional up the aisle of the church.
Cornelia was buried in Mt. Olivet Cemetery next to her father.
The inscription on her footstone reads "Killed in the Service of
Her Country." Fort was the first woman pilot to die on active
military duty in U.S. history.

Love didn't speak at the funeral—she couldn't. She felt inca-
pable of handling such an ordeal. But she wrote a letter to Cornelia's mother. "My feeling about the loss of Cornelia is hard
to put into words—I can only say that I miss her terribly, and
loved her. She was a rare person. If there can be any comfort-
ing thought it is that she died as she wanted to—in an Army
airplane, and in the service of her country."[7]

Rob Simbeck interviewed Fort's first flight instructor, Aubrey
Blackburne, who shared and commented on a letter Nancy Love
later wrote to him. "She said she felt she owed it to me to tell
me that the military investigation following the midair collision
completely exonerated Cornelia of any blame in any way," Blackburne said. "She also said, 'If it'll be of any consolation, Cornelia
was at least unconscious, if not dead, from the collision, because
she was too good a pilot not to have cut the switch and turned off
the gas before crashing.' And I agreed with her because Cornelia—she wasn't afraid. If the last thing she was conscious of was
that she was going in, she still was absolutely not afraid."[8]

"Nancy lived in an ordered world. Everything she did was
well thought out and concise. Those who worked with her assumed the same position," says Barbara London. "She did not
emote, she handled herself and the situation calmly."[9]

"A commander often appears to be cold," WASP Iris Critchell (43-2), who knew Love, observes. "Nancy had an aloofness about her. She cared, but she couldn't remove the control. This is what happens if you're willing to be a leader. You have to handle the situation and stay detached. Most of the women flying came from flight instructing or from air show experience. They hadn't progressed to the point of taking on such a big responsibility. But Nancy had."[10]

When the funeral was over, Erickson, Love, and Major Dunlap flew to Washington, D.C. They had aboard two crates of oranges for General Arnold and they had to deliver them. This gave Nancy a chance to see Bob. The C-47 they were ferrying was not due in Maxton, North Carolina, until March 27. Erickson took advantage of the RON and rode the train to Wilmington to visit her old squadron mates.

Nancy and Bob had less than twenty-four hours together, but she had lived and aged a lifetime since she last saw him. He helped her through some needed soul-searching. The WAFS, unlike men in combat, did *not* live with death as a constant companion, unless one looks at the element of chance. Anyone can die tomorrow—or today. But they were *not* serving in a foreign country, they were *not* near the front lines, they were *not* under fire. What they were doing was ferrying airplanes from one place to another. Given the fact that accidents happen, any one of the ferry pilots—male or female—could crash and be killed at any time. However, the fact that they were professionals and good at what they did went a long way in protecting them. That is why Colonel Tunner insisted on accepting only the most qualified—the best. He wanted impeccable credentials, he wanted the most hours and experience he could get from his people *before* they set foot in one of his airplanes—*before* those expensive airplanes were placed in those pilots' care.

In March 1943, the women ferry pilots were on the threshold of flying the Army's newest, hottest, airplanes off the assembly line. Nancy Love didn't want to "think" about the possibility of an accident happening; the possibility of one of her pilots dying.

✈ 11 ✈
Transport and Transition

To date, there was no transport system in place to return ferry pilots to their home base after they delivered a plane, which meant that days could be wasted as these pilots made their way home by any means possible. Male ferry pilots were allowed to hop—or hitch—a ride in a military airplane. WAFS were required to return via commercial airliner, train, or some other mode of public transportation.

The regulation specified that WAFS were not "to solicit rides in bomber-type aircraft either for local flying or for cross-country flying without specific authority from the Group Commander." This was to protect their reputations. The problem was *not* concern over the moral character of the WAFS, rather that the newspapers would publicize this fact and give gossip-mongers a chance to question the women's reputations.[1]

"If the WAFS are to succeed, our personal conduct must be above reproach," Nancy Love told her women pilots early on. "There cannot be the faintest breath of scandal. Among other things, this means you may not accept rides with male pilots. If a male pilot and a WAF were seen leaving a plane together there would be suspicions that they were playing house in government property."[2]

Until March 1943, the ability to hop rides was the only real distinction between male and female ferry pilots. On March 17, the Ferrying Division forbade women to fly copilot with male pilots on bombers. On March 25, the women of the 3rd Ferrying Group in Romulus found themselves even more severely limited in what they could fly. Down came four policy changes:

- The women of the 3rd would be allowed to fly only light trainer aircraft. This meant no transition into basic or advanced trainers or twin-engine aircraft;
- Women would not be given assignments as copilots on bomber ferrying missions;
- Women would not be allowed to transition on any high-powered single-engine or twin-engine aircraft. Numbers two and three meant women couldn't "build time" or work on transition in different airplanes as copilots to male pilots other than their instructors;
- In order to further protect their morals, women would make their deliveries on alternate days from the male pilots. AND, they were to be—if at all possible—sent in opposite directions.[3]

The Director of Operations for the Ferrying Division penciled the following comment on a copy in the Ferrying Division files: "Mrs. Love objected to this directive."[4]

More than likely, Nancy Love was livid when she read it.

Then on March 29, ATC headquarters sent a letter to group commanders stating that no woman was to be assigned to flying duty when pregnant and that women were not to fly one day before, through two days after, their menstrual period.[5] The restriction meant a wasteful eight or nine days of non-flying time a month per WAFS.

Male staff had become concerned about the physiological problems of women in relation to flying activities. Should a woman fly when pregnant? Should a woman fly during her menstrual period?[6] By then one of the original WAFS, Esther Manning (Rathfelder) was pregnant. However, Betty Gillies, Esther's squadron leader at Wilmington, already had solved the problem. Gillies let Esther fly until she couldn't get the stick back in the cramped confines of the PT-19s she was ferrying. Then Gillies grounded her and put her to work as Operations Officer, thus allowing Gillies and her executive officer Helen Mary Clark to get out of the office and fly more.[7]

Nancy Love had no problem with the morals protection issue, but the restrictions in transition went against everything she had hoped to accomplish. Now this latest order oozed Victorian absurdity. She went over the heads of both Group and Ferrying Division Commanders and appealed the menstrual period ban and the prohibition on transition to her friend Gen. C.R. Smith, Chief of Staff of the ATC. She risked Colonel Tunner's ire by ignoring the chain of command and was, in fact, not in his good graces for a period of time after that.[8]

General Smith, in a letter dated April 17, 1943, addressed Nancy Love's concern about the transition restrictions. The Ferrying Division, he said, had imposed certain flight limitations on women pilots without consideration of individual professional qualifications. "It is the desire of this Command that all pilots, regardless of sex, be privileged to advance to the extent of their ability in keeping with the progress of aircraft development."[9]

Love had achieved an important victory. The WAFS *would* be allowed to transition into bigger, more complex airplanes. This put the WAFS program in line with the practice of Britain's ATA, which required its pilots (male and female) to begin on the lightest and simplest aircraft and work up through progressively more difficult types of aircraft to the highest level suitable for each individual pilot. Pilots progressed as far and as fast as their skills and temperament allowed without them being under any compulsion to keep pace with other pilots or being subjected to the fear of washing out.[10]

The fact that Love's WAFS had an almost perfect accident record certainly drove the decision. By then, Cornelia Fort had been exonerated of any blame in her fatal accident. And the only other accidents had been a couple of bent propellers following ground loops.

The ATC Flight Surgeon thought pregnancy was a disqualifying condition for flying, but he agreed with Love that the menstrual period should be regarded as an individual problem to be regulated by the local WAFS leader and the station Flight Surgeon "when his assistance was required."[11] Obviously, Love's talk with C.R. had convinced him. He had listened to her complaints and moved to rectify them. She had stepped in on the side of reason and won her point.

On April 26, Colonel Tunner withdrew the March 29 directive relative to WAFS not flying during menstruation and the March 17 order forbidding a woman to fly copilot with a male pilot. The WAFS now could transition on multi-engine and high-powered single-engine aircraft in keeping with their individual experience and ability. Still tiptoeing around the morals issue, the directive did say that *normally* the WAFS would be given transition on cross-country checkouts by other fully qualified WAFS "when and if available."[12] Love's concern about a "playing house" allegation remained.

Bob Love, on an ATC assignment in England in April 1943, wrote to Nancy regarding her visit to their friend C.R. Smith. "I do hope you made out all right in the talk with C.R. and that you got your way without getting your head chopped off."[13]

A few months later B.J. Erickson in Long Beach dealt with Barbara Towne (Dickson) the same way Betty Gillies had dealt with Esther Manning. Towne, who was married to an AAF pilot, checked out on the P-51 the summer of 1943, before her pregnancy began to show. She flew the hot pursuit until she, like Manning, couldn't get the stick back, and then went home to have her baby. Towne rejoined the squadron for a short time, but eventually stayed home to care for her son. Manning rejoined the squadron in Wilmington after she gave birth to a son in summer 1943 and continued to serve as Gillies's operations officer until fall of 1944.[14]

Nancy Love's leadership in transition was paying off. By mid-February 1943, the women stationed in Dallas and Long Beach had begun to fly the BT-13. In Wilmington, the women still flew only PT-19s and PT-26s. In Romulus the women ferried only primary trainers and liaison planes, and the weather often kept them grounded.

The ferry pilot's mission was very different from the combat pilot's mission. "The job of a combat pilot is [to risk] his life and his ship in order to inflict serious damage upon the enemy," Colonel Tunner wrote. "But in the Ferrying Command we had to have different standards. The mission of our pilots was ... to fly skillfully and safely and deliver those planes in good condition."[15]

A fledgling Air Transport Command had learned in 1942 how to best train ferry pilots, the men who eventually would ferry four-engine bombers and fully-loaded, four-engine cargo planes over oceans, deserts, and mountains all over the world. "We could hardly expect our new pilots to step into four-engine planes and fly them over long distances on instruments, but the problem answered itself," Tunner wrote. "I set up a program of on-the-job training in which the pilots actually performed the mission of the Command at the same time they bettered their flying. Thus those at the bottom of the ladder would deliver the simplest forms of aircraft, such as artillery spotting planes and primary trainers. As they built up their flying time in these basic types, they would also be going to ground school and instrument-flying school, preparing themselves for the next step up. Gradually ... they worked their way from short hops in trainers on clear days to delivering the largest aircraft all over the world."[16]

This solution worked for the women ferry pilots as well. They started out flying cross-country in little single-engine liaison planes and PTs. However, the Ferrying Division soon realized that if it allowed the women ferry pilots to remain static, flying only the smallest airplanes at the bottom of the transition ladder, the men who needed to begin at that level in order to work their way up would be denied that valuable training. Keeping the women on the lowest level would create a bottleneck.

The solution was to let them transition up as well. This way, the women gradually would gain the confidence, experience, and skills necessary to be ferry pilots capable of the swift and safe delivery of any airplane placed in their charge. That was what the training school down in Houston and then Sweetwater was designed to accomplish. That was what the ATC found it needed to do with the women ferry pilots it employed.

In April 1943, Colonel Tunner and his Ferrying Division staff established their pioneering pilot classification system for rating pilots as to the type of airplanes they were qualified to fly. All ferry pilots—male and female—carried a card stating their classifications, which were:

> Class I—qualified to fly low-powered single-engine airplanes (examples, PT-17, PT-19, PT-26, Cubs);
> Class II—qualified to fly twin-engine trainers and utility planes (examples, UC-78, AT-9);
> Class III—qualified to fly twin engine cargo/medium transport planes and on instruments (examples, C-47, C-60);
> Class IV—qualified to fly twin-engine planes in advanced categories, such as attack planes, medium bombers and heavy transports (examples B-25, A-20, A-24, A-25);
> Class V—qualified to fly the biggest airplanes, four-engine bombers and transports (examples B-17, B-24, B-29, C-54) and able to deliver them overseas;
> Class P-i—qualified to fly single-engine (P-51, P-47, P-40, P-39, and P-63) and twin-engine (P-38 and P-61), high-performance pursuits or fighters. The small "i" after the P denoted instrument rated.[17]
> The P-class was a special class. *These fast and hard-to-handle planes required skill and experience, but the flying of fighters was not, in itself, of great experience value in working up to the big four-engine planes.*[18] (Emphasis added.)

When Colonel Tunner explained the new classification system at a staff meeting on April 28, 1943, he specified that women pilots would be classified the same as the men.[19]

What also became apparent was the fact that since ferrying pursuit did *not* further a male ferry pilot's movement up the classification ladder to qualify for overseas duty, why have him transition into pursuits? Why not let the women, who *were not* going overseas and who *were* qualified, ferry those airplanes? That is exactly what began to happen after April 1943, a critical point to remember in the light of later developments.

The ATC also established its own airline. Twin-engine transports and the pilots who flew them performed the personnel transport job for the ATC, primarily taking ferry pilots back to base. The airline was nicknamed SNAFU—situation normal all fouled up. That was the polite translation.[20] Each base typically had only one airplane for such use.[21]

April saw many problems ironed out and May became a month of significant firsts. Betty Gillies delivered her first P-47 on May 8, 1943. Helen Mary Clark became the second WAFS to check out in the "The Jug." By the end of June, the two of them had accounted for the delivery of seventeen P-47s. A new era of ferrying was dawning for the WAFS. They were beginning to deliver the Army's glamour ships, the swift, powerful pursuits.

Some reluctance remained when it came to the women flying the hottest pursuit of all, the P-51. But Colonel Tunner stuck to his guns when questioned by his staff. "The WAFS [will] fly everything they are capable of flying."[22]

Stationed in Long Beach where she could fly just about everything the AAF offered, Love had the best of all worlds. Her administrative duties necessitated flying around visiting her other squadrons periodically to check up on how smoothly they were running. She wanted to fly airplanes, not a desk. Between December 1942 and June 1943, she notched checkouts in twelve aircraft—single and twin-engine, including the P-51 and the B-25 twin-engine medium-range bomber—and she had flown copilot in a four-engine B-24.[23]

On May 1, the first twenty-three women from the training school in Texas arrived, split equally among the four WAFS squadrons. Overnight, the WAFS nearly doubled in size. Colonel Tunner eyed his doubled strength of women pilots—forty-nine—

Nancy was the first woman to check out on the B-25.
Photo NCAAB Public Relations Office, courtesy the Love family.

looked over his shoulder at Jacqueline Cochran's continued activity, and decided that he needed Nancy Love at headquarters.
By early June, the number of WAFS had climbed to ninety-two
with the arrival of the second class at the ferrying bases. Love
reported to Ferrying Division headquarters, now located in Cincinnati, Ohio, June 25, 1943.

Jackie Cochran, of course, knew that the women in flight training in Texas were destined to serve in the Ferrying Division—Love's
domain. Surely this didn't sit well. However, General Arnold's November 3, 1942, directive to the Training Command emphasized
that women pilots could be considered for a variety of jobs.[24] Cochran began to look for other flight-related jobs the women pilots
could perform, just as she had envisioned back in 1939.

In May 1943, Cochran sent a lengthy letter to General Arnold listing all the reasons why she should be in charge of the
entire women's flying program. The following are excerpts:

> The group of women Ferry pilots has been more than
> doubled by the first small class graduated ten days

ago. The next class ... will make the Ferry group about 500 percent it's [*sic*] original size. By the end of the year, there will be nearly 1000 in flying service and in training....

My own idea is that before this group of girls is militarized, they should be moulded into a smooth running unit with problems relating to them in operations discovered and solved, and routines established.... [and] when they are militarized [the Army Air Forces] should leave them a separate unit directly under the Air Force.... You need eyes and ears in whom you have confidence to follow this women pilot program for you. They must be experienced, qualified eyes and ears, and they must be feminine. That's the job I would like to do, and which I think I can do well.... You and I had this job in mind for myself from 1941 on.[25]

General Arnold agreed with her.

On June 28, 1943, the Office of Special Assistant for Women Pilots was established and Jacqueline Cochran was named Director of Women Pilots. Her duties were to decide where the women pilots could best be used and place them accordingly; establish acceptance and graduation standards; set rules of conduct and see to the women's welfare; draw up plans for militarization; and make regular inspection visits to the women's units.[26] The official announcement of Cochran's title was made to the press July 5, 1943.

Neither the ATC nor Colonel Tunner was notified as to what this announcement meant to Nancy Love and the women ferry pilots. Tunner's response was that the intent appeared designed to interfere with the Ferrying Division Command regarding women pilots and that he disliked the idea of having to explain his reasons every time he found it necessary to issue orders.[27] Tunner made an appointment of his own. On July 5, the War Department also announced the appointment of Nancy Love to the position of Executive for WAFS on Colonel Tunner's staff.[28]

Cochran believed her position gave her the power to administer the assignments, activities, and regulation of *all* the women pilots flying for the Army. Tunner and the ATC believed it was their prerogative to regulate their own people, and that included treating male and female personnel in like manner. The latter became an increasingly larger bone of contention.

The July 5 announcements unleashed the press. The newspapers had been on constant lookout for a way to get news about the two experimental programs involving women pilots. After all, that was the kind of juicy stuff the public wanted to know about. Tunner had put a lid on publicity about the WAFS after several erroneous articles appeared the previous winter. Cochran had done the same regarding stories on the girls in training. The press was anxious for fresh fodder.

Now they had it. *Newsweek's* July 19 article, with photos of Love and Cochran, was headlined "Coup for Cochran."

> Last week came a shake-up ... even the Air Forces weren't agreed on which of the photogenic female flying chiefs would outrank the other. The ATC maintained that Miss Cochran's job was merely advisory and not superior to Mrs. Love's executive post. But officials at Air Forces headquarters insisted that Miss Cochran had "highest authority" over women pilots: "If the Air Transport Command is not already aware of this, they will have to be made aware of it."

Under their photographs ran the caption: "Miss Cochran and Mrs. Love: which one bosses women fliers?"[29]

WAFS Del Scharr writes in her memoir: "The media took the opportunity to exploit the tussle for supremacy between the two women and to toss out just enough half-truths to make their stories more saleable."[30]

Marianne Verges agrees: "The newspapers and magazines had a field day with the shake up in the women pilots' program, playing up the rivalry between Jackie and Nancy. They made Jackie's appointment seem like a victory in an ongoing war. Up until now this war had been undeclared, but from July 1943, onward, the careful guarding of command prerogatives versus the aggressive attempts for headquarters-staff control often overshadowed the accomplishments of the women pilots—and in the long run contributed to their doom."[31]

Nancy and her commanding
officer, Gen. William H. Tunner.
Courtesy Love family; electronic image
NAHF.

Colonel Tunner's promotion to brigadier general came a week after the July 5 announcements. His second memorandum, on July 14, further spelled out Nancy Love's duties. She was to advise the Ferrying Division Headquarters as to the best use of the WAFS; plan the allocation of the WAFS to the various Ferrying Groups; plan and supervise training standards and a progressive air-training program; and "formulate rules and regulations governing conduct, morale and welfare of the WAFS." This was intended to counter the listing of Cochran's duties as Director of Women Pilots.[32] The memo also was designed to stimulate interest among WAFS to fly the more advanced aircraft coming available for ferrying and thus avoid stagnation on lighter types of airplanes.

The other shoe dropped on August 5. All the Army's women pilots—the original WAFS and the WFTD graduates now serving as part of the Ferrying Division's WAFS, and those recently transferred to Camp Davis in North Carolina as well as the WFTD trainees down at Sweetwater—would now go by the name of Women Airforce Service Pilots or WASP. The acronym WASP bore Cochran's PR-savvy touch and it encompassed all the women pilots, no matter where and for whom they were serving.

"We went to bed WAFS and woke up the next morning WASPs," said Betty Gillies.[33]

All along, Cochran wanted to use women pilots for more than ferrying and successfully convinced Hap Arnold of that plan's feasibility. Once she was named Director of Women Pilots, she activated her plan. In early July she took several graduates of Class 43-3 away from the Ferrying Division and sent them to Camp Davis to learn to tow gunnery targets.[34]

That was only the beginning. More graduates would be sent to other commands to fly a variety of airplanes and missions. The name "ferrying squadron" no longer accurately described what the many women pilots flying for the Army were doing. In changing the name, Cochran brought a more comprehensive name to the services the women pilots were now performing.

Nancy Love, now spending a lot of time behind a desk in Cincinnati, wondered what was next. Other than a desire to fly more, she was, at that point, doing what she wanted to do. In an interview years later, she described her job this way: "My duties involved administration of six WASP ferrying squadrons [two were still to come as of summer 1943] and planning of operational and training procedures. In addition, and this was the 'fun' part, I went through transition on each type of military aircraft and ferried at least one of each kind before that particular class of airplane was released for WASP training and subsequent ferrying."[35] The explosion of numbers in the squadrons proved to be manageable, though with the added personnel she had added headaches. Love was adept at handling these. The confidence of Generals Tunner and George in her was rewarded.

Uniforms were now a point of contention. General Tunner had written to the Secretary of War concerning a proper uniform for the newly arrived graduates of the Texas training facility. He noted that more than sixty new women pilots on the job in July wore whatever they pleased on duty—"attire dictated by individual taste." He suggested that a uniform slightly different from that of the original WAFS would be appropriate and that the original WAFS then could continue to wear theirs.

Cochran considered the WAFS' uniform too drab. The newly designated Director of Women Pilots hired a fashion designer from Bergdorf Goodman in New York to come up with something for the WASP. The result was the now familiar dress uniform of Santiago Blue—a sharp looking, lightweight wool gabardine jacket and skirt of an attractive shade of dark blue, accompanied by a matching beret and a pair of silver wings. The work uniform consisted of a waist-length battle jacket and slacks of blue wool gabardine to be worn with a blue shirt—cotton in summer and flannel in winter. In addition, the women would have blue cotton coveralls. Accessories included a black calfskin utility bag, black calfskin shoes with buckle, and black calfskin gloves. A putty-colored trench coat of weatherproof wool gabardine topped off the outfit. It had a removable dark blue lining.[36] Tunner never did like the new uniform because his WAFS were being forced out of the uniform he knew they wore with pride.

Coinciding with the name change and the proposed new uniforms came Nancy Love's one-year anniversary at the helm of the WAFS. Though the Ferrying Division doggedly held on to the name WAFS after August 5, the usage began to disappear as the name WASP gained both official sanction and general popularity. Up until this point, Love had fought to keep her concept and her command viable. Though Love's position with the Ferrying Division never changed—she was now referred to as the Executive for WASPs in the Ferrying Division—Cochran was calling the shots for the growing WASP organization. Some 500 women were in training at Sweetwater at any one time and the number on active duty grew with each graduation.

The year of the WAFS was over. The year of the WASP had begun.

✈ 12 ✈
A B-17 Bound for England

In his memoir *Over the Hump*, General Tunner recalled that in early summer 1943, the Command was getting static from male pilots who objected to ferrying B-17s over the North Atlantic to the United Kingdom. "These flights had become almost routine and there was no reason for complaint. I decided to let a couple of our girls show them just how easy it really was."

Before his promotion to brigadier general in July, Tunner called Nancy Love into his office and told her that he was assigning her and Betty Gillies to ferry a B-17 to England. "Our number one and number two pilots leaped at the chance to be the first women to ferry a plane overseas. We had scheduled a blitz movement of two hundred B-17s and I assigned the two women to one of those planes."[1]

Though he liked both women and respected them as pilots, Tunner was not out to make heroines of Love and Gillies. That was the farthest thing from his mind. Already he had used the women ferry pilots to prove to the men how routine most jobs in the Command could be. Four WAFS had ferried PT-26s from

Hagerstown to Alberta, Canada, in record time. In another coup, two women had just checked out on the problematic P-39, the pursuit the men called the flying coffin. Once again, Tunner was going to use women to prove his point.

The ATC had begun to make plans for massive deliveries of B-17s and their crews to England via the route known as Snowball. This route—from Gander, Newfoundland, or Goose Bay, Labrador, to Prestwick, Scotland—was used in 1941 during Lend Lease to deliver goods and airplanes to Great Britain (like Cochran's June 1941 flight). Now, in 1943, the U.S. used it to deliver its own airplanes to the AAF squadrons stationed in England.[2] In July 1943, at their commanding officer's direction, Love and Gillies began the biggest transition of their aviation lives.

The Boeing B-17 was characterized as "rugged, stable and easy to fly, it carried the war to the heart of Germany and was universally loved by its crews for bringing them home despite extensive battle damage." The wingspan is 103 feet and the airplane is 74 feet long. Empty, it weighs 32,720 pounds. Loaded, 55,500 pounds. Powered by four Wright 1,200-horsepower radial engines, it has a maximum speed of 300 miles per hour at 30,000 feet, and its range is 1,850 miles.[3]

Love and Gillies faced extensive preparation. Betty kept a daily diary throughout the war. Here are some of the notes she wrote in July and August 1943 about events leading up to their B-17 transition and a flight across the Atlantic.

July 11—Got number one typhoid shot and vaccinations.

July 12—[The following is underlined in red in her diary.] Received TWX from HQ: Commanding Officer, 2nd Ferrying Group, NCAAB—It said: "Commanding General desires that Mrs. Gillies be checked out in B-25, both day and night, and that she be sent to instrument school at your group." Signed Tunner.—Began sandbagging in a B-25 each day at Wilmington. [Sandbagging is observing in the cockpit from behind another student pilot and an instructor. The two student pilots change seats part way through the flight.[4]]

July 19—Received letter from Cincinnati HQ. Ordered to drop everything for instrument school. Began instrument school.

August 3—Received Army instrument rating. Got ninety percent on written. Did extremely well in flight check. B-25 transition follows.

August 8—Awaiting orders to head for Cincinnati HQ. Ordered to Fort Myers. P-47 delivery with Teresa James. [Teresa James checked out on the P-47 on July 5, 1943.]

August 9—Arrived Cincinnati HQ. Met Nancy Love at the field. We sat in a B-17 and refreshed ourselves with systems and cockpit layout.

August 10—Nancy and I will be pilot and co-pilot with Captain Forman as our instructor, Lockbourne Field, Columbus, Ohio.[5]

Love's logbook for the same time frame shows the following:

July 24-29—Instrument School, Romulus, Michigan: 11 hours 45 minutes under the hood in a single-engine BT-13 and then a twin-engine C-78.

July 30—Local check, instrument, Romulus: C-73—one hour under the hood.

July 30—Cross-country check, Romulus-Cincinnati: C-73—two hours under the hood.

August 6—Cincinnati-Evansville-Cincinnati: C-73—2 hours 45 minutes.

August 9—Cincinnati local: B-17E—copilot—one hour with Capt. Forman.[6]

Love and Gillies were ready to begin cross-country training, including night flying, night landings, instrument operations and full operation of the B-17, all under the careful tutelage and watchful eye of their instructor, Capt. Robert D. "Red" Forman. Their training took place at Cincinnati and at Lockbourne Army Air Base the B-17 base in Columbus, Ohio. Tunner and Forman had met when Tunner commanded the Memphis, Tennessee, Air Corps Detachment in 1939. Tunner was recruiting Reserve pilots and Forman was one of the best. He got him in the Reserve and when war was declared, Forman went where Tunner went. He was, among other things, Tunner's copilot on the Hump in 1944–1945. Forman eventually became Brigadier

General Forman who commanded Military Air Transport in Europe in the 1960s.[7] Tunner trusted him implicitly, which is why he turned Love and Gillies's training over to him.

In her logbook for August 10, Love lists a sequence of landings and a short flight that ordinarily wouldn't attract attention. However, August 10 in Middletown, Ohio—a town located about 100 miles southwest of Columbus and 30 miles north of Cincinnati—was a most important day in that town's history. She and Forman flew B-17E #41-2550 to Middletown and landed the big bomber on the 3,500-foot grass runway at the local airport on State Route 4.

Two newspaper stories told of the big day.

Middletown's Aeronca Aircraft Corporation and its employees were scheduled to receive the coveted Army-Navy "E" Award—presented for excellence in the production of war equipment. An Army Air Forces general was the guest speaker and a Navy lieutenant commander presented "E" award lapel pins to every man and woman employed at Aeronca. The "E" pin was a sign of distinguished service, something war workers wore with pride. In addition, the company received a large "E" flag to be flown over the plant signifying their excellence in furthering the war effort.

"Huge B-17 Bomber Lands at Local Airport for First Time in the History of the Municipal Airport," one headline proclaimed.

"It was a gala day for the citizenry of Middletown as well, for the entire town seemed to have turned out to pay tribute. The high-ranking Army and Navy officials plus an assemblage of leading lights in the aviation field—builders of sky giants—plus an imposing list of invited guests added luster to the resplendent and decorative grandstand," the *Aeronca Wing Tips* reported, and went on to add this noteworthy piece of information: *"A guest in the form of a Flying Fortress, which alighted on the field during the ceremony, was a messenger of additional good will."*[8] (Italics mine.)

Seated on the banks of the hydraulic canal adjacent to the airfield—watching the action much as they did from the bleachers at Cincinnati's nearby Crosley Field when the Reds were at home—was sixteen-year-old Wally Baldwin, along with some of his high school buddies. From their privileged perch, they watched in awe as the big B-17 came in for the landing. "It was the biggest thing we'd ever seen," said Baldwin.[9]

Baldwin's father Bert worked for Aeronca and he, too, was there August 10, in the audience waiting to receive his "E" pin. The ceremony began at 3 p.m. and, according to the newspaper account, lasted twenty-six minutes, though it seemed much longer to Wally. The newspaper said that the ceremony was short because the workers had to get back to their jobs, "more anxious than ever to add the stars to the 'E' flag."

Aeronca, builder of the L-3 liaison plane, as well as PT-19 and PT-23 primary trainers during the war, was the first "light plane company" to receive the "E" award, making the day and the celebration even more special. The company also built elevators for Boeing to be used on the B-17. And that, says Baldwin, is why the Army sent the B-17 to Middletown that day.

It so happened that the day before, Nancy Love had made her first B-17 flight with Red Forman. Likely, Forman used the short flight to Middletown to give his student needed cross-country experience and cockpit time.

Baldwin's father and others in Middletown were convinced that Love herself flew the big bomber in—alone—landed it, and took off because, apparently, Forman never got out of the plane. The only pilot people saw alight from the B-17 was a woman, Baldwin says. That woman was Nancy Love. Considering the B-17's lack of bathroom facilities, she probably needed to use the restroom.

Because of the length of the runway, the B-17 had to make a short-field landing. This meant it had to be at minimum fuel and weight. The bomber came in on a southwest approach over the Miami River and landed southwest to northeast to avoid wires at the northeast end of the grass runway. When they left, they took off the opposite direction—northeast to southwest, again to avoid the wires. The river curves around the airfield to the southwest and the flat riverbed offered no obstructions other than a low-lying levee.[10]

Boeing B-17 Flying Fortress lands at Middletown, Ohio, for the Army-Navy "E" Award ceremony August 10, 1943.
Courtesy the late W. O. "Wally" Baldwin private collection.

Love had not been checked out on the B-17 at that point, nor would she have had the necessary experience to make the short-field landing in the big airplane. But of such things are legends made. It's hard to convince those who were there that she didn't personally land the B-17 that day.

August 13, Gillies's diary entry reads: "Tunner wanted to go to Ludington in B-17."[11] What followed can only be put together based on what Betty Gillies wrote in her diary and also what she related to Delphine Bohn some forty years later, after both Love and General Tunner were gone. Bohn then wrote about the incident in her memoir. But Bohn and Gillies are now gone as well.

Love and Gillies were passengers for part of the flight that carried their boss General Tunner and some of his staff officers on an administrative cross-country flight. They started to land at Ludington, Michigan. Close inspection revealed the runway was too short to take the fully loaded B-17. Red Forman pushed the throttles forward to generate full power and aborted the landing.[12]

Gillies writes: "Number four engine detonated on pull up. Captain Forman feathered it."

Bohn writes the following: "Close by was the Navy-occupied Traverse City airport. This airport was selected as an alternate. Although they did get in, the Navy was inexplicably unwelcoming. So unfriendly were they that it was not only suggested but ordered that the B-17 group make an immediate departure from the field, that they make a three-engine takeoff, in fact. They did. They could not do otherwise, since several jeep loads of armed sailors escorted them to the runway."[13]

Gillies's exact words in her diary are: "The Navy was most inhospitable!"

They headed for next nearest airfield that could handle their airplane and the necessary repairs, the AAF base at Alpena, Michigan. From there, they flew back southwest, again across the state, to Muskegon, which was, like Ludington, on Lake Michigan. Love apparently flew the Alpena-Muskegon leg because she recorded in her logbook that she made the landing in Muskegon. She also flew the next leg to Nashville where they all spent the night and where, most likely, number four was checked out again at the ATC's Nashville facility. Love does record making a night landing in Nashville.

Why the Navy's paranoia? Delphine Bohn points out that General Tunner's B-17 bore "plentiful United States Army Air Forces insignia, as did all aboard." Nevertheless, General Tunner and his entourage were simply told to "git." Turns out the Navy was involved in the top-secret developing, building, and testing of guided missiles at Traverse City. There were German spies about and no one was allowed in.[14]

August 14 found them back at Lockbourne practicing landings. On August 15, they got a new airplane, a B-17F. Sixteen landings, practicing first with three engines and then with only two, were followed by some cross-country time.

Hydraulics or no, flying the heavy Fortress was hard work, particularly without the full power of four engines. Love's and Gillies's endurance and physical strength were being tested. They underwent thirty-two hours of intensive training, refusing offers of help from Forman. "We have to find out if we can fly this plane by ourselves," Nancy wrote to Bob.

Nancy in the cockpit of the Queen Bee.

Courtesy Love family; electronic image NAHF.

On August 16, Love, Gillies, and Technical Sergeant L. S. Hall were signed off as "Competent crew to fly B-17 type aircraft on domestic deliveries. They will be permitted to make such deliveries between factories and modification centers, and modification centers and final domestic delivery points on operation orders of your Group. For the Commanding General."[15]

Then beginning August 18, Love and Gillies, accompanied by T/Sgt. Hall, ferried a series of B-17Fs, finishing up on August 24 and toting up twenty-four hours of ferrying time.[16]

On September 1, 1943, Love and Gillies left Cincinnati in B-17F (No. 42-30624) on the first leg of a trip that would take them across the cold, ominous North Atlantic. With them were 1st Lt. R. O. (Pappy) Fraser, navigator; T/Sgt. Stover, radio operator; T/Sgt. Weintraub, aerial engineer; and T/Sgt. L.S. Hall, assistant aerial engineer. The plane was destined for the U.S. Eighth Air Force in Great Britain.

Love carried in her B-4 bag a letter of introduction to Maj. Roy Atwood, executive officer of the ATC European Wing in London written on official Air Transport Command letterhead.

The writer also asked that Atwood "receive and take care of the bearers of this letter."

> They should arrive in Prestwick presently and due to the shortness of time will bring this letter. I have known these people for a good while and they are thoroughly competent as pilots, as well as having a background in aviation activities. They are being sent to perform a certain amount of liaison with the ATA and other agencies interested in the ferrying of aircraft to the UK.
>
> I am sure you will find these two personalities pleasant, if not unusual, in that they arrive as they did, and sincerely hope you will give them your highly accredited effort in showing them around.
> Very sincerely yours,
> Robert M. Love
> Colonel, G.S.C.
> Deputy Chief of Staff
>
> P.S. Incidentally one of them is my wife and the other a good friend.[17]

The crew RONed in New Castle, where they picked up the fleece-lined flight suits and oxygen masks required for the North Atlantic air route. On September 2, they flew to New York's La-Guardia Airport for an overnight briefing and proper clearance. From there, on September 3, 1943, the bombers flew to Presque Isle, Maine, to the staging point for the trans-Atlantic flight. They RONed there, received their briefing and clearance and left the following day under instrument conditions for Goose Bay, Labrador, once a tiny Eskimo village on the tip of Lake Melville. Early in the war, the Canadian government had decided to build an air base there and invited the United States and the British to share the use of it. The base now served as air cover for trans-Atlantic flights and as a staging field for ferrying bombers to Britain.

The story that everyone would like to believe happened is that the two women pilots and their crew took off the following day and successfully crossed "the Pond" to Scotland and delivered their B-17F to the Eighth Air Force. That, of course, didn't happen. A telegram arrived at the eleventh hour from Hap Arnold ordering them to stand down and turn the airplane over to a male pilot and copilot.

Gen. C.R. Smith, thinking the two women and their crew were well on their way, sent a wire to England alerting the commander of the ATC European Wing, Brig. Gen. Paul Burrows, that the plane flown by the two women pilots was on its way, and to notify General Arnold. Paraphrased, it read: Routine delivering flight arriving in your wing will be B-17 number 30624 in few days. For Burrows and Atwood from Smith. Airplane is piloted by WAF crew first pilot Nancy Harkness Love and second pilot Betty Gillies. First instance of overseas ferry of four-engine military aircraft with women pilots also first instance overseas ferry any type military bomber with women serving both as pilot and copilot. In previous flights with woman pilot male second pilot has been utilized. Desire General Arnold be informed and that other contacts be made for proper liaison with ATA and other interested agencies. For definite time of arrival follow this airplane by number.[18]

The telegram was delivered while Burrows was having dinner with his boss, Hap Arnold. Burrows handed the telegram to Arnold who immediately ordered the flight stopped.

Weather had delayed their departure a day. The word reached the two crews in Goose Bay as they sat in the mess hall finishing dinner, September 5. Betty Gillies had this to say in an interview more than fifty years later: "What did I say? 'Damn!'

"Arnold didn't think about the personal disappointment. That wasn't his concern. His responsibility was for domestic flying. The B-17 was going to England. We were flying into a war zone. He didn't want women flying into the war zone.

"We weren't taxiing out on the runway, though that is the story everyone tells. We were at supper the night before. We had plenty of time to go to the bar and drink our sorrows and get up the next morning with a hangover."[19]

The following is Arnold's message: "Just have seen message from C.R. Smith … indicating that a B-17 with women crew

"Caught by the higher ups." Nancy and Betty with their crew in Goose Bay, Labrador.

Courtesy of the National Museum of the U.S. Air Force.

will leave for England shortly.... Desire that this trip be cancelled and no women fly transoceanic planes until I have had time to study and approve."[20]

There was nothing for them to do but step aside.

While they awaited the arrival of the replacement male pilot and copilot the next morning, a photographer snapped several photos of Love, Gillies and the male crew standing in front of their B-17. Thirty-two years later, Love wrote to WASP historian Marty Wyall telling her how the airplane got its distinctive name: "We'd just been 'caught' by the higher ups and were sadly awaiting a male replacement pilot and copilot.... Incidentally our loyal (and brave!) male crew had named the airplane and painted 'Queen Bee' on her during the night, trying I suspect, to raise our very low morale. That was September 1943."[21]

Nancy Love and Betty Gillies boarded a C-52A as passengers the morning of September 6, 1943. The flight was bound for

Presque Isle—the opposite direction from their original destination Prestwick. Two male pilots took their places and ferried B-17F No. 42-30624 on to Scotland.

After the war, both Nancy and Bob Love put to rest the question of "why?" in interviews and an exchange of letters with official AAF historian Lt. Col. Oliver La Farge, the officer who wrote the second and accepted draft of the WAFS' story entitled "Women Pilots of the Air Transport Command."

When he was preparing his draft of the history of the women ferry pilots with the ATC, La Farge wrote to Bob Love on November 7, 1945, asking for further clarification of the facts on Love's thwarted trans-Atlantic flight. Following are excerpts from Bob Love's answer. The letter is dated November 10, 1945.

> Here is the actual dope—C.R. decided to give Tunner the go ahead on his own and all the preparations were started, special checking, etc. One day in a casual way he mentioned to [General] Giles (probably item 34 on a long list) the fact that he was planning to let the girls go. Giles ... nodded and said "Really? Good idea," and nothing was done until the girls were well on their way.
>
> After they had been out of Presque Isle for over two days and we had no word—no position report because the Northern Lights were playing hob with Goose Bay's sparker—C.R. decided pretty much on my assurance I'm afraid that they were really clear of the USA and that it was the news story of all time.
>
> So he snapped out one of those typical world shaking promotional wires and shipped it off to Burrows to give to Arnold then in London. Arnold personally, from the dais of a "state" dinner in London, told Burrows to use his name and send an immediate wire to Giles telling him to ... stop them and send the crew back! So the only part Giles had to do with it was carrying out [Arnold's] orders. That's the whole and I believe accurate story.[22]

Lt. Col. La Farge also interviewed Nancy Love extensively in order to write the official history. His notes from his October 3, 1945, interview with her state that "had General Tunner not ordered her B-17 routed via Goose [Bay], Mrs. Love would have succeeded in flying the Atlantic. The regular route via Gander would have had her over the ocean in time."[23]

"I had always wanted to fly a B-17 and wondered if I'd be capable of handling an airplane of that size," Love wrote in 1955. She described preparing for the trip and concluded with the following:

> ... we started for Prestwick, Scotland, with a crew of three enlisted men and a lieutenant navigator. This dream was shattered for us when we were held overnight by weather in Goose Bay Labrador. Someone high up, who apparently disapproved of us in particular, heard about it and stopped the flight. Betty and I, raging and frustrated, were sent ignominiously home, while a male replaced us as pilots. That disappointment is still with me though later I managed to fly around the world, about half of the trip as pilot.[24]

✈ 13 ✈

Change in the Air

On September 7, 1943, Brig. Gen. C.R. Smith wrote a memo to Maj. Gen. Barney M. Giles, Chief of the Air Staff, justifying the Love-Gillies trans-Atlantic flight. Such flights were considered routine, he said, and given the number of women pilots in the Ferrying Division, more were probable in the future. Both women were capable pilots with no qualms about making the flight. And he thought it wise to reconsider sending the two women pilots over the Atlantic in another of the badly needed B-17s.[1]

Jackie Cochran took particular note of the cancelled flight. If she had felt—in the light of her own troubles with the gear of the twin-engine Lockheed Hudson—that a woman couldn't fly a B-17, she knew now that a woman could. Marianne Verges writes in *On Silver Wings*, "The woman who made her mark with individual aviation records and who was forever proud of being the first—and only—woman to deliver a bomber to England during World War II, reported on her agenda for the WASP, 'Individual comet-like achievements should be avoided, graduation into important new assignments should be not by exceptional individuals but by groups.'"[2]

With that in mind, Cochran acted. She asked the commanding officer at Avenger Field for the names of his biggest and best among the trainees about to graduate. She wanted women big enough to handle a B-17 and who also were considered both exceptional pilots and mature young women. She selected nine from Class 43-6 with the highest scores in twin-engine AT-17 transition. They graduated October 9. To those nine, she added eight graduates of 43-5—who had just been assigned to the Ferrying Division—and sent them all to B-17 transition school at Lockbourne. They reported October 15, 1943.[3]

Thirteen of those women graduated as first pilots, four of whom initially were assigned to engineering flying and delivery work out of Lockbourne and the other nine as copilots of B-17s on gunnery missions.[4] Some of the nine eventually flew missions as first pilot.[5]

"By July [1944] the WASPs had proved themselves capable of handling the Fortress and were authorized to fly as first pilot with another WASP on all B-17 flights except on the heavily loaded (10 gunners and ammunition) B-17Gs on gunnery missions over the gulf [of Mexico]," WASP Yvonne Pateman (43-5) wrote in *Aviation Quarterly* magazine. Pateman quotes WASP B-17 pilot Julie Ledbetter (43-5): "We had to have a male first pilot when we first flew gunnery missions, since the characteristics of the gunnery B-17s were different than the planes we flew in training, especially the B-17G.... Our ships at Lockbourne were stripped down types with no turrets except in the tail and no guns or ammo and fewer people. Eventually, they let us fly them without a man on board."[6]

B.J. Erickson flew two orientation flights on the B-17 on October 8 and 9, 1943. The following spring, she checked out as first pilot in the aircraft and ferried several as copilot and then as pilot in command.[7] The ATC really didn't need women to ferry B-17s, Erickson-London says. However, the Ferrying Division treated its male and female pilots the same and had no problem with qualified women pilots checking out in the Fortress. "Gender didn't matter. They were allowing the women pilots to check out in more complex airplanes at their own rate based on individual skill—just like the male pilots."[8]

Publicity claiming that the women learning to fly B-17s at Lockbourne were the first women to fly the Fortress prompted General Tunner to write to the War Department's Bureau of Public Relations on November 20, 1943:

> It has been brought to the attention of this Headquarters that statements have been made to the effect that the first WASPs to fly four-engine aircraft are at present being trained at Lockbourne.... This Command wishes to state that two of the women pilots employed by the Ferrying Division have been qualified as first pilots on the B-17 aircraft since August 15.... It is requested that prior to release of news stories involving the WASPs of the Ferrying Division, the accuracy of statements be checked with this Command.

He sent a copy of the memo to Director of Women Pilots Jackie Cochran.[9]

The differences in Love and Cochran's methods surfaced again in their approach to transition. Love's premise was that when she, as the leader of the WAFS, checked out in bigger airplanes, she paved the way for her pilots to follow suit. Cochran preferred to send large groups—like the seventeen B-17 pilot candidates—into transition at the same time.

A fitting postscript to the aborted B-17 flight arrived on Love's desk in October. Love and Gillies's navigator on the Atlantic flight, 1st Lt. R.O. (Pappy) Fraser, wrote October 16, 1943: "I thought I would be getting a call from you for another trip, long before this, so would like to remind you that I am liable to get stale if I sit around too long. If you see the General and can work it in, remind him that on the 1st of September he too promised me a trip." Fraser tells her that the crew was able to collect some of her and Gillies's personal items left on board the *Queen Bee* when it took off from Goose Bay for Scotland without them— her shoes, some papers, and two Mae West life preservers among them. He adds that "the rest of the trip was uneventful and we were fortunate to catch the last plane back before they started sending the crews back by boat." He concludes with, "I hope it will not be long before I get a call from you or the General. How about cooking up a deal to deliver the first B-29?"[10]

Love buried herself in her work, dealt with the disappointment of the thwarted B-17 flight, and moved beyond it. If she had problems dealing with disappointment, frustration, or depression—and quite probably she did—she hid them well.

Following Love's lead, the original WAFS were already moving up in transition. Between July 29 and August 6, 1943, B.J. Erickson made four, 2,000-mile deliveries—three of them pursuits—in slightly more than five days. B.J., who had checked out in the P-51 earlier in July, also held multi-engine ratings and therefore was at the top of the duty roster at each stop. In addition, she had perfect weather.[11]

Such a series of deliveries in that short a time was remarkable, even with all the elements in her favor. Word of Erickson's feat was passed on in the Ferrying Division's weekly report to ATC and eventually made its way to Air Staff in Washington, which recommended her for an Air Medal for her performance on duty. The intent was to commend all the women ferry pilots by pointing out what they were doing, but the result still was perceived as singling out one person for recognition. In truth, the award embarrassed Erickson. She maintains, to this day, that she was doing her duty as any of the WAFS would have done under similar circumstances.

Love's four squadrons were well settled. Betty Gillies ran the Wilmington group with an artful mixture of discipline and tender loving care. The women loved her, but she could be tough. Helen Mary Clark was her executive officer and Esther Manning Rathfelder, grounded from flying because of pregnancy, served as operations officer until June and then left to have her son. After the baby was born, Esther left him with her family and returned to her operations duties.

Del Scharr led the Romulus squadron until summer 1943, went briefly back to Wilmington, and was reassigned to Long Beach in the fall. Love named Barbara Donahue squadron commander in Romulus, Lenore McElroy became the executive officer, and Margaret Ann Hamilton, WASP Class 43-2, handled operations. Florene Miller led the squadron in Dallas until December 1943. Delphine Bohn was transferred from Wilmington to Dallas in March 1943 to work with Florene when Love moved from Dallas to Long Beach. Bohn was named operations officer. B.J. Erickson headed up the Long Beach squadron throughout its entire twenty-two months of operations. All of B.J.'s staff were graduates of the flight training school in Texas.

Before Cochran was named Director of Women Pilots and began to assign the graduates to other than the Ferrying Division, Nancy Love accompanied Colonel Tunner on a visit to Avenger Field. The date was June 16, 1943. Love wanted to talk to the future graduates about what to expect in the Ferrying Division.

"You will have the same privileges as the officers," she told them. "You will be entitled to use the Officers Club. It is a very military life. When you are assigned and arrive for duty you will have indoctrination for about one week in order to learn the necessary paper work you must file when delivering an airplane. You are on duty seven days a week. When you return from a trip you are given a reasonable length of time off to take care of your personal affairs, and your laundry, which has proved to be quite a problem.

"The trips are long, averaging about 1,000 miles. On the trip you are completely responsible for the ship assigned to you, including having a guard and sending an R.O.N. to your home base. This R.O.N. states where your ship is each night and why, so that your office may know where every ship is every day and every night.

"You will start on PTs and BTs. After you fly a PT 2,000 miles cross country without a radio you will learn a lot about navigation. Then you will go on to AT-6s and AT-17s. It's entirely up to you and your own hard work how fast you progress."[12]

Love was in Cincinnati to stay—away from day-to-day contact with the other WASP. She made trips to the other bases, but mostly she flew her desk. She became General Tunner's troubleshooter in any matter dealing with the women pilots. She was good at getting to the bottom of things and then handling them in a delicate, equitable manner.

Flights in her logbook are sparse following the return from Goose Bay through the end of the year. She took transition in an A-20 twin-engine, single-cockpit attack airplane in Long Beach on September 27, then took a C-47 to Dallas. No flights are listed between October 4 and November 28.[13] But a look beneath the surface of what was going on at Ferrying Division headquarters reveals an active and involved Love—not out front, but working with the command structure to keep the women ferry pilots functioning efficiently.

In the fall of 1943, the two opposing views of organizing and controlling the women pilots once again clashed. Cochran wanted to appoint a special assistant and several WASP "establishment" officers and field representatives. She sought an AAF regulation to give herself that power. The proposed regulation would replace the Memorandum of June 28 (1943) that established Cochran as Director of Women Pilots and gave her vague powers over the women flying for the Army. The "establishment" officers would represent the Director of Women Pilots on nontechnical administrative matters, maintain WASP discipline, and supervise welfare, conduct and morale on the bases where they were assigned. The field representatives' job was to check up on WASP "doings" at the various bases and make sure things were running according to the wishes of the special assistant and Director of Women Pilots.[14]

As of fall 1943, most of the active duty women pilots still were assigned to a Ferrying Group at an ATC base and served under that base commander. That meant an establishment officer would be assigned to the ATC bases where women served. Nancy Love, as leader of the women in the four ferrying squadrons and with her own able lieutenants heading up each of those squadrons, considered both the establishment officers and field representatives little more than spies. Tunner once again took Cochran's action as an attempt to wrest control of the women's squadrons from the ATC. He sent Major Teague and Nancy Love to Washington to prepare an answer.

Their strongly worded reply, which General George in turn sent to the AAF on November 3, 1943, said:

> The proposed regulations and organization of the WASPs are a direct violation of established military chains of command, and of policies established throughout the Army Air Forces ...
>
> Women pilots should be considered on the same basis as men pilots. The Air Transport Command has operated with women pilots for over a year, during which time we have learned by experience that the present organization in use in the Ferrying Groups, based on strictly military lines, is the most efficient. The proposed regulations would set up two methods of administration, one for men, one for women; not only our own experience, but all military teaching is to the effect that uniformity is mandatory.
>
> Any system such as that proposed which directs administrative control from Headquarters, Army Air Forces directly into the squadrons would be intolerable. It is axiomatic in the Army that when a commanding officer is given a mission to perform, he must have full and complete responsibility, and must have command control. The proposed regulation violates this rule ...
>
> Since it is believed that only confusion and conflict can result if this regulation is adopted, *it is the belief of this Command that it would be far better not to use WASPs in the Command than to have them operating under the proposed terms.*[15] [italics added]

"[Nancy Love] came to Washington with Teague to help draft the comment on the proposed WASP regulations," Lt. Col. Oliver La Farge writes in his notes on his interview with Nancy on October 3, 1945. "The final remark [italicized above] that it was better to have no women pilots than have them under the proposed regulation was hers."[16]

ATC also reminded the AAF that the WASP were civilian not military employees and should be handled accordingly. When the official regulation was issued December 21, 1943, that to which the ATC and Tunner objected had been eliminated.[17]

Once again General Tunner and the ATC were able to thwart an attempt by Cochran to control the inner workings of the women's squadrons in the Ferrying Division. That was Nancy Love's prerogative as executive. Once again, Love was part of the decision-making team.

Oliver La Farge, who wrote the accepted Army Air Forces history of the women of the ATC—"Women Pilots of the Air Transport Command"—presented his personal assessment of the problems in his book about the ATC, *The Eagle in the Egg*:

> From this point on [fall 1943] there was a steady push and pull between the Ferrying Division, through ATC, and Miss Cochran over the clash between its sole desire to get on with its mission of delivering aircraft and training pilots, and hers to conduct a large experiment. Again I feel that some of this conflict could have been avoided if Air Staff had been blunter with its Director of Women Pilots in regard to the limitations of a staff officer's command functions. In order to carry out her experiment most effectively, she desired and perhaps needed to exercise a control over all WASPs, which ran head on into the rights of command control of the operations organizations. Air Staff seems to have preferred to let the lower organization—in this case ATC—carry the burden of setting her straight. From Miss Cochran's point of view, this meant that the Command seemed rebelliously intransigent; from the Command's point of view, that Miss Cochran seemed a wild imperialist. Extremely hard feelings developed all around.[18]

Army historian Capt. Walter J. Marx writes in his AAF history, "Women Pilots of the Ferrying Division," that in November 1943—because nothing was happening with regard to the militarization of the WASP—General Tunner personally urged that the WASP be put into the WAC with commissions. Still trying to head off Cochran's attempts to override the Ferrying Division's command prerogative, he had Nancy Love write to Colonel Hobby outlining his proposal. The letter, signed by

General Tunner, was dated November 22, 1943, and carried the subject heading "Militarization of WASP."

Love listed in the letter the various adjustments that would be necessary if the WASP became part of the WAC and asked Colonel Hobby for her opinion on each of the proposed adjustments. But Tunner never received an answer because, according to Marx, his letter never reached Colonel Hobby. "It was stopped by the A-1 Air Staff and pigeonholed." The Ferrying Division's request never surfaced and, consequently, was never considered.[19]

Captain Marx wrote the first history of the women ferry pilots, by order of the AAF, as the WASP were being shut down the fall of 1944. It was based on interviews with Jackie Cochran, Nancy Love, James Teague, and "many of the other officers who had something to do with the women pilots of the Division," Marx states in his Preface. He says that he had access to the complete files of the WASP office at Ferrying Division Headquarters in Cincinnati as well as General Tunner's WASP files. However, Cochran rejected the Marx manuscript as too critical of her and her project. She had enough clout to get it revised.

Marx, in a February 28, 1946, letter to Nancy Love says: "First, you recall that ATC made me cut out whole sections of my original manuscript as irrelevant or biased.... Miss Cochran got her hands on the volume and for a long time would not give it back to the Air Staff. She tried in every possible way to discredit it. Finally, the Air Staff got it back with the understanding that it would be rewritten. I was not trusted with the job but Colonel La Farge took it over personally."[20]

La Farge rewrote the history using "large sections of my volume ["Women Pilots in the Ferrying Division"] word for word," Marx says in a follow-up letter to Love on April 5, 1946. "It is much condensed and of course more critical of the [Ferrying] Division than mine was. And he adds, "The La Farge history does have a few more documents cited that we did not have access to."[21]

Lt. Colonel La Farge wrote Bob Love on October 29, 1945:

> The Women Pilots' history is about finished. We had
> a lucky break on that. Miss Cochran, having read
> Marx's original job, took and wrote about fifty pages
> of rebuttal to it. She really should learn not to put
> things down on paper.... Also, I am sorry to report,
> she made some statements which are demonstra-
> bly not so. These deal with matters of some impor-
> tance.... it was necessary for us to take formal no-
> tice of her statements in our histories, and to show
> why we could not accept them, since the questions
> involved were important. This necessity, we agreed,
> was most unfortunate, since it would give readers the
> impression that Miss Cochran was inaccurate.[22]

In the April 5, 1946, Marx letter to Nancy Love, he mentions
that he just that morning received "the FERD (Ferrying Division) copy of the La Farge WASP history."

Love read the La Farge volume prior to its being accepted as
the official history of the women pilots in the ATC. Previously,
she had also received a copy of the Marx history, which she
squirreled away. Marx in his April 5, 1946, letter to her mentions that her copy of his work was supposed to be destroyed,
but the manuscript was found years later in her private papers.

✈ 14 ✈
Pursuit School

Production of trainer airplanes dropped thirty percent in May and June 1943 and continued to decline.[1] Pursuit planes were rolling off the factory assembly lines in ever-greater numbers. General Tunner still needed ferry pilots, but now he needed pilots capable of handling pursuits, because pursuit ferrying had become the number one job of the Ferrying Division. One potential source was the WFTD graduates.

By the end of June, the Ferrying Division had received sixty-five WFTD graduates—the total number of women trained in the first two classes in Houston. On June 26, 1943, Nancy Love wrote to General Barton Yount, commanding general of the Flying Training Command, that the flight training of those early graduates had been "thorough and well adapted to their duties as ferrying pilots. Their attitude and conduct have been generally excellent." The Ferrying Division did request additional training related to cross-country flying and in group flying as many Ferrying Division deliveries still were made in groups of five to nine. Also requested, additional practice on crosswind landings.[2]

The women in those first classes were experienced pilots, some of whom could have qualified for the original WAFS but were committed to instructing jobs and could not get away until their contracts were up. Others were some hours short of the 500 initially required of WAFS, but had more than 200 when they entered training and would have more than 300 hours by the time they graduated. In its two-year existence, the Ferrying Division had learned that ferry pilots needed a minimum of 300 hours. That level of experience was necessary to fly the 150 different types or models of planes—from trainers to four-engine bombers—they could be called on to ferry. The women of those early classes fit quite well into the Division's needs and into the WAFS structure already in place.

However, by April 1943, Cochran had succeeded in lowering the number of hours required for acceptance into the WFTD program. Two hundred gave way to seventy-five, and by spring 1943, was reduced to thirty-five.[3] Estimates now indicated that the Ferrying Division would have approximately 500 women ferry pilots on its rosters before the end of 1943.[4] Yet, by the end of August 1943, as his number of women ferry pilots continued to grow, General Tunner was becoming concerned about an increase in accidents and mishaps among the women pilots.[5]

In his September 14, 1943, report to General George, Tunner expressed the need for all of his ferry pilots to be qualified to deliver at least the AT-6 "without personal supervision or additional training." To address that, he recommended that requirements for WFTD graduates be raised.

As of September 21, 1943, the Ferrying Division had 180 WASP in its four women's squadrons. Twenty-two were original WAFS. The remaining 158 were graduates of four classes from the Flying Training Command school. Class 43-5 had graduated September 11[6], but had not yet reported for duty. Also on September 21, the Ferrying Division formally requested that it only be assigned fifteen training school graduates per month. The mission of the Division was changing. They needed pilots who possessed the skills to fly high-performance single- and twin-engine pursuit and attack planes, not trainers.[7] To fly pursuit, a pilot had to have instrument training. In the fall of 1943, the Ferrying Division began to prepare its women pilots for pursuit transition by sending them for instrument training. Upon successful completion, the women would be issued the Army's white instrument card.

Nancy Love had to have felt considerable satisfaction. Her efforts in early 1943, against almost overwhelming odds, had paid off. She had fought the sexist belief that women couldn't handle high-performance and/or heavy aircraft. She had, with the backing of the ATC Air Surgeon, overcome the inherent male lack of understanding of menstruation as a basic physical function, not an illness. And she had waited out any latent resistance the men had to letting women fly pursuit airplanes. Her willingness to listen but also to offer her opinion to the men in the command structure kept the give and take of daily operations upbeat and one built on cooperation. To Nancy Love fell the job of coordinating the women ferry pilots, placing pilots newly arrived from the training school, assessing their capabilities, and getting them moving on the path that led to pursuits.

Delphine Bohn writes: "Mrs. Love's enthusiasm for these duties and her knowledge of military rules and regulations, as well as her highly developed organizational and administrative abilities had preceded her.... One of many valid reasons for Love's popularity was the background that enabled her to walk into any Operations office and to give help wherever needed. It was with finesse she would suggest remedies to alleviate pileups and mix-ups."[8]

Bohn has this to say of the WAFS' loyalty to Love.

> Already the talents and successful careers of several so-called "Originals" had assured they were of a stamp to render it difficult that they could be impressed by unusual individuals/personalities. Every member of the group was a strong persona who walked "tall." Yet each WAFS, other than in one or two occasional strange reactions, acknowledged the leadership of Nancy Harkness Love! They followed her happily: they followed her with grace.
>
> All were pleased to note the respect accorded her by the high-ranking military. There was realization among a few that without Mrs. Love, without her level of association with the military, without her ef-

forts and her ability to share the officers' problems
with enterprise, in all probability, there would not
have been any women accepted to serve in any part of
the Air Forces. Nancy's administrative excellence reflected her formal education and reflected even more
her business background and partnership with her
husband Bob. She provided us guidance by example
as well as otherwise.[9]

On October 7, General Tunner submitted the names of fifty-
six women ferry pilots qualified to go to pursuit school and to
transition to more advanced type aircraft.[10] Already the Ferrying
Division was working on plans for its pursuit transition school.
Both male and female fledgling pursuit pilots would be trained
in Palm Springs, California. There, they would learn to fly the
four single-engine pursuits—P-47, P-40, P-39 and P-51—in a
focused, four-week training period.

In the fall, with pursuit school in the works, the Ferrying Division ordered its base commanders not to allow members of
their squadrons to attempt pursuit transition. Pursuit school
would soon take care of that need.

November also brought Nancy Love and General Tunner disturbing news in the form of a report from the Air Inspector that
addressed "Utilization of Women Pilot Graduates." Jackie Cochran had requested an investigation after hearing complaints
from some of her flight school graduates about unfair treatment
regarding transition.[11] The women pilots at Wilmington and
Dallas were being discriminated against with regard to transition, said the report. Flight checks at Love Field were said to be
obstructive and unfair at the hands of check pilots resentful of
the women's program. The base commander at New Castle was
said to be slow at allowing transition.[12] The latter was nothing
new. It was why Nancy Love had left Wilmington in January.
Women's squadron leader Betty Gillies also had complained of
slow transition there.

The planes available for ferrying by Wilmington-based pilots
were: the Fairchild primary trainers that the women already
were ferrying; the Martin B-26 bomber; and the P-47 built on

Long Island. The B-26 was termed "too important in the men's upgrading program to permit any large-scale training of women pilots for ferrying this type of plane" and the women needed pursuit training in order to ferry the P-47s.[13] However, by early July 1943, three of the original WAFS stationed in Wilmington—Betty Gillies, Helen Mary Clark, and Teresa James—had checked out on the P-47 and were actively ferrying them.

The situation at Wilmington was a known quantity, but Dallas was not. Dallas was *not* lacking in airplanes needing to be ferried, so General Tunner ordered Love to check out Love Field. One of the youngest of the Originals, Dorothy Scott, had joined the program as number twenty-five in November 1942 and had been sent to the 5th Ferrying Group in Dallas in January 1943. Scott was a bright, articulate, capable young pilot who enjoyed having a good time, believed in fair play, and was deadly serious about flying. She, too, was concerned over transition and the attendant gossip, and wrote to Love on November 26, 1943: "The way I see it is that you get all the 'official' information and I get some of the undercurrent gossip, so if I tell you what I learn it might help you out. Darn if I like to appear as a stool pigeon, but if you don't know some of this stuff and should, this is OK." [14]

Several of the women in Dallas had heard they were going to pursuit school—Scott among them. A lot of rumors were flying around WASP quarters. The girls were getting mixed messages. How many were going—when—who? Hoping Love would come to Love Field and answer their questions, Scott also wrote: "My main worries are that some of the girls refusing to go may spoil things for all of them, and too, that perhaps they aren't using the best methods of finding out who would be best to send. No one seems to have thought of asking the checkout pilots in A-24s and A-25s, (rumor has it they're betting on how many will live thru [*sic*] it all)." [15]

What Love was to discover was that some of the Dallas women were receiving "bootleg" transition in the P-47—instruction and cockpit checks by male pilots without the commanding officer knowing about it.[16] One such flight ended up in the newspapers.

Dallas Love Field, back in late 1943, was girdled by a series of utility lines strung from steel poles. These lines transmitted power to the field and also to a large area of Dallas surrounding the field. The Civil Aeronautics Authority and the military had tried to have the poles removed and the lines placed underground, but to no avail.[17]

Sunday afternoon, November 28, WASP Florene Miller took a P-47 aloft and did some maneuvers to get the feel of the airplane. When the late afternoon haze worsened, the tower closed the field and told her to come in. Miller's approach was into the sun, her visibility reduced by haze. In her words: "As I came in, I knew exactly where I was except that I was about ten feet lower than I intended to be. I flew straight into a steel utility pole. It was strong enough that, as I found out later, I didn't knock it down but it made an awful, screaming metal-tearing-against metal sound. The collision caused the airplane to shoot straight up and start to roll."[18] With that began Miller's battle to stabilize and fly the stricken airplane.

"Circling Love Field for nearly an hour at dark Sunday after the undercarriage of her heavy fighter plane sheared the power line, leaving the field in darkness [and] knocked out radio communication, Florene Miller, commander of the Women's Airforce Service Pilots, landed right side up, uninjured," wrote the *Dallas Morning News*.[19]

With help from the ground, a series of emergency radio transmissions, and jeep headlights illuminating the darkened runway, Miller was able to land the plane. When she was down and safely parked, the first man to clamber up on the wing was her commanding officer. "I knew he was going to fire me or kill me or worse," Florene recalls. But he was so relieved that she was down safely that he congratulated her on landing at all.[20]

Sixteen of Nancy Love's original group went on to fly pursuit. Nine of those, including Love herself, did not go to pursuit school. Betty Gillies, Helen Mary Clark, Teresa James, Delphine Bohn, Del Scharr, B.J. Erickson, Barbara Towne, and Evelyn Sharp did their transition at their local bases.

Sharp, Erickson, and Towne began P-51 transition in the summer of 1943 at what was then the 6th Ferrying Group's satellite base and fuel stop at Palm Springs. First, they flew the AT-6 from the backseat, a regular training procedure for flying the tail wheel pursuits because the big engine up front blocked forward visibility. Sharp made her first P-51 flight on June 13, 1943.[21] Erickson and Towne followed in July, Erickson taking her first flight on July 24, 1943.[22] Then they returned to their home base, Long Beach, and began ferrying P-51s.

Stationed at Long Beach, these three were most likely to fly the P-51 built at the nearby North American factory, which was the reason for their transition. The other single-engine pursuits the WASP would fly were built back East. As the opportunity arose, Erickson and Sharp checked out in them. Towne, who by then was pregnant, was grounded before she had the opportunity to fly any of the other pursuits. No longer could she get the stick back in the confines of the small cockpits.

Gillies, Clark, and James had transitioned in the P-47 at Wilmington. Those three and Scharr, who was stationed in Romulus and was the first to fly the P-39, then checked out in other pursuits on an as-needed basis. Bohn, in Dallas, also checked out on pursuits as the opportunity presented itself.

Eight women and thirty-five men reported to Palm Springs November 30 to begin pursuit transition on December 1. Among them were four of Nancy Love's originals: Dorothy Scott, Florene Miller, Helen Richards, and Gertrude Meserve.[23] Originals Nancy Batson and Helen McGilvery from Wilmington and Barbara Donahue from Romulus arrived a week and a half later.[24] During the summer of 1943—before the Ferrying Division's pursuit transition moratorium was issued—Donahue had checked out in the P-39 at Bell Aircraft in Buffalo, New York, and Meserve had flown the P-47 in Wilmington. But they were sent to the school in Palm Springs to learn to fly the other three single-engine pursuit aircraft. Tapped for the first two classes of pursuit school along with the seven original WAFS were several Houston graduates.

Nancy Love had scheduled two flight checks in Long Beach the end of November, after which she planned to fly on to Palm Springs and meet with her incoming pursuit pilot trainees. On November 29, she flew a B-25 from both the left and the right seat. Next, she planned to check out in the twin-engine pursuit, the P-38 Lightning built at the nearby Lockheed plant. If she proved capable of handling it, some of the women who graduated from pursuit school eventually would get to check out in and ferry P-38s to the East Coast for shipment to Europe or North Africa.

Her first P-38 flight was on November 30.[25]

Suspended in the bubble of the narrow Plexiglas-canopied single-seat cockpit, between and slightly above the streamlined twin engine nacelles, the pilot—Nancy Love in this case—had a commanding view of the Long Beach runway and taxiway complex. This airplane was quite different from sitting in the tail-dragger P-51. The P-38 was equipped with the new tricycle gear. Thanks to her extensive work with Joe Gwinn and the Aircar as well as the Hammond Y plane, Love felt very much at home.

She executed the sequences in preparation for takeoff. To call the tower for clearance she pressed the button in the center of the yoke (a half steering wheel) to activate the microphone. She sat at the end of the runway, her toes pushed hard against the brakes. The airplane shook as the twin 1,475-horsepower Allison engines roared their readiness to fly. She thrust the throttles full forward and, with that, Nancy Love once again was ready to make history—this time as the first woman to fly the P-38.

The Lightning surged forward, pressing her back in the seat. Then she was airborne, the ground falling away beneath her. Love flew for fifty-five minutes and made two landings. On December 1, she was back for more. This time she spent two hours and twenty minutes in the air and logged five landings in the P-38.[26]

Iris Critchell recalls when Love was in Long Beach to check out in the P-38. "That's when I gained my appreciation for how gracefully she handled people and situations—quietly and wisely. For just a few moments, I was privileged to see her open up a bit and smile and speak warmly about flying, ferrying, and subsequently, the P-38. She allowed herself to show her warmth and respect for B.J. and those of us present at that particular moment. She showed the sparkle and then moved on to her cool business-like bearing which served her so well."[27]

That cool bearing and firm self-control were about to be tested again.

WAFS original Dorothy Scott, in a letter home datelined Palm Springs, December 1, 1943, described the army facility in the desert oasis:

> Helen [Richards] and I are roommates, and there are eight of us girls with thirty-five fellows. We spent to-day getting passes and entrance red tape then went to town. I'm surely sold on Palm Springs for its warm sun, beautiful mountains and quaint shops in town. This is on my "post-war living" list.
>
> Our barracks are two-by-four with outside plumbing (building adjoining though modern interior). No hot water and sand sand everywhere.
>
> Tomorrow we start flying. It will be dual in BC-1s (AT-6 type). Then in order, the P-47, 39, 40 and 51. We are divided in flights A and B, fly half day, school half day. I'm in A flight and must be on the line at 7:15 each a.m.
>
> We have to wear skirts at evening mess—dern it.[28]

Scottie, as the girls called her, and the others settled in for the long-anticipated four-week course to become pursuit pilots. Love wanted to wish them well. She also needed to talk to Florene Miller and get her side of what had happened on that ill-fated P-47 flight. She left Long Beach and headed for Palm Springs, ninety miles as the crow flies, but over the imposing twin peaks of the San Jacinto Mountains.

Love and Miller met on the flight line at Palm Springs on December 3. As Florene recalls, the two of them waved to Dorothy Scott as she and her instructor took off in a BC-1 (AT-6) trainer. Florene was due to go up next. While Scott was flying, Love and Miller talked.[29]

A high thin overcast limited the visibility to thirty miles. The desert temperature was a pleasant seventy-six degrees and the wind was a light four miles per hour out of the west northwest.

Scott, flying from the back seat with her instructor in the front, had already made several landings. Once again, she set up and entered her final approach, establishing a normal gliding attitude. Above and behind her, a P-39 pilot swung from a shorter base leg into his final approach. Apparently the student in the P-39 could not see Scott because of the position of the low winter sun and the banking attitude of his airplane. He was above her and descending faster than she was. They were on a collision course.

The tower shouted a warning, but it came too late. The P-39 came down over the trainer. The two planes collided in mid-air. The tail section of the BC-1 was severed. Both ships crashed into the ground a short distance from each other with the BC-1 bursting into flames upon impact. Dorothy Scott was killed, as was her instructor, 2nd Lt. Robert M. Snyder. The P-39 pilot died as well.[30]

Later, Love would remember, with sorrow and regret, the earnest face, the absolute dedication to flying, the youth and promise of her twenty-fifth Original, Dorothy Scott. Here was the girl who had cared enough to write her commanding officer—a courageous feat in itself—about her concerns over transition practices.

No one can know what Love went through in private, but, publicly, the stoicism she had exhibited at Cornelia Fort's funeral manifested itself and she managed to focus on what had to be done. The very existence of the women's ferrying squadron was on the line. Now two of Love's original WAFS were dead—Cornelia Fort and Dorothy Scott—both in mid-air collisions, but in neither case was the woman pilot at fault. There was no question of pilot error on Scott's part. The P-39 pilot and the tower were assigned the blame.[31]

The accident report noted, "It is also believed that the camouflaged aircraft in this area (Palm Springs) is a contributing factor to the accident." Among the recommendations listed on the form: "All aircraft used in Pursuit Transition be painted yellow."[32]

In the aftermath, Love ordered Miller to accompany Dorothy's body home. Florene recalls, "Because I had been Dorothy's squadron commander at Dallas—and she and I had gone to Palm Springs together for pursuit school—I had to call her father and twin brother and tell them. I'll never forget that."[33]

On December 6, Love flew to Dallas with two tasks to perform. General Tunner wanted her to check on the Air Inspector's assertion that the women pilots there were being denied transition. And she needed to check the reports on Miller's accident. Regarding transition, what Love discovered was just the opposite from what she expected to find. Rather than being denied transition, some of the women in Dallas were being pushed too quickly through transition before they were fully qualified.[34]

The Dorothy Scott tragedy had changed the dynamic. But for Miller's safe landing of the stricken P-47, Love could have had two dead pilots on her hands in less than a week. She was in a tough spot. She had the reputation of her women's Ferrying Division squadrons—by now nearly 300 strong—to uphold. If, because of two back-to-back accidents, questions were raised about the women's fitness to fly pursuit, all of her hard work could come tumbling down around her. The less ruckus raised, the less attention called to the incident, the better.

Nancy Love had a reputation for coolness under pressure, of getting the job done without a lot of fanfare, and of keeping her mouth shut. With one of her pilots dead and another barely escaping with her life, she exercised the restraint for which she was famous, coped, and moved on. The women continued to do their job—ferry airplanes—and women pilots continued to be assigned to pursuit school. The last two women pilots to graduate from pursuit school did so on October 15, 1944.

Love officially relieved Miller of her command in Dallas, put Delphine Bohn in charge of the 5th Ferrying Group's WASP squadron, and transferred Miller from Dallas to Long Beach. Byrd Granger writes, "It is a rule that any pilot who washes out an airplane must be transferred or discharged."[35] When

Miller graduated from pursuit school, she reported for duty to squadron commander B.J. Erickson at the 6th Ferrying Group in Long Beach.

Love, the women ferry pilots, the Ferrying Division, and the ATC had been shaken to the core.

On December 14, 1943, after investigating the status of preparation for the women pilots for pursuit school, Love wrote to General Tunner.

> [I recommend] that the transition department be much more thorough, first, in selecting suitable applicants for transitioning, and second, in instructing these students both on technical aspects of the airplane and on the proper flying of the ship. If a student does not display good judgment, thorough understanding of the airplane and good flying technique, she should be returned to her squadron for further time on less complicated aircraft.
>
> That no quota for pursuit school be required of any WASP squadron. When a pilot is judged by transition to be superior, every effort should be made to give her an instrument course and to make her a thoroughly competent Class 3 pilot after which she should be sent to pursuit school. These pilots who are judged borderline cases should be given further ferrying duties until such time as their ability is considered sufficient to fly more complicated aircraft.
>
> That investigation be made by this Headquarters of the transition policies and procedure at Dallas since the situation observed with regard to the WASP seems to be a general one which affects all the pilots at the Group.[36]

Based on Love's recommendation, General Tunner immediately took steps to upgrade WASP training at all the ferrying bases. Ferrying Division pilots needed a minimum of one and a half hours as first pilot in a C-47 or fifteen hours copilot time in order to qualify for pursuit school. Some of the women had been sent to pursuit school without meeting this requirement.

The problem, it turned out, was the old March 1943 restriction on women copilots flying ferrying missions with male pilots, which was intended to protect the WAFS' reputations. Times, and the needs of the Air Transport Command, had changed. Still, women pilots destined for pursuit school were having trouble getting required checkouts in twin-engine cargo and medium transport planes.

In addition, on December 14, 1943, General Tunner sent a letter to the 2nd Ferrying Group in Wilmington, telling the command to "immediately" implement the policy, already in place, allowing unlimited advancement of women pilots.[37]

In a January 8, 1944, letter, Tunner reminded his group commanders that delivery flights could be considered training flights. Qualified WASP were to receive copilot training on specified twin-engine planes—with male pilots—in order to fulfill eligibility for pursuit school. All this was to be done after consultation with the WASP squadron leader.[38] The Ferrying Division needed all the qualified pursuit pilots it could find.

Not every WASP, not even every original WAFS, wanted to fly pursuit. Nancy Love didn't think a woman should be compelled to fly pursuit if she didn't want to. Nevertheless, on January 10, she put in an eloquent plea to the Ferrying Group commanders to encourage their WASP ferry pilots to begin transition to pursuit. She wrote: "Those WASPs who are capable of flying these types, will be performing the greatest service for their country and for the Ferrying Division."[39]

In the meantime, six of Love's originals—Nancy Batson, Barbara Donahue, Gertrude Meserve, Helen McGilvery, Florene Miller, and Helen Richards—proved their mettle and graduated from pursuit school in Palm Springs. Also graduating were those Houston graduates who attended with them. Eventually one more original, Sis Bernheim, would join that exclusive group. Pursuit school was moved to Brownsville, Texas, in April 1944 and Bernheim was sent there. She graduated on July 15, 1944, and immediately was assigned to ferry mostly P-47s out of Farmingdale, New York.

Nancy Love now had a growing cadre of women pursuit pilots—the 134 who eventually qualified were divided among five squadrons.[40] Another Ferrying Group, the 21st, would be formed in Palm Springs in April 1944 when pursuit school moved to Brownsville. And in August 1944, Love placed a small rotating contingent of women ferry pilots in Evansville, Indiana, to service the pursuit modification plant there.

Nancy Love's successful checkout in the P-38 opened that door. The records of the P-38 museum located at March Air Reserve Base (in California) list twenty-three WASP who ferried the P-38, including Love and seven of her original WAFS: Batson, Clark, Erickson, Gillies, McGilvery, Richards, and Sharp.[41]

And Dorothy Scott was not forgotten. Her twin brother Ed wrote his thoughts to the rest of the Scott family in a letter dated December 22, 1943: "I guess a lot of American families have to give. It must be just an act of God. We have to pay, ever so dearly, for what freedom we can get out of life. And my sister was always one to be out in front and I guess she just was cut out to lead the Scott family into eternity. God made her that way and perhaps just for that reason. She'll be up there waiting, just like we last saw her."[42]

Nancy Love received the following letter from Ed Scott, dated February 10, 1944: "Our birthday is the 16th of this month and on that day I do hope you will be thinking of her. I want to thank you now for that grand Christmas card and also the new hall, which has been named in her honor at Love Field, Dallas, Texas."[43] The letter arrived at Ferrying Division Headquarters in Cincinnati on February 14, 1944: Nancy Love's thirtieth birthday.

Nancy received yet another letter on her thirtieth birthday—this one from her father: "Dear Nance." After some chit-chat about working on income tax, he gets to the meat of his letter:

> I again tackled the matter of getting your scrapbook consolidated; it is really quite an exhibit and some of it is too good to be brushed off lightly though, Thank God, you have not taken it too seriously—ol' feet on the ground. I have what I considered a good scrapbook for the clippings—if one can call a 14 x 10 inch blow-up a clipping—but have come to see that looking through it would mean unfoldings and careful handling enough to take the joy out of it. I have it all ready for the book but am now negotiating

for a larger area if not so good looking a book. This was for your birthday—I hope to have it ready for Christmas.

The Army business looks pretty good from your report earlier in the week—you've certainly done a good job of restraint there—sitting on a powder keg and buying yourself a cigarette. The story would have been more entertaining if it had exploded.

Having vented the above parable—now to continue with the Sermon: never do today what you can put off 'til tomorrow; [a family friend] is sitting on the edge of her chair scowling at me because my daughter has not written an acknowledgment of a well-meant Christmas greeting.

What follows is family news, then Dr. Harkness ends the letter, "Happy birthday and love from your mother and me," signing it,

Affectionately, Dad

February 12, 1944—30 years ago. Don't let that figure 30 bother you.[44]

✈ 15 ✈
The Quest for Militarization

ilitarizing the women ferry pilots by making them part of the WAAC was the original plan. However, the WAAC was not yet militarized when the WAFS squadron was formed. The WAAC was an auxiliary and the legislation that created it lacked provision for flying status or ratings. Next, in the spring of 1943, the idea of commissioning the WAFS directly into the Army of the United States was suggested, but went nowhere.

Why militarize the women pilots? Military status would give them military insurance, death benefits, hospitalization, and pensions. And continuity of their service would be ensured.

Consequently, when the WAAC was militarized and became the Women's Army Corps (WAC) on July 1, 1943, General Tunner contacted Colonel Hobby and requested the WAFS be incorporated into the WAC. Jacqueline Cochran, named Director of Women Pilots June 28, 1943, opposed the incorporation of the women pilots—soon to carry the name WASP—into the WAC. She recommended that "militarization be withheld until the WASPs' absolute worth was proved by performance," despite the fact that the precedent now had been established that American women doing military work would be militarized and subject to military control. She felt the AAF should have its own organization for women pilots. More important, General Arnold concurred.[1]

Jackie Cochran did not like WAC director Col. Oveta Culp Hobby. In her autobiography, Cochran refers to Hobby as "the woman I love to hate."[2] Cochran resisted all attempts to put the WASP under Hobby. She did not want to be subordinate to her and the WAC could have only one colonel.

On September 30, 1943, Congressman John Costello of California introduced a bill in Congress calling for the militarization of the WASP (by then the name change was official). The bill went to the House Committee on Military Affairs for study. Subsequently it was amended to include the appointment of female trainees (the women at Avenger Field in Sweetwater, Texas) as aviation cadets and was reintroduced on February 17, 1944.

The Ferrying Division played no part in the sponsorship of this bill nor was it consulted. But naturally it was concerned with the outcome. The Ferrying Division favored militarization of the women pilots, but not under Jackie Cochran.[3]

The entire tenor of the war had changed by the time 1944 began. Two years of uncertainty fell away as the military might of the United States began to roll. Production by American industry was, in the words of one editorial cartoon, "Putting the screws on the Axis."[4]

Some headlines from January 1944:

January 2—"American troops land on New Guinea taking port and airfield; January 7—Allied forces go on the offensive in Italy"; January 10—"Allied troops push forward in Burma"; January 22—"Allied forces land at Anzio and set up beachhead"; January 31—"Allied forces attack Marshall Islands."[5]

The Allies—almost overnight, it seemed—were winning the war.

The bill to militarize the WASP was on the horizon and would soon be re-submitted to Congress.

Pilot casualties had been far fewer than anticipated. General Arnold had overestimated the number of pilots he was going to need, based on earlier RAF losses. In the early days of the war in England, a novice RAF pilot was given, at best, three months to live. But American pilot casualties never were that high. On January 15, 1944, the CAA WTS program for training flying personnel was terminated and the AAF began to cut back on its own pilot training program.[6] The after-shock ultimately would bring the WASP program to its knees. The availability of pilots had done a one-eighty. Now rather than a dearth of male pilots, there was a surplus. A year earlier, as Nancy Love's WAFS were just beginning to stretch their wings and ferry airplanes—albeit single-engine trainers—the demand for more pilots was loud and insistent. The women were needed. Now, as a result of the cutbacks in pilot training, the WASP became increasingly aware that their presence was not looked on as the saving grace it had been.

Before the big push toward militarization in Congress and just prior to the announcement of the release of the male flight instructors, four of the original WAFS—without Nancy Love's sanction—took the matter of WASP militarization into their own hands. Betty Gillies, in her February 8, 1984, memo to Delphine Bohn, recalled the events using notes in her diary.

Love held a conference of WASP squadron commanders and their assistants in Cincinnati on January 5, 1944. Present, says Gillies, were: Barbara Erickson and Bea Medes, Long Beach; Delphine Bohn and Avanell Pinckley, Dallas; Lenore McElroy and Ann Hamilton, Romulus; Betty Gillies and Esther Rathfelder, Wilmington. "The subject of militarization has been painfully avoided. Off the record, B.J., Delphine, Esther and I are going to go to Washington and see what's what. We got orders for B.J. and Delphine to proceed to NCAAB "to coordinate WASP affairs." And we are leaving here tomorrow a.m. planning to delay in Washington enroute."

Gillies writes that on January 7, 1944, they saw Jackie Cochran "to feel her out. Spent about two hours in her office and got nowhere. But it was an interesting experiment!"

On January 8, they visited the Navy. The Navy was interested in using women ferry pilots. Then, back at the Pentagon, Gillies met with Brigadier General William E. Hall, Deputy Chief of Air Staff. "Asked him if it were possible for us to ask for and receive a commission in the Army of the United States (AUS) and service pilot rating. 'By golly,' he said, 'if you can, that would solve all our problems.'"

Erickson, Bohn, Rathfelder, and Gillies spent January 9 in Wilmington "working up a proposed regulation permitting us to apply for a commission in the AUS as service pilots. We checked all the Army regulations and AAF regulations and can find no snags."

On January 10, three of them went back to Washington to see General Hall, who "seems to approve of our ideas" but needed more time to work on the proposal. Bohn and Erickson called their base commanders to get permission to remain a couple of days longer. Gillies returned to her duties at Wilmington.[7] General Hall did look into whether the matter might be resolved without legislation. In a memo dated January 11, 1944, he asked Air Staff Personnel to "look into the legality of commissioning women pilots directly into the Army on the basis of their qualification as service pilots, stating that if such legal basis could be found, General Arnold would be highly pleased because it would be the answer to militarizing the WASP and at the same time keeping them out of the WAC."

Unfortunately, the reply two days later stated, "the authority required extended only to men and could 'not be regarded as authority for commissioning women as officers in the Army of the United States.'"[8]

Delphine Bohn, in her memoir, recalls two visits she made, one to Speaker of the House Sam Rayburn (a fellow Texan) and one to General Somerville, Commanding General, Army Services Forces. She notes that Somerville "had under his command military personnel of the Women's Air Corps category."

But by then, she and Erickson had high profiles in Washington. When Love found out what her trusted lieutenants were up to, she knew she had to put a stop to it. The Arnold-Cochran plan to militarize the WASP was nearly ready. Too much was at stake. Bohn says: "Someone, helpfully, notified Cincinnati and Nancy Love. Since we were registered at the Hay-Adams Hotel and the whole of the military community had become familiarized with our many visits about town, she had no difficulty locating us."

Love telephoned them in Washington and—in a voice that belied the empathy she felt and yet underscored the authority she carried—according to Bohn, "very gently, but very firmly, ordered us back to our bases."

So ended the only grassroots attempt by the women ferry pilots to militarize.

The trouble really began when Erickson and Bohn got back to their bases. "Sadly, in our complete lack of thoughtfulness, we had caused our admirable base commanders trouble," Bohn writes. The culprits were reprimanded for their "illegal use" of Transportation Requests. They had to repay the cost of their unauthorized fares, which says Bohn, they intended to do anyway. "But these reputable officers had to accept from headquarters a share in our reprimands. For a week or so following our return, our commanders could not decide whether to smile, laugh or frown heavily whenever they ran into us on base. We attempted to avoid them."[9]

"Most of the women ferry pilots didn't want to be militarized under Jackie Cochran," says Erickson London. "But we were interested in militarization as individuals. Militarization would provide the benefits we knew we needed. But we didn't fit anywhere as a group. That had already been tried when they wanted to put us in the WACs. So I applied for a commission to become a Service Pilot. I had the qualifications. Using my initials, B.J. Erickson, they wouldn't know if I was male or female.

"It was a good idea, it was logical. The women ferry pilots were for it. But it fouled up Jackie Cochran's idea to make us a separate group under her command. She wanted equal status with Oveta Hobby and the other women commanders of military units—the SPARs, the WAVES, the Women Marines. She needed the thousand-member WASP for that. Jackie's influence was unbeatable—her wealthy husband, both Roosevelts, Arnold. And Nancy thought she could bring it off."[10]

Nancy and Bob managed to schedule re-checks—his on instruments, hers the B-17—at Long Beach at the same time late in February. Then Bob headed west for an ATC assignment in the Pacific. Nancy flew home via Sweetwater for the awarding of B.J. Erickson's Air Medal.

The occasion was the graduation of WASP Class 44-2, March 11, 1944, at Avenger Field. Hap Arnold, himself, pinned the

General Hap Arnold flanked by Jackie Cochran (left) and Barbara Erickson. Nancy Love is behind Cochran. Class 44-2 graduation at Avenger Field. Arnold awarded Erickson the Air Medal.

A *Fort Worth Star Telegram* photo, used with permission.

medal on Erickson's brand-new WASP uniform jacket. Both Nancy Love and Jackie Cochran were seated on the platform.

The hearings began in March 1944. What the Costello bill said was this (paraphrased): For the duration of the war, women would be commissioned as flight officers or aviation students in accordance with existing regulations. No woman would be appointed to a grade above colonel and there would be no more than one officer of that grade. Female flight cadets, upon successful completion of the prescribed course of training, would be commissioned as second lieutenants in the AUS. All commissioned women would receive the same pay and allowances as male members of the Army and they would be entitled to the same rights, privileges and benefits according to their rank, grade and length of service.

"On March 22, 1944, General Arnold testified about the WASP before a friendly House Armed Services Committee, flanked by three lovely ladies in new Santiago blue uniforms: Jackie Cochran, Ethel Sheehy—and Nancy Harkness Love," Marianne Verges writes. "Nancy had become alarmed by the uproar in the press. No matter how she felt about Cochran, the entire AAF women's program might be in jeopardy if everyone didn't pull together." The Armed Services Committee, after listening to Arnold in yet another session—this one closed—recommended the proposed WASP bill "favorably" to the House.[11]

General Arnold was the only witness heard.

When the news of the WASP bill reached the streets through the nation's newspapers, congressmen began to receive angry protests from civilian flying instructors now out of jobs and threatened with the draft; from the American Legion and other veterans' organizations; and from mothers of boys who had been transferred from aviation cadet training to the infantry. Congress was far more interested in the plight of the male trainees and instructors— who at this time were being released by the AAF—than it was in a handful of women pilots. The anti-WASP forces made far more noise and politicians pay attention to the squeaky wheel.

Molly Merryman suggests in her book *Clipped Wings* that other, equally important factors were at work in support of the

Nancy Love had to put her WAFS uniform aside and don the new WASP uniform.

Courtesy the Love family; electronic image courtesy the National Aviation Hall of Fame.

anti-WASP forces. She maintains that returning combat pilots also saw the WASP as a threat: "combat pilots who had returned to the United States were eager to perform any utility flying so that they could continue to receive flight pay. (AAF pilots received a greater monthly salary the more hours they flew. However, civilian pilots hired by the AAF, such as the WASPs, did not receive greater pay for their flight time, regardless of how many hours they flew.)"[12]

The other factors were the media with its ability to spin a story and how that story meshed with public opinion in 1944. The laid-off flight instructors and the veterans' organizations mounted a publicity campaign that produced countless stories denigrating the WASP, their skills and their work, but had the public not been receptive, the campaign might not have had the effect intended.

Merryman points to the wartime articles and photos that graced the pages of the popular magazine, *Life,* to make her point. "Just as depictions of men and women in general received differing constructions within the pages of *Life,* the magazine also depicted female pilots differently than male pilots," she writes. Stories about men are couched in bold terms: "masses of airplanes," "rigid training." One WASP story talks of "girls who so joyously scramble into silver airplanes."[13]

Nancy Love could easily identify with the rhetoric. Flowery language cropped up in countless articles about her and her flying career before and during the war. In the 1930s and 1940s, reporters and editors gave the public what they thought it wanted to read about young women flyers: how feminine and attractive they were and how they dressed. Nothing changed as World War II revved up. Articles showed young women, in the flush of patriotism, rushing to do their bit. But their bit usually was done on the sidelines and in support of their men—even Rosie the Riveter and the WASP—because that is what the U.S. public expected.

"Beneath her overalls, Rosie was still 'wearing her apron,'" says Jean Bethke Elshtain in *Women and War.*[14] Doris Kearns Goodwin, writing about 1944, makes similar observations in *No Ordinary Time:* "Ignoring poll after poll that suggested that the majority of women wanted to continue working, the women's magazines focused almost exclusively on those women who were ready to quit. 'My position is to go,' said one. 'My man wants me home and I want to be there. And we want kids.' Said another, 'It will be grand to get back to normal living again.'"[15]

That was one side. Then there were the seventy-nine percent of the working women who said "yes" they enjoyed working more than staying at home. Says Goodwin, "Of this total, 70 percent were married with children. For some, the best part of work was the sociability of the workplace versus the isolation of domestic responsibilities. For others, the best part was the financial independence, the freedom from having to ask their husbands if they could buy a new dress or clothes for the kids, the knowledge that they were contributing to the family's economic welfare." One Rosie the Riveter said, "At the end of the day I always felt I'd accomplished something. It was good—there was a product, there was something to be seen."[16]

Goodwin points out that Eleanor Roosevelt, through her columns and her speeches, tried to present a balanced view of women's work, reminding her audience that different women worked for different reasons. And Walter Reuther, United Auto Workers Union president, told the first national women's conference December 1944, in Detroit, "Industry must not be allowed to settle the employment problem by chaining women to kitchen sinks." But "even as Reuther was speaking, women were losing their jobs with unseemly haste; their layoff rate was 75 percent higher than for men."[17]

By 1944, the tide of the war had turned in favor of the Allies. The tide that brought women into the factories and munitions plants, into a multitude of jobs formerly filled by men, and most certainly that brought women into the military and into the cockpits of military airplanes, had turned as well. The WASP were caught in it. They became, in fact, a most visible pawn in the struggle to return to what was normal, and "normal" meant prewar.

The Committee on the Civil Service of the House of Representatives, led by Robert J. Ramspeck—a Georgia Congressman and a former deputy U.S. Marshal—launched an investigation of the WASP program. The WASP were under Civil Service; therefore public funds were being expended on their program, which Congress knew next to nothing about. Nancy Love was asked to give a deposition. She did so on Sunday, April 16, 1944. Her conversation was with a Colonel McCormick and a Mr. Shillito, investigators for the Ramspeck Committee in Washington, D.C.

Love wrote a brief report on the type of questions asked of her and the answers she gave.

Q. What do you think of the qualifications of the girls who come from the training school [Avenger Field, Sweetwater, Texas]?

A. They are good pilots. They are on a par with what I know of the male graduates of the Training Command.

Q. What is the policy on pursuit pilots?

A. We need pursuit pilots.

Q. (He) was very interested in the relationship between Miss Cochran and myself. Wanted to know if there was a battle between us.

A. (I) said Miss Cochran's was an administrative job and mine was an operational one, and there was no battle between us.

Q. Do the girls want militarization?

A. The majority do.

Q. Why do the girls want to be militarized?

A. For recognition and protection. A civilian girl going into a modification center to pick up an airplane is open to suspicion as a spy. Also, compensation and insurance for the families would then be available to them.

Q. How much do you think, off the record, that the uniform is worth?

A. I have no idea. I have never been interested in clothes.

Q. What items are issued and what are purchased?

A. We are issued two winter and two summer uniforms. We purchase accessories, etc.

Q. What is the pay of the other operational WAFS?

A. $250 per month, plus overtime, which comes to about $280. [Love had already answered that her pay was $142.08 every two weeks.]

Q. Who are the girls who are competing for the Air Medal?

A. I have no idea what you mean. It has been awarded to Miss Erickson.

Q. How did she make those deliveries so fast?

A. The weather was good; she is a good pilot and a hard worker; and she had fast airplanes.[18]

Love signed the six-page document dated April 17, 1944.

The WASP bill would not go to the floor of the House until June.

In the meantime, the WASP were hit with charges of favoritism. The women, their detractors claimed, were flying more frequently than the men, had better assignments, and men sat on the ground while the WASP were kept busy.

Nancy Love and WASP Ann McClelland ferrying.
Courtesy of the National Museum of the U.S. Air Force.

ATC commander General George asked General Tunner to compile a complete report of the WASP performance on the job in the Ferrying Division: "Make it thorough and make it good." General Tunner sought input from the commanders of the Ferrying Groups and from pursuit school, all of whom had daily dealings with the WASP ferry pilots. He knew he would get an accurate report from them.[19]

Some resentment did exist among a minority of the male pilots and that particular minority was quite outspoken, Tunner's report said. But the supervisory and operational personnel, whose sole interest was the efficient operation of the ferrying mission, did not share this resentment. "Those personnel are familiar with the pilot shortage in the Ferrying Division and appreciate the WASPs' contribution."

As for favoritism: "The WASPs flying time has consistently averaged slightly less than the flying time of male pilots." The women pilots took their turn in frequency and type of assignment. The Ferrying Division, as Tunner pointed out, had been extremely busy with domestic operations and all pilots, regardless of sex, had been utilized without anyone waiting an undue length of time for assignment. Some pilots were qualified only on a few types of airplanes and had sat on the ground while other pilots who were qualified on many types got to fly because of the kind of airplane that needed to be ferried. That was true among WASP and among male pilots. "And he added, "in this report, it must be noted that during the last three-month period all leaves to Ferrying Division pilots were cancelled due to a pilot shortage."[20]

General George submitted General Tunner's report. Apparently—and sadly, considering the outcome—it was never presented to the concerned members of Congress.[21]

The concern of the Ramspeck Committee, it appears, was *not* the use of women as pilots but the further recruiting of inexperienced personnel. The Ramspeck Committee contended that training women pilots, from scratch, cost too much. There were male pilots out there, including combat veterans now returning having flown their maximum number of missions, who could be retrained to ferry much more quickly and cheaply than women who had just managed to fly the thirty-five hours necessary to be admitted to the WASP training program.

A year earlier—when the WAFS were beginning to ferry in earnest and more of them were needed—those combat pilots were training for overseas bombing missions and couldn't be spared for ferrying. The plan had worked.

Congressional debate on militarization continued and the press coverage, most of it anti-WASP but some in their favor, continued to churn until the bill finally would come to a vote in the House on June 21, 1944.

✈ 16 ✈

In Pursuit, Coast to Coast

lying pursuits was dangerous duty. Those women who qualified to fly them knew this. Some of the women ferry pilots
opted not to take pursuit transition. But 134 of those who
tried, qualified. Included in the 134 were 124 pursuit school graduates, 9 original WAFS who did not go through pursuit school,
and Helen Richey—an experienced pilot who flew Spitfires for
the ATA in England before entering the Flight Training School in
Sweetwater in 1943. She was exempted from pursuit school.[1]

On January 6, 1944, the ferrying of pursuit planes became
the number-one priority of the women assigned to Nancy Love's
squadrons. When Love met with her squadron commanders
January 1944 in Cincinnati, the main topic of conversation was
pursuit training. "The ships we are most needed to fly are P-47s,
51s, 39s, 40s, P-38s, and A-20s. So we are setting our training
program with that in mind," Betty Gillies noted in her diary.[2]

The first fourteen WASP graduates of pursuit school returned
to their squadrons in January ready for pursuit ferrying duty.[3]
At that point, Nancy Love and General Tunner placed eight of

their Wilmington-based pursuit pilots at the Republic factory in Farmingdale, New York, where the P-47s were built. Each pursuit pilot would spend two weeks there then rotate back to Wilmington for other duty. Original WAFS Batson, McGilvery, and Meserve, along with several Houston and Sweetwater graduates, joined Gillies, Clark, James, and Richey on the schedule for rotation in and out of Farmingdale. Their duty was to ferry the P-47s from the Long Island location to the docks at Newark, New Jersey, fifty miles west as the crow flies. Given the short distance, and if the weather cooperated and depending on how quickly the airplanes came off the assembly line, each pilot could move several airplanes in one day.

Betty Gillies secured for them the use of a C-60 to follow the P-47s and their pilots to Newark, pick them up, and bring them back to Farmingdale so that they would spend less time getting back to the factory and, therefore, could make more deliveries. Batson, James, and Meserve subsequently were checked out in the C-60 and traded off as pilot and copilot on those runs.

Love's women pilots became so good at what they did that, as of June 8, 1944, they took over all the ferrying out of Farmingdale. Betty Gillies ran that squadron as she ran Wilmington, like clockwork. Male ferry pilots were assigned elsewhere.

As the Romulus-based pilots returned from pursuit school, they went to work ferrying Curtiss P-40s out of Buffalo, and P-39s and later P-63s out of the Bell Aviation plant in Buffalo, New York. Those were delivered to Great Falls, Montana, where male ferry pilots took them on to Alaska to be handed over to Russian pilots. Some Romulus WASP also served two-week stints at Farmingdale when needed. The women in Dallas ferried a variety of airplanes and, of course, the women in Long Beach had the biggest number of different types of airplanes available to them because so many of the aircraft factories were located in the Los Angeles Basin.

Nancy Love's trouble-shooting for the Ferrying Division in December 1943 centered on clearing up the misunderstandings and miscommunications at Ferrying Group command level that were keeping the women out of the cockpits of the airplanes they needed to fly in order to transition up and be eligible to go to pursuit school. Following Love's December groundwork, General Tunner sent a pursuit incentive letter to the Group commanders on January 8, 1944: "It is desired to progress qualified WASPs as rapidly as possible consistent with safe practice, so that they may be eligible for Pursuit School. Copilot training will expedite transition on Class 3 and Class 4 aircraft. You are reminded that you are authorized to assign WASP co-pilots with male pilots on delivery flights. It is desired that this practice be instituted after careful consultation with your WASP Squadron Leader."[4]

Two days later, on January 10, Love also wrote to the commanders of the bases where her women were stationed. Though there was a definite need for pursuit pilots, the Ferrying Division did not compel WASP to undergo pursuit training. Love simply asked that any WASP willing to go to pursuit school sign a statement to that effect *before* she was given the necessary Class III transition and instrument training:

> It is felt that it is of the utmost importance that WASPs be made to understand the need for their service as pursuit pilots. The Ferrying Division training plan is designed to progress male pilots toward 4-engine overseas delivers and transport flights. Pursuit training is not a necessary step in this progression. Thus there is a genuine need for WASPs in both the single and twin-engine pursuit categories (A-20 and P-38 types), and those WASPs who are capable of flying these types will be performing the greatest service for their country and for the Ferrying Division.[5]

Considering the makeup of those fast, complex pursuits, their quirks and unpredictability, it was only a matter of time before a woman pilot would die at the controls. In all, three women would lose their lives ferrying pursuit aircraft; another disappeared in the P-51 she was ferrying and neither she nor the plane, to date, have been found. And two—Dorothy Scott and Alice Lovejoy—died while in training learning to fly them.[6]

The P-51 was the Long Beach WASP's major responsibility. But, beginning in 1944, several eventually flew the Lockheed P-38

Lightning as well. On March 5, 1944, Evelyn Sharp wrote to a friend that she was scheduled to check out on the P-38. Though only twenty-three when she joined the WAFS, Evelyn already had 2,968 hours. Once Evelyn had checked out in the Lightning late in March 1944, she was assigned to deliver a P-38J to Newark. The afternoon of March 30, she took off for Palm Springs. Long Beach, located on the Pacific Ocean, frequently was socked in until mid afternoon. Ferry pilots routinely took off when the fog lifted and flew east to Palm Springs where they could RON and get an early start the next morning to head east.

Amarillo was Evelyn's destination the second night, then on to Cincinnati April 1 to meet with Nancy Love. The following day she hoped to make Newark, but landed at the New Cumberland, Pennsylvania, airport near Harrisburg to RON because of bad weather over the Allegheny Mountains. The morning of April 3, she was back at the airport ready to take off a little after 10 a.m.[7] At breakfast in the hotel that morning, she mentioned to a young second lieutenant that she had been having trouble with one of her engines.[8]

After preflighting the aircraft, she climbed into the cockpit, settled herself down in the seat and began the engine run-up and pre-takeoff cockpit check. When everything was a go, she taxied out to the departure end of the runway. Another series of check offs completed, she fastened her safety harness. The tower cleared her for takeoff. She turned onto the runway and lined the nose wheel up on the centerline. She was wheels up at 10:29.

Black smoke poured from the left engine. The pilot and the airplane tried valiantly to fly. But the P-38 stalled, hung in the air, the left wingtip caught a cluster of trees, and the sleek silver aircraft hit the ground flat, skidded ten feet, and stopped. The Plexiglas canopy lay upside down a few feet ahead of the right prop.

The stopped clock on the instrument panel read 10:30.[9]

"I was at the Republic factory in Farmingdale waiting to take a P-47 over to Newark when Helen Mary Clark came up to me in the Alert Room and told me Evelyn had been killed," Nancy Batson remembered. "I was stunned. Evelyn was such a good pilot. Of course, later, we heard what happened to her.

"Then Helen Mary said, 'you have orders from Nancy Love to return to Wilmington, immediately. You're to go to Harrisburg to pick up Evelyn's body from the undertaker and accompany her home on the train to Ord, Nebraska.' Nancy Love never attended a funeral after Cornelia's. We think she was so broken up over Cornelia that she couldn't face another one. Remember, she sent Florene home with Dorothy Scott. And she sent me with Evelyn."

Dressed in a Santiago blue WASP uniform—the new uniforms, by then, had been issued to the original WAFS as well as to the Houston and Sweetwater graduates—Nancy Batson left Wilmington with $200 collected from the WASP who were members of the 2nd Ferrying Group, many of whom were Training Command graduates and did not know Evelyn. Her instructions were to give it to Evelyn's parents when she arrived in Ord.

Nancy Love was waiting in Wilmington when Nancy Batson returned a few days later. "How did it go?" she asked.[10]

Neither shed a tear, nor had Batson cried throughout the trip out and back. Both Nancys did their crying in private. But Evelyn's death painfully reminded Nancy Love, once again, that the women pilots who flew for her had no insurance or other benefits provided by the Army because they were not militarized.

Now three of Nancy Love's Originals were dead.

Sharp had been scheduled to take over as commander of the new women's ferrying squadron ready for placement at Palm Springs as part of the 21st Ferrying Group. Pursuit school had been moved to Brownsville, Texas. Now Love had to decide on someone to take Evelyn's place. She summoned Byrd Granger and Mary Lou Colbert to Cincinnati for a conference. Both were 43-1 Houston graduates and early pursuit school graduates now stationed at Love Field, but assigned to the new Palm Springs squadron.

They met with Love in her apartment on April 4. Love placed Granger in command, appointed Colbert executive officer, and assigned Vivian Cadman (43-5) as operations officer. While in Cincinnati, Granger experienced the beginning of a severe hip problem that landed her in the hospital back in Texas. With Granger disabled, Colbert took over the command.[11]

"Viv [Cadman] and I went to Palm Springs together to start up the squadron from scratch," says Mary Lou Colbert Neale. "Byrd was in the hospital and then laid up a long time. She didn't join us until very late."[12]

General Tunner no longer had sufficient trainer-type airplanes for the less qualified WASP to ferry. In April, he told Love and Cochran to work out the transfer of non-pursuit-qualified pilots back to the Training Command.

Love was due in Orlando, Florida, April 19, to begin Officer Training School (OTS). Cochran had succeeded in securing officer training for the WASP in consideration of their expected militarization, and Love was to take part in the first class. Cochran invited Love to be her houseguest the weekend of April 16, knowing Love was due in Washington for her deposition. Their meeting marked the beginning of several reassignments of women pilots that would occupy considerable amounts of both Cochran's and Love's time and energy over the next four months.

From Washington, Love headed to OTS. The first class of twenty-four included the squadron leaders and several other Originals—Gillies, Batson, Donahue, Erickson, Bohn, Miller, Batten, and Scharr in addition to Nancy Love—as well as training school graduates who had been on active duty the longest.[13] A new class of twenty-four students would begin every first and third Wednesday of the month. Later classes had fifty students. Four hundred-sixty women pilots graduated from OTS before the school was closed to women in the fall of 1944.

Nancy Love, as if she didn't already have enough pressure, studied the class material before she went to Orlando and focused on pulling down the top score in the class. As the executive officer, she felt she had to. The curriculum consisted of military discipline, courtesy and customs, chemical warfare, as well as the organization of the army and staff procedures. She kept a notebook that contains some of her class notes.[14]

The first OTS class gathers in Orlando.
Photo from the Nancy Batson Crews collection, in the author's possession.

The timing couldn't have been worse. The WASP program and the fate of the women pilots were being debated daily in the press, yet here were the women being treated to a four-week training session to prepare them to be officers. Right then, the Ferrying Division desperately needed every pursuit ferry pilot it could lay its hands on to move airplanes and could ill afford the loss of several of them for four weeks at a time. Though it wasn't publicly known then, D-Day was less than two months away when Love and her group reported to Orlando.

Nancy Love and her women pilots had several visitors in Orlando—columnists from east coast newspapers among them. Jacqueline Cochran herself flew in to greet the first class and invited Love, Gillies, Bohn, and others to dinner. Another to call on the first attendees was the chairman of the House Civil Service Committee, Representative Robert Ramspeck, who also extended an invitation to dinner. "He invited Nancy Love and three or four of us to have dinner with him, all the while he queried us as to the WASPs," Delphine Bohn writes.[15]

The Originals weren't too keen on being militarized under "Colonel" Jacqueline Cochran. Already, they were upset at having to give up their familiar gray-green uniforms for the newly arrived Santiago blue uniforms worn with such pride by the WASP who had graduated from Houston or Avenger. They resented Cochran, feeling she had interfered with their mission and taken the command prerogative away from their leader, Nancy Love.

At Orlando, "there was a beautiful meeting of minds between Nancy Love and the first WAFS she had gathered for the Ferrying Division, especially apropos the joys of flying," Bohn writes. "Our gossiping had been marvelously good.

"One subject at various times had been the Douglas A-20 medium bomber. Nancy had marked the A-20 as a favorite. None of us had flown the airplane, but all of us were eager to do so. Her remarks as to its specialness had helped to develop that eagerness. This desire, Nancy understood."[16]

The Douglas A-20 (also known as the DB-7) was an attack bomber with twin 1600-horsepower Wright engines and a service ceiling of 25,000 feet.[17] Love offered Delphine Bohn, Nancy Batson, Barbara Donahue, and B.J. Erickson the opportunity to take A-20 transition in Orlando. Once checked out, they were each to deliver an A-20 to the West Coast. The other three were able to rearrange their schedules, but Bohn was not. Batson, Erickson, and Donahue took off early the following day, May 14.

A solid bond of affection existed between Nancy Love and "her girls" and manifested itself under a variety of circumstances. While enroute on that cross-country A-20 delivery, Batson, Erickson, and Donahue wrote a series of post cards to Nancy, addressed to her at Ferrying Division Headquarters in Cincinnati. From Louisiana they wrote:

> 1st stop. It's still the most terrific ship of them all.
> Whee!!!
> The three of us.[18]

Nancy Batson saw that plum assignment as validation of her work as a ferry pilot. "Nancy Love was saying to me 'you've done a good job.' That was her way of patting you on the back and saying thanks for all your hard work and dedication. Because, you see, Nancy Love didn't say things like that to you in person. She expected you to do your job—the job we were hired to do, fly airplanes—and to do it right, no questions asked. She was a wonderful person to work and fly for."[19]

In April 1944, just as OTS classes commenced, the number of women pilots in the Ferrying Division reached its high point: 303.[20] However, Nancy Love and Jackie Cochran already had begun to work out the logistics of what would become known as "the Great Transfer." Byrd Granger uses that term in her book.[21]

First, forty WASP were transferred out of the 2nd Ferrying Group to non-ferrying bases. Shortly after, on April 27, Betty

"Nancy was smiling," Iris Critchell says of the photo she took of Nancy with Nancy Batson and Betty Gillies at OTS.

Photo courtesy Iris Cummings Critchell.

Gillies was told she was to get seven of the May 23 (Class 44-4) graduates. Because of the recent transfer out, Gillies and her commanding officer asked that the seven not be assigned to the 2nd because there were a limited number of light aircraft to be ferried at Wilmington.[22]

In a telephone conversation between Nancy Love and Jackie Cochran on July 3, 1944, the main topic of conversation was the transfer of more than 123 women out of the Ferrying Division into the Training Command. At this point, the two leaders were trying to stop the Training Command from sending several new Avenger graduates to Ferrying Division squadrons because they would have to be reassigned and sent elsewhere.

"Do you have all the girls you'll ever want, or do you have too many now?" Cochran asked.

"We can use more if they're qualified. You remember we suggested that the fifteen a month we get be qualified for pursuit—to be sent to pursuit school? That part's all right with us," Nancy answered. "We have sixty nine qualified on pursuit. As a matter of fact we have more than that now because twelve just graduated. So we've got eighty-one pursuit pilots and we have ten going into this next class."[23]

Love recently had returned from the Brownsville, Texas, Municipal Airport and the Air Transport Command's 4th OTU (pursuit school) where she had attended the graduation of the largest pursuit class yet. She told a reporter there that she was pleased with the progress of the WASP assigned to the school in Brownsville.[24]

On August 15, 1944, the Ferrying Division released the 123 non-pursuit-qualified women pilots to the Training Command for reassignment.

Iris Critchell, a pursuit pilot, and one of B.J. Erickson's squadron staff leaders in Long Beach, remembers very well the transfers the summer of 1944 and the many women who were sent back to the Training Command. "The girls had to be able to ferry pursuit, because that is what we had to fly. The Ferrying Group at Long Beach still had a place for women who had qualified to ferry the P-51s and high-performance twin-engine aircraft like the A-20, the P-38, and the P-61."

Critchell points out that the women qualified to do this, like the men, had to have a Class III-P rating to ferry single-engine pursuit or a Class IV-P rating to ferry twin-engine pursuit-types. To qualify for pursuit school, a pilot first had to transition in a twin-engine C-47 or similar aircraft. This was to provide experience in a heavier airplane with more complex systems. Many of the women pilots who had come into the Ferrying Division from the later classes simply had not had time to move up in transition in order to be considered for pursuit school.[25]

Byrd Granger writes: "[Some] historical reports attempt to make it appear that the girls who were transferred out of the Ferrying Division in August 1944 were unqualified or inexperienced or unsuited for the work for which they were trained. [The] ... ferrying of trainer type airplanes was falling off rapidly ... women pilots would be utilized almost altogether in pursuit

Nancy attended a Pursuit School graduation in Brownsville, Texas, June 1944.
Courtesy Love family; electronic image NAHF.

work.... This lack of qualification in many cases was due only to lack of time to gain flying experience."[26]

"The transfer the summer of 1944 was very simple," says B.J. Erickson London, WASP squadron leader in Long Beach. "The girls who had not qualified in pursuits were sent to the Training Command. There were no other airplanes left in Long Beach for them to fly. By sending them to other assignments, they got to fly airplanes they were qualified to fly, doing other jobs at other bases."[27]

Women included in the transfer were those who had no desire to ferry pursuit; had been eliminated from pursuit school; had failed in transition to other classes of airplanes; were not considered pursuit material; or had insufficient experience.[28]

A few non-pursuit-qualified women pilots stayed in the Ferrying Division by moving into administrative positions and a few continued to ferry Class III twin-engine cargo and transport planes. By then a new category of deliveries had been added: war-weary airplanes that had to be ferried to the graveyard. This included everything from beat-up trainers to shot-up pursuits and bombers. Obviously, these too took extra care and expertise in handling.

If a woman did not want to go back to the Training Command, she could resign. Because the WASP were not militarized, they were free to leave any time and several did over the organization's two-plus-years existence—for reasons of marriage, health, pregnancy, and the necessity of caring for children. Some left giving no specific reason. A few left to join other services like the WAC. After the Great Transfer, the strength of the Ferrying Division women averaged around 140.

Fifteen of Nancy Love's Originals were still ferrying. That number included Lenore McElroy, an experienced Class III pilot who had opted not to fly pursuit because she was the mother of three teenagers. Also, she was Barbara Donahue's second-in-command at Romulus and virtually indispensable. Originals Bernice Batten and Betsy Ferguson were transferred to the Training Command. Esther Manning Rathfelder Shively, a Class I pilot, continued to serve as Betty Gillies' able operations officer in Wilmington.

✈ 17 ✈

Militarization Denied

On June 5, 1944, the day before D-Day, the Ramspeck Committee presented its report to Congress. The committee's verdict was that the WASP program was "unnecessary and unjustifiably expensive." The committee was opposed to militarization and recommended "the recruiting of inexperienced women and their training as pilots be terminated immediately."[1] On June 21, fifteen days after the Allies landed in Normandy and began the push that would end the war in Europe eleven months later, Congress voted down the WASP bill. Militarization was denied. That did not mean that the WASP were out of a job. Not yet anyway.

Five days later, General Arnold announced that the recruitment and training of all additional WASP would cease. No new classes were to begin after July 1, 1944. Young women already on their way to Sweetwater for the class scheduled to begin July 1—designated 45-1—were to be sent home. There was, however, more to Arnold's statement. Those women already in training at Avenger Field would be allowed to finish. The WASP operations would continue and the women already on active duty would continue to serve.[2]

On July 5, a board made up of Jackie Cochran and Generals George, J. H. McCormick, H. A. Craig and R. W. Harper was appointed to submit recommendations as to the future of the WASP program. On July 8, Cochran, who had begun the process of writing her report, submitted her recommendations. Militarization was important, she noted, but putting the WASP in the WAC was not acceptable. Then on August 1, her report finished, she recommended to General Arnold that the women pilots either be militarized or "serious consideration should be given to inactivation of the WASP program."[3]

On August 7, her report was released to the media and the story appeared in the nation's newspapers on August 8. In the meantime, efforts were brewing to generate support for the WASP and campaigns were underway to get Congress to reconsider. One such effort was begun by the Ninety-Nines and another by a group of citizens from Sweetwater, Texas, the home of the WASP Avenger Field training facility.[4]

WASP Class 44-6 graduated August 4, and the women were assigned to duties around the country other than with the Ferrying Division. The women in WASP classes 44-7 through 10 continued to train at Sweetwater. On August 15, the 123 non-pursuit-qualified women pilots were transferred out of the Ferrying Division. The 142 women pilots remaining continued to ferry mostly P-47s, P-51s, P-38s, and P-63s to embarkation points to be shipped overseas. They also ferried their share of war wearies to the bone yard.

On August 24, Allied troops retook Paris, setting off a celebration on both sides of the Atlantic.

The four-week WASP training course at the AAF School of Applied Tactics in Orlando was shut down in September.[5] On October 2, General Arnold announced the total casualties suffered by the Army Air Forces since the outbreak of the war. They were far fewer than the numbers for which the Army had planned. General Arnold was able to state, positively, that the AAF now had sufficient pilots for present combat needs.[6] The following day, Arnold made public his decision on the WASP. They would be disbanded on December 20, 1944, "unless there are unexpected and much higher combat losses in the air war over Germany.... Reduction in training made several thousand civilian flyers available to be trained and assigned the routine service pilot jobs now being done by the WASP.... The date fixed permits the transitional training of male replacements ... and will permit the WASPs to reach their homes by Christmas. Until December 20 current WASP activities will be continued without change."[7]

In his letter to each of the WASP, which accompanied a letter from Jacqueline Cochran, Arnold told the women how proud he was of them and explained his decision to shut down the program. And he added: "The situation is that if you continue in service, you will be replacing instead of releasing our young men. I know that the WASP wouldn't want that."[8]

Why were the WASP shut down? Contrary to rumors, it was not because Nancy Love and Jackie Cochran had fundamental differences on how the organization should be run. Nor was it because Jackie Cochran asked Arnold to militarize them or shut them down. For all practical purposes, and given the turn of the tide of war, disbanding the WASP seemed the expedient thing to do.

Army historians tell it this way:

> To the casual observer, unacquainted with the course of military events the summer of 1944, the AAF would appear to have made an about-face on the WASP question. In June, General Arnold was pleading for the induction of women pilots into the Army as a military necessity. In October [when the WASP were officially notified of their deactivation] he was stating that unless the program was deactivated these pilots would be keeping men out of the air. The explanation for this rapid change in view apparently lies in the phenomenal military successes of the intervening months and in an AAF attrition rate much lower than had been expected.[9]

In his memoir, General Arnold wrote: "The WASP did a magnificent job for the Army Air Forces."[10]

In his December 7, 1944, address to the WASP Class of 44-10, the last to graduate from Avenger Field, Arnold would tell them of his initial doubts as to a woman's ability to fly military air-craft and what had made him change his mind.

> You, and more than nine hundred of your sisters, have shown that you can fly wingtip to wingtip with your brothers.... The entire operation has been a success. It is on record that women can fly as well as men. We will not again look upon a women's flying organization as experimental. We will know that they can handle our fastest fighters, our heaviest bombers; we will know that they are capable of ferrying, target towing, flying training, test flying and the countless other activities which you have proved you can do. This is valuable knowledge for the air age into which we are now en-tering.... We will never forget our debt to you.[11]

General Robert E. Nowland, who succeeded General Tunner as Ferrying Division commander, wrote to General Arnold on November 1, 1944, pointing out problems that would be en-countered by the Ferrying Division when the women pilots were let go. He went on to point out a dollars-spent estimate on what replacing the women ferry pilots would cost. And he asked that he be allowed to retain the women until their replacements could be trained and brought on duty. At that point, he suggested, the women would be let go gradually over a period of time.

General Nowland was told: "Inactivation of the WASPs was based upon a policy decision which has a vital effect upon the AAF as a whole."[12] He also was told: "Evaluation of this pro-gram in terms of dollars and cents is not the immediate issue at stake and personnel under your control should scrupulously avoid any discussion along this line."[13]

The decision to deactivate was devastating to the WASP. They felt they still were needed. The women pilots in the Ferrying Division by then were ferrying more than sixty percent of all the pursuits coming off the assembly lines. Other base commanders around the country who had WASP working for them asked to keep them on because the women performed their jobs so well.

The WASP wanted to see the war to its victorious end. But they accepted the decision and the reasons they were given as to why it was made. Unfortunately, the "we" to whom General Arnold referred in his speech *did* forget the debt owed the WASP. What the WASP had accomplished faded into obscurity for more than thirty years and came back to light only when women, once again, climbed into the cockpits of military airplanes in the 1970s. When that happened, those young women, mistakenly, were hailed as the first.[14]

The WASP *had* been forgotten—until then.

For years it was assumed that the decision to deactivate and disband the WASP had nothing to do with the intrinsic value of the women pilots or the job they had done or were capable of doing. However scholarship that has come out of the Women's Movement suggests a more complicated answer to the question of "why were the WASP shut down?" Molly Merryman, who holds a Ph.D. in American Culture Studies and teaches at Kent State University in Ohio, published her findings in *Clipped Wings, The Rise and Fall of the Women Airforce Service Pilots (WASPs) of World War II* in 1998. She writes:

> Perhaps the most important factor leading to the demise of the Women Airforce Service Pilots program was a negative media campaign precipitated in part by the return of combat pilots from overseas and the release of Army Air Forces cadets and pilot trainers into the "walking Army" for service in anticipated large-scale ground assaults against Japan's military. The male civilian pilots organized a lobbying group and discovered in the WASPs a target against whom they could articulate claims of preferential treatment, thus deflecting attention away from their real intent of refusal to serve as combat soldiers, the role in which the military had deemed that these men were needed.[15]

Why didn't the media and the public in general see through that? Merryman maintains that the mindset of the media and of the public was such that it wasn't ready to see the value of women in the kind of work flying military airplanes represented. "The WASPs were the first American wartime service unit comprised entirely of women who performed functions traditionally associated with men. WASPs were involved in activities considered both dangerous and adventurous for the men who performed them; thus, a high level of status was associated with their roles and missions.... [F]lyboys were the elite of the U.S. military."[16]

Women, by excelling on "a terrain that was very much a proving ground of masculinity," upset the accepted natural order of things. The other military women of World War II did not do that. Merryman continues: "[T]he WASPs directly questioned the purportedly natural and expected status of men within the military by serving in one of its most desired roles—desired both because pilots were the elite of the military and because the WASPs were assigned to domestic, noncombat positions, which were the safest flying positions in the Army Air Forces.... By taking on roles and missions previously associated with the masculine, WASPs challenged assumptions of male supremacy in wartime culture."[17]

There was no way for the media to soft-pedal what the WASP were doing. They weren't doing "women's work"; they were flying military airplanes. When the media wrote stories about them, they couldn't be depicted in traditional or accepted women's jobs, as the WACs or WAVES could be.

As World War II geared up, industry needed women, Leila J. Rupp writes. "By 1943 the shortage of labor had become acute.... Because the prewar image ignored already working women and because propaganda concentrated on industry, the war transformed the image of American women. That the ideal woman in 1943 worked at all was a change ... [and] that dominated the wartime public image."[18]

The WASP were heroines in 1943. But by 1944 the Allies were on the offensive. That changed the impetus from patriotism and a general acceptance of doing anything one could to help win the war to preparing to return to a normal way of life, which included getting the women out of the factories—and airplanes—and back to the kitchen. Unfortunately, the attempt to militarize the WASP came about after the war began to go our way.

Cynthia Enloe writes: "Wars have beginnings and endings and this provides us with clearer sign posts for monitoring the changing conditions of women's lives…. Rosie [the Riveter] was celebrated because she was an anomaly and a short-lived one at that…. Government propaganda geared up [in 1945] to persuade women that their natural place was back in the kitchen."[19]

Given that, in the eyes of the public, the women pilots already were considered to be a temporary solution, then it would make sense that the attitude would also be that the men were entitled to have those jobs when they were once again available to take them. Despite what General Arnold said to them in his October letter, the WASP generally did not agree with that premise. They thought they should be accepted on their own merits. But they had no choice in the matter, nor was their case defended until it was too late. An AAF ban on publicity about the WASP was in effect throughout the congressional hearings.

"We were highly trained, proficient women pilots and we were badly needed to ferry those pursuit planes that were coming off the assembly line," says B.J. Erickson London. "It was politics that sent us home and that was tragic."[20]

"It wasn't the right time," says Iris Critchell. "The political atmosphere wasn't right. Society wasn't ready for a separate women's Air Force."[21]

Nancy Love was not blind to these realities. She knew some male pilots were prone to easily deflated egos and were "looking for cases of favoritism whereby WASPs got better assignments and opportunities to transition to desirable types of airplanes. [She] did all that was possible to counteract male pilot antagonism, first of all by seeing to it that the girls did a thorough job and without fanfare and secondly by deliberately avoiding all possible occasions that might lead to antagonism," Captain Marx writes. On occasions she protested when General Tunner asked for women to be placed on assignments that might arouse jealousy among some male pilots.[22]

WASP Jean Hascall Cole, in the conclusion to her 1992 book about her Class 44-2 classmates at Avenger Field, ponders the question of why they flew and why they accepted the fate the Army handed them.

Young people of the 1990s, who have read this account, tell me they find if difficult to see how these WASPs could happily accept the adjustment from their flying careers back to their old roles as housewives and mothers. It was not an easy adjustment ... but it was accepted, and I suppose for many of us that was how it had to be....

Some of the women seemed to think of the whole experience as almost illicit ... as though they had no legitimate right to fly.... Well, back then things were really quite different.... I can only report what really happened back in the forties.[23]

Lt. Col. Mattie E. Treadwell, one of the highest ranking WACs and the author of that service's official history, writes of the bigger picture of incorporating women into the military of WWII:

It must be recognized at the outset that the problem of integrating women into an army was merely a part of the larger problem of their evolving status in civil life, accelerated by the industrial revolution and affecting every phase of modern society.... This was particularly true of the public skepticism and masculine hostility into which the WAC ran headlong in its first year. Admittedly, the Army had its share of a conservative element that had scarcely recovered from the shock of the mechanized horse when confronted with the militarized woman.[24]

✈ 18 ✈
Denouement of the WASP

Nancy Love had known for some time that General Tunner was to be reassigned. He left Cincinnati to take command of the ATC's Hump Operation in the China-Burma-India Theater on August 1, 1944. Before he left, he wrote the following commendation for her: "I wish to express my appreciation for the loyal, devoted, and cooperative efforts which you have put forth in the interests of the Ferrying Division since 12 March 1942."

Tunner emphasized that Love was responsible for the organization, supervision and operation of a unit for which there was no precedent in military annals, and which necessarily involved duties with which she was unfamiliar at the time. He noted that she devised policies and procedures that not only served the immediate present, but became a standard for similar organizations during succeeding years. He praised her work on his staff as Executive for WASP and her familiarity with the mission policies and operations of the Ferrying Division. He concluded with the following:

> In all these tasks you demonstrated ability, good judgment and superior executive qualities. You have dependably and efficiently performed every assignment given you. Your splendid service and your loyalty have been a source of deep satisfaction to me.
>
> William H. Tunner
> Brigadier General, USA
> Commanding[1]

Tunner's dogged support was key to Love's ability to achieve the success she did with her women pilots and the women's ferrying program as a whole.

Fortunately for the WASP, Tunner's replacement, Gen. Robert E. Nowland, totally supported the women flyers. And Tunner's transfer turned out to be a blessing in disguise for Bob and Nancy Love.

The war put a tremendous strain on marriages. Bob and Nancy Love were no different from the countless other couples who had to endure long separations mixed with uncertainty. Their logbooks prove that only on rare occasions did they spend even an abbreviated amount of time together, and those were occasions when their work schedules put them in proximity to each other.

Bob's wartime letters to Nancy voice three major concerns: one, he does not like living apart from his wife; two, he is disturbed when Nancy lets Cochran upset her; and three, by spring 1944—while on assignment in Australia—he became increasingly conscious of Nancy's heightened interest in a military career that wasn't there before the war.

In wartime, there wasn't much the Loves could do about living apart. As for dealing with Cochran, Nancy was not prone to public temper flare-ups. That cool control took over. But she was apt to vent her frustration after the fact to Bob—in person, on the phone, or via the mail if he was out of the country. Control, keeping those kinds of feelings private, was extremely important to her. She was safe with Bob.

On one occasion he wrote to try to calm her: "I felt like hell after that conversation last night, as no doubt you did. What I really wanted to say wasn't gotten across at all and, sweetie, you must listen ... when you begin to rant and rave about her [Cochran] or lose your composure at all and admit that you can't deal with her, you are playing into a neat trap that every tabloid, newsmagazine and cheap reporter has carefully set for you." [2]

He was her leveling influence.

Nancy's daughters characterize their mother as the classic slow burn. She also had a sarcastic side along with a keen, sometimes biting wit. She was always handy with the wisecrack around trusted friends and family. Though she had learned to control the iconoclasm of her youth, she still was her father's daughter, needing proof that something was truly what it purported to be. That didn't help her when she was pushed to take Jackie Cochran on faith. But Nancy's circumspect approach—in keeping with her vigilant approach to flying—was the public face she exhibited. Whatever boiled under the surface, she kept hidden there. This same iron control, coupled with a tenacious devotion to duty, also helped her keep her tendency to depression at bay.

Bob understood all of this about his wife and he doggedly dealt with the first two concerns. What he found hard to understand was his wife's turn-around from mere utilitarian interest in the militarization of the WASP to what he perceived as a new direction, an interest in climbing that career ladder herself. This seemed to be leading her away from the life they had planned to return to when the war was over. Between March 27 and April 11, 1944, Nancy's letters began to arrive in Australia and Bob found the contents disturbing. The congressional hearings were in full swing and the smear campaign against the WASP was on. Nancy vented her distress over the proceedings.

He had dealt easily with her fame. He was secure in his own self and not threatened by his wife's achievements or her abilities. However, her new interest in WASP militarization and pursuing it not only for her pilots but for herself now surfaced in her letters to him. Bob absorbed three blows in her letters that arrived during those critical two weeks. One, Nancy had contracted, and was now recuperating from, the chicken pox. Two, she had run out of money and, from Australia, he had to scramble to get funds transferred to her so that she could pay their bills. But number three—her seeming change of direction on militarization—was the big one.

On April 11, 1944, he wrote back to her:

> Add to this your sudden change on the subject of the Army and I'm really about to disintegrate into a shower of sparks.... I'm so afraid you're working un- consciously toward an independence of thought and soul that might forever preclude what I'm struggling for when this mess is done.
>
> On this Army deal, I sure hope you're right. People out here assume you are in already, paining me no end. The only [underlined] thing I am really worried about in your judgment on this subject is your some- times indiscriminate confidence in people you think you know well but don't. When you're caught with a commission you are caught for at least three years and we'd look funny with me out and you still in.[3]

Two other factors influenced Nancy along with the allure of a military commission. For the first time in her life, she was liv- ing alone, in Cincinnati, and she found herself to be quite self- sufficient. It was a validation of self. This didn't mean that she was turning her back on her marriage. It simply meant that she was growing in many and unexpected ways and she wanted to try those new wings.

Second, Nancy was not immune to ego and the seduction of power. She knew she was good at what she did; she knew she had solid backing in the right places. Being given the opportunity to acquire the rank of lieutenant colonel in the U.S. Army was no small achievement. Power, prestige, position, a good income, benefits, pride in accomplishment. Who wouldn't be tempted? What Bob could see and what he was afraid Nancy couldn't see—or didn't want to see—was the downside. His concern was for their marriage. "We'd look funny with me out and you still in," said it all. Bob Love had been on active duty with the Army for three years at that point. He had traveled all over the world on behalf of the United States and its armed forces in an effort to win the war. Most of what he had done was secret and would remain so. His daughters say he never talked about it.

Now, the U.S. was about to enter the home stretch in the race to end the war. He knew that. He also knew by then that he wanted no part of a military career after the war. Bob feared that if Nancy accepted a commission in the spring of 1944, she was "in" for three years while he was looking to get out the minute the war was over. Bob wanted to get on with their life. They were still young. Nancy had just turned thirty. There was still time to have children and to once again enjoy things together. The thought of his wife holding down a commission in the Army Air Forces indefinitely was anathema to him.

It wasn't that Bob was old-fashioned, and he certainly proved that he believed marriage to be a fifty-fifty proposition. He liked being married to a strong woman. She was who she was. But he also was a man who desperately wanted to put the madness of war behind him and for the two of them to move beyond it and once again live what he—and he thought *she*—considered a normal life.

Bob, thoroughly disgusted with the long separations from his wife, had been lobbying for reassignment in order to be near her. When General Tunner left for India, Cincinnati and Ferrying Division Headquarters fell into his lap. Col. Robert M. Love—stationed since December 1941 in Washington and living with five other ATC officers—was named deputy commander of the Ferrying Division. On August 31, 1944, he left for Cincinnati. He wrote "PERM CHANGE STA!" in bold cap letters in his logbook when he landed at Lunken Field to stay. He and Nancy were together again.

On July 17, Bob had been offered a Douglas A-20 for his personal use. Soon after, the same A-20 appears in entries in Nancy's logbook. This one was a stripped-down G model that she classified as "sensitive on the controls" and "had long range with a fuselage tank, and a spirited personality all of its own."[4] The A-20 was her hands-down favorite airplane.

When Bob left on August 4 for a three-week fact-finding trip to South America for the ATC, he left the A-20 in Cincinnati in Nancy's possession. While Bob was out of the country, Nancy logged fourteen cross-country trips in the A-20.[5] In an interview years later, she referred to the A-20 that she used for several months as her personal transportation when she needed to visit one of her squadrons.[6]

Beginning in August 1944 and through to December 20 marked the *denouement* of the WASP. Everything moved toward the inevitable conclusion. On September 4, 1944, Nancy wrote a letter to her ailing comrade and friend, Delphine Bohn. Bohn, the commander of the 5th Ferrying Group's women's squadron in Dallas, was on medical leave recuperating from pneumonia and Love was filling in for her. The letter sums up Love's current state of mind and what she was doing to keep her 140 ferry pilots' attitudes and performances sharp. Bohn included parts of Love's letter in her memoir.

> The WASP situation remains in its usual SNAFU state, but I've acquired a new slant on it, and have tried to transmit same to the gals, i.e., we are now the long-sought-for, small select group. We've got a heck of a good record behind us and an even rosier one ahead, or should have with this bunch of good pilots. So forget the newspapers, the Training Command, J.C., WTS/CAA and the whole damned mess—and fly!
>
> If the WASPs are abolished, we're still civilian pilots, and darned good ones, and though I've out-grown optimism in the last two years, I have it on pretty good authority that we who are left in the Fer-rying Division are not to worry, but to keep mouths shut, eyes on the ball, stop arguing and fly the pants off any and all airplanes assigned to us—from L2s ... to A-20s or B-17s.
>
> I haven't seen J. C. in months, and have assidu-ously avoided her. Our airplanes were both on Long Beach at the same time, but there's no use arguing with her—she only twists statements.
>
> So that's the deal and I still have hopes.
>
> Anyhow, there's no use in getting het up and hav-ing a nervous breakdown over the deal. When you get

back, you'll find your squadron small and self-sufficient, and there's no reason squadron leaders can't get out and have fun—only one responsible person need be there. We've all gotten so violent about this that I think it's broken down our health—you and Esther Manning with pneumonia, I've had flu and now have trench mouth, of all things. So let's stop worrying and have fun—and see what happens.

Nancy—you know, POLLYANNA—Love[7]

And Bohn, recalling the physical toll all the stress and uncertainty took on Love and her ferry pilots, wrote the following:

Even the female of the human species began to wilt, to lose energy and strength. There was a greatly evident lack of all vitamins. We were subjected to debilitating psychological pressures. The questions of militarization or nonmilitarization and with whom as primary director were wrapped round with and buried in too much desire for personal glorification by too many people. Also, there were too many questionable decisions to be made as to our own grading of various female abilities and disabilities, inclusive of flight.[8]

The rumors were true. On October 8, when the letters from Cochran and Arnold were delivered, the WASP knew it was over. They were stunned. Their work, however, was not finished. For the women in the Ferrying Division, the pace had picked up. If they thought they had been busy delivering airplanes before, now they were constantly on the go.

"Production was so heavy that we frequently had rows of P-51s stored in the middle of the Long Beach Airport," B.J. London recalls. "If you got back to base by noon, Operations sent you right back out that day. You picked up the airplane and headed for Palm Springs so that you could leave from there the following morning to ferry the plane to Newark. If you got back to base later in the afternoon you didn't have to go back out until the next morning."[9]

Iris Critchell remembers:

> The P-51s were such a high priority, in the fall of
> 1944 after we delivered to Newark, we no longer
> were allowed to detour and pick up a P-39 or P-40 on
> the way back to Long Beach. Instead, we were under
> orders to return to base immediately on the airlines
> or military transport—the fastest way possible.
> At the Newark airport where we landed, the har-
> bor was right there. The ships were pulled into the
> slips where they waited for our airplanes. We'd land
> the P-51 where the men were ready to load the aircraft
> onto the ships. Sometimes they were in such a hurry,
> they'd start to pull it by the tail to be loaded—with us
> still in the cockpit! They wanted them on their way to
> England or Italy as fast as possible.[10]

One of the least publicized facets of the work all ferry pilots
did in the second half of 1944 was to move war-weary airplanes.
These planes had either been manhandled by students at training bases or had actually been flown back from overseas where
they had been shot up. Mostly, these sad ships were destined
either for "the bone yard" or to be used for ground instruction
or target practice. These planes were referred to as "Class 26."
The women of the Ferrying Division moved their share.
On October 16, 1944, Nancy Love and B.J. Erickson picked
up a beat-up B-17 at Patterson Field in Dayton, Ohio. They
were assigned to ferry it to Amarillo, Texas. Flying with them
was engineer M/Sgt. O'Neill. Grease and oil stained the concrete under each engine. The ship was dirty and much patched,
but—they soon discovered—she had a proud heritage. On the
instrument panel, Love and Erickson found a plastic plate with
the following inscription.

> "Genevieve"
> First Airplane Repaired By
> Rome Air Depot
> Please Advise of Her Escapades
> Rome, N.Y., U.S.A.

Love and Erickson decided to take special care of this tired old
lady of the air. But when they fired up the four engines, they real-

ized that would be harder than they had hoped. Three of the four engines needed immediate attention. Number four poured oil on the already saturated concrete ramp. The repairs took most of the afternoon. Finally, the ship was ready. Heeding a large red sign on the instrument panel that warned them NOT to try to retract the landing gear, they filed a clearance to Scott Field near St. Louis with a true airspeed on 150 mph. That meant that, enroute, they were bothered by, and did their best to ignore, aircraft that flew by them signaling "in a superior manner" that they'd forgotten to pull the landing gear up. When a squadron of P-47s whizzed by, the pilots laughing and gesturing from inside their bubble cockpits, "we strongly suspected that the epithet 'women drivers' was being directed at us along with the hand signals."

Ever-increasing vibrations in engine #1 caused concern. They reduced power but feathering proved to be inadvisable if not impossible. "Upon arrival at Scott Field #1 was now emitting a noisy series of irregular but sensational explosions, causing some interest on the part of spectators." They RONed at Scott and after overnight repairs, "Genevieve" was ready to fly on to Amarillo, her sad destination.

"We became very fond of her," Love admitted. "We felt a certain spiritual kinship with her, since we share a common and ignominious fate, we being bound for our 'figurative' grave on 20 December 1944, when the WASPs are to be inactivated."

On November 9, 1944, Love wrote to the commanding officer of the Rome Air Depot, Rome Army Field in Rome, New York: "We hope that this account of the final escapade of 'Genevieve' will be of interest. Her saga in combat was an honorable one, as discovered in her battered form #1 A.

> Nancy H. Love
> Special Assistant to Commanding General"[11]

Not all of Love's flights that fall were Class 26 airplanes bound for the graveyard. She finished on a high, checking out on and then ferrying several Douglas four-engine C-54 transports. "This was fun, as there were always large numbers of hopeful military personnel thumbing their way on leave or change of station and my WASP copilot and I filled the plane on every trip. Playing airline pilot fulfilled another of my ambitions!"[12]

Love told the following story of her first C-54 delivery, with a WASP copilot. They carried seventy-two passengers and a black puppy from San Francisco to New York's La Guardia.

> The plane was to be delivered to American Export Airlines, and was the first DC-4 to be assigned to them. So the chief pilot and high officials were at the field at 1 p.m., waiting. They had never had such big ones before and were much impressed by the size of the plane. They hurried aboard, walked up the long passenger aisle, opened the front cockpit door with expressions of triumph and welcome on their faces.
>
> They stopped in a sort of frozen shock as their minds finally grasped the fact that the two happily grinning pilots were—women! Without a word, they turned and walked out again.[13]

In all, Love flew twenty-seven military airplanes during the war, four of them—C-60, C-71, AT-23, and B-24—as copilot only. Most notable of those she flew are the P-51, P-38, A-20, B-25, B-17, C-47, and C-54. She logged the most hours in C-47s: sixty-two; the least, fifteen minutes in a little L-2.[14]

In mid-November 1944, Love was trying to find jobs for some of her women ferry pilots. She corresponded with a Mr. Traylor, from the Reconstruction Finance Corporation, about the possibility of the women being hired after deactivation.

> I am very anxious to see these pilots given an opportunity to utilize the flying skill they have acquired in the service, since they have worked hard and conscientiously for the Army, and now find themselves without jobs…. If you will advise me as soon as possible of your requirements, I will advise the WASP Squadron leaders at our Ferrying Groups, and can

assure you that they will select highly qualified pilots
upon whom you can depend.
Nancy H. Love
Special Asst. for CG [Commanding General] for
WASP
Ferrying Division, Air Transport Command[15]

The contractors the government used to sell its surplus warplanes had to supply their own pilots to fly the airplanes to the
eight sales centers across the U.S.

With the end approaching, WASP who were not a part of
the Ferrying Division began to talk up, among themselves, an
organization of their own named for Fifinella, the winsome lady
gremlin mascot Walt Disney had designed for them. The WASP
Staff Executive, headquarters Eastern Flying Training Command, Clara Jo Marsh wrote to Love asking for a roster of the
women in the Ferrying Division. She explained "The Order of
Fifinella": "Many WASP ... have felt a strong need for main-
taining contact with each other, personally and professionally."
She added that the group was establishing an unofficial newsletter and concluded by saying: "Many of us in the Training Command have felt isolated from the ATC WASP. We've not wanted
to be. A newsletter should keep us informed about our friends
in any situation."

Love was invited to attend the final ceremonies at Avenger
Field, to take place as part of the graduation of the last WASP
class on December 7, 1944. A celebration of the WASP's accomplishments was planned. Both Hap Arnold and Jacqueline
Cochran would be in attendance.

Love chose not to attend the graduation.[16]

In retrospect, it seems shortsighted of Love not to have attended. But she was, by then, at the end of her energy, as were
most of the women of the ATC. Neither Love nor the other
women ferry pilots were looking forward to celebrating their
demise. As she had told Bohn three months earlier, "I've out-
grown optimism."

Love was, by then, in a withdrawal mode. She opted not to join
the efforts to establish the Order of Fifinella. The fact that Love

was not a joiner contributed to her decision. The other Originals followed her example. They still resented being placed under Cochran's authority and having to give up the WAFS uniforms they wore with pride. They believed that if Cochran hadn't meddled in the work they were doing for the Ferrying Division, they would not be looking at deactivation and the loss of their jobs.

The women ferry pilots were hurting. Absolute bewilderment best describes how they felt at being dismissed December 20 when pursuit planes that they were capable of delivering sat on the ground. There were not enough pursuit-qualified male ferry pilots to move them. The women retreated into their respective shells, ignored everything else—as Love had suggested—and flew on as assigned until deactivation.

On Love's final flight as a WASP on December 14-15, 1944, she and WASP copilot Bea Medes left the Douglas plant in Chicago to deliver C-54B #42-72389 to the West Coast.[17]

In the fall of 1944, a handful of Love's Long Beach WASP, who already were qualified on the P-38, got to check out in Northrop Corporation's high-altitude, twin-engine night fighter the P-61, also known as the Black Widow. "My very last trip was in a P-61 to Sacramento on December 19," B.J. Erickson London remembers. "After delivery, we were picked up by military transport and brought back to Long Beach.[18]

"What was so sad was, when I left for home the following day, there were sixty-six new P-51s sitting beside the runway waiting to be delivered. And they wouldn't get delivered that day or the next because the qualified women pilots who had been ferrying P-51s to Newark—and who were still so badly needed—had been dismissed and sent home."[19] A similar dilemma existed at Farmingdale, Buffalo, Niagara, Dallas, and Evansville. By the end of November 1944, the last full month of WASP operations, the number of women ferry pilots under Nancy Love's command stood at 140, of whom 113 flew pursuit.[20]

"The 303 WASPs assigned to the ATC delivered 12,652 aircraft between October 1942 and December 1944 and, by September 1944, were delivering three-fifths of all pursuit aircraft

Nancy waves from cockpit of C-54 she and Bea Medes are getting ready to ferry.
Courtesy the Love family.

coming off the assembly lines," Betty Gillies told a Ninety-Nines' gathering years later.[21]

Banquets honoring the Ferrying Division WASP were held at the ferrying bases the evening of December 19. Nancy Love chose to return to where it all began: Wilmington. Eight Originals still actively ferrying airplanes gathered along with the rest of the women of the 2nd Ferrying Group on December 19 at the New Castle Army Air Base Officers Club for what that group termed "the last supper." Dressed in their blue WASP uniform jackets and skirts, the eight sat at the head table with squadron commander Betty Gillies and Nancy Love in the center. To Nancy's right were Nancy Batson, Helen McGilvery, and Gertrude Meserve Tubbs. To Gillies's left were her executive officer Helen Mary Clark, Teresa James, and Sis Bernheim. The rest of the squadron, thirty graduates of Houston or Sweetwater, sat at tables down each side of the head table.

The "Last Supper" at Wilmington, December 19, 1944.
Photo from the Nancy Batson Crews collection, in the author's possession.

What went through Love's head that night? As those eight friends who had been through so much together looked around them, faces were missing. Not just Evelyn and Dorothy and Cornelia—though those were the ones that hurt too badly to talk about. But because of the nature of the assignment that brought them together in the first place, they were always destined to go their separate ways whether through the lonely job of delivering airplanes or by being reassigned to a remote ferrying base in another part of the country. She had created a small cadre of women—dedicated professional pilots—who had volunteered to serve their country in wartime and perform tasks not done before by women.

American women had long heard men talk reverently about the team and a tight feeling of togetherness focused on a winning effort, and about their wartime experiences and the buddies with whom they shared life and death situations. Now, for the first time, women shared with each other the kind of experiences only men had previously shared and the resulting bonding became a female experience as well.[22]

The WAFS and the WASP had raised the bar.

That last night, Nancy Love was there to enjoy herself and share the pleasure of being back together with friends. Just like the oth-

Betty Gillies and Nancy Love (kneeling center) and the 2nd Ferrying Group's women's squadron.

Photo from the Nancy Batson Crews collection, in the author's possession.

ers, she raised her glass in toast, smoked her cigarettes, laughed, and reminisced. They were women relaxing after a job well done. And for a few hours that night, they didn't think about the hurts and losses of yesterday or the challenges to be faced tomorrow.

Chicken a la king was the entrée with sweet potato croquets, fresh fruit, chocolate éclairs and rare French wine to help with the toasts, which were sometimes long and often teary. Finally, the thirty-eight weary WASP found the exhaustion of emotion was too much and they said goodnight for the last time and went back to BOQ 14 to finish packing.

Not long after that, a male voice outside shouted, "Fire!" Out they ran, clad in bathrobes or coats, into the cold December night. The women joined the crowd of male officers outside the Officers Club that had been their haven for twenty-seven months and where they had just eaten their last meal as active-duty ferry pilots.

Nancy Batson looked at the building as it went down in flames. "Let it burn!" she hollered, and added a Rebel yell. "Let it burn!"[23]

✈ 19 ✈
Flying the Hump

On November 14, 1944, Gen. C.R. Smith wrote to General Nowland: "Before Mrs. Love gets out of the service, if that comes to pass, I would like to see her get a trip to some of our foreign stations. This should have been done a long time ago, as we wanted some of the WASPs to make foreign ferries, but you know the reason why that could not be done."

On November 20, 1944, General Smith wrote to General Tunner at his headquarters in Hastings Mill outside of Calcutta, where he now served as commander of the Hump Operation. He wrote: "Would like for Nancy Love to go to Calcutta for the purpose of looking over our operation. Will be necessary that permission of Theater Commander be secured. Would you secure that permission and inform us."[1]

General Smith, Deputy Commander of the ATC, was on his way to India for a one-month inspection tour during the end of December 1944. He wanted to send Love on a concurrent fact-finding tour of the new Crescent supply route to India and the airlift support from there to the American and Chinese forces fighting in China. The Hump airlift was C.R. Smith's baby from the beginning.[2] He wanted information a general could not get

220

and he knew who could get it for him. Just as when the ATC sent Bob Love to India in the fall of 1942 to check out the then fledgling Fireball route operation through the eyes of an actively engaged pilot, now the ATC was asking for the same kind of fundamental observation of Crescent from Nancy Love.

To do this, Love could not accompany General Smith and his party in the general's C-54. She had to travel Crescent to India alone. Armed with security clearance and passport and with orders in hand to fly halfway around the world, Nancy Love reported to the New York Aerial Port of Embarkation at La Guardia Field on December 27, 1944. There she boarded an ATC transport. Destination Calcutta. Her assignment, as stated in secret orders issued by General Nowland, was "for purpose of coordinating Ferrying Division matters and upon [completion] thereof will [return] to Cincinnati, Ohio."[3] General Smith's November 20 note to General Tunner states that he needs permission from the Theater Commander in order for Love to make the trip. On paper this sounds like a routine matter, but considering that Theater's ban on women in the area, it was not a given.

The legendary Lt. Gen. Joseph W. ("Vinegar Joe") Stilwell, CBI Theater commander since early 1942, had been relieved on October 18. Stilwell had a rule of no women in the theater.[4] There had been few exceptions to date, but the transition brought about by Stilwell's departure assured changes. Now, women would be allowed in both theaters. Some women already were there despite Stillwell's order. The Office of Strategic Services (OSS) (precursor to the CIA) had women serving in India and on the island of Ceylon (now Sri Lanka) beginning in the spring of 1944—among them Julia McWilliams who, as Julia Child, later would become famous as television's "The French Chef."[5] At least five OSS women were flown to Chungking in late 1944.[6]

Maj. Gen. George E. Stratemeyer, the commander of the U.S. Air Forces in India, had brought in WACs in July 1944 to work at AAF headquarters in Calcutta. Stilwell approved this only because Stratemeyer promised the women would never be assigned other than to headquarters.[7] Ninety Army nurses had entered the CBI Theater as early as May 1942 as part of the

59th Station Hospital. They arrived shortly after Stilwell's re-treat from Burma "in the face of an overwhelming Japanese offensive."[8] And in late 1943, flight nurses began to assist with the air evacuation of sick and wounded from the CBI Theater—primarily in ATC airplanes—and were probably the first Ameri-can women to make flights over the Hump.[9]

So other American women, either military or government employees, had preceded Love into the Theater. Love's assign-ment was different and was temporary.

Enroute to India, Love discovered several problems on the Crescent run, and took note of them. Passengers were delayed for lack of a reliable schedule and the Ferrying Division was getting a bad name. Crescent had been dubbed the "when, as and if airline." Far more care was taken with runs to Paris and the United Kingdom than to India. Planes failed to show up when expected. When they did arrive, many had mechanical problems and were sent back to the States for repair rather than being sent on to India. Coordination and communications were sorely lacking.

In Calcutta and elsewhere, she saw and talked to several old acquaintances—former Ferrying Division pilots now flying C-46s on scheduled runs for the North Africa or India-China Di-visions. The men liked flying the C-46, felt they had been well trained for it, and were doing a good job. Love also learned that General Tunner and his staff were in dire need of radio opera-tors, and, the most obvious, more pilots.[10]

Love visited the other Assam Valley ATC bases at Misimari, Chabua, and Jorhat, and then flew to Delhi and also to Agra. She logged sixteen hours in the cockpit over India, all duly re-corded in her logbook. On these flights she flew a staff B-25.[11]

The opportunity to fly General Smith's C-54 over the Hump route rather than go as a passenger on this flight was not part of her assignment.

And though Love wrote nothing of her experiences on the flights over and back, her part is recorded in her logbook, she spoke of it when interviewed in later years, and she acknowl-edged the trip in later correspondence. From that information and stories she told her daughters, the flights on January 8 and 10, 1945, can be pieced together something like this:[12]

January 8, 1945: Cruising altitude was 16,000 feet, high enough to safely clear the 14,000-foot crests of the mountains on this route. The temperature aloft was on the far minus side of zero.

No freakish weather buffeted the plane and Japanese patrols were a thing of the past. When terraced rice paddies ringing the mountainsides came into view, Kunming lay beyond. The flight pattern took them into a long low approach between craggy mountains—Mount Tali was 12,000 feet—and over Lake Tali which sat at its base. The descent into Kunming was hazardous. "Circle in a figure eight over the radio beacon and let down 500 feet at a time" were the standard instructions.[13] This was to let the planes stacked in the landing pattern below land as their turn came. Elevation of the runway was 6,000 feet. Length of the red clay runway also was 6,000 feet.

Most runways in wartime China were gravel, built by the toil of thousands of Chinese laborers. Native men and women crushed stone with hand-held hammers, carried it by the basket load on their heads, dumped it out, and then spread it by hand on the leveled ground that was to be the runway. A massive roller, usually powered by the muscle of 200 workers rather than by steam, pressed the gravel flat so that airplanes could land on it.

At the various bases in India, Love had watched elephants load fuel drums aboard transports. Now scores of Chinese coolies flocked to the C-54 to unload the cargo that would help keep the Chinese and U.S. armies fighting a little longer. Every flight over the Hump carried drums of precious aviation fuel in addition to other cargo and any passengers.[14]

Flight time from Calcutta was four hours, thirty minutes.

Love and the men she accompanied found the high-altitude, wintery air cold and crisp, not teeming with the wretched humidity of Calcutta. They made their way to Operations and then to the mess hall. The traditional meal of fresh eggs fried in butter and lots of good hot coffee awaited the VIPs.[15]

Their party spent two nights in Kunming. What did they talk about?

Chances are they discussed the damage left in the wake of the worst storm ever to hit the USAAF forces flying the Hump. On the night of January 6–7—a day and a half prior to their arrival—the CBI route had been battered and damage reports were still coming in. Final total: ten airplanes carrying thirty-eight pilots, crew, and passengers had been lost. An investigation was being launched and the clean-up operation had begun. The incident came to be known as Black Friday.[16]

And where was Love, the lone woman in a contingent of ATC visiting brass, billeted in Kunming? Whether she was lodged in a guesthouse in town or slept on an Army cot in some officer's hastily vacated quarters, Love didn't ask for special treatment.

The morning they were to head back to Calcutta, Love and the crew made the trip to Operations to get a weather briefing for the trip home. They were routed by way of Myitkyina (pronounced "Mish-in-naw"[17]), a Burmese village with an airfield that had been recaptured from the Japanese in August 1944, thus opening the southern and much lower Hump route over which Love had flown two days earlier. By January 1945, the Japanese Army had been driven from most of Burma. Now flights could be made from Calcutta across the central part of Burma to Kunming without fear of attack from Japanese Zeroes and without having to cross the higher Himalayan crests farther north.[18]

Just before climbing back into the big airplane to leave, Love—like any woman boarding an Army war plane in those days—would have made a quick trip to the lavatory. The toilet facilities on military aircraft consisted of a relief tube. There was a lavatory on board General Smith's C-54, but a woman first would have to remove her flight jacket, struggle out of the upper half of the bulky zip-up flight suit, and then remove the upper half of her one-piece long johns—all this in high-altitude, subzero temperatures.

January 10, 1945: The route took them further north, over rugged, ice-encrusted crags, the jungle and the gorges of the Mekong and Salween Rivers to Myitkyina where two streams meet to form the Irrawaddy that flows on to Mandalay and Rangoon. On this trip, they flew at 18,000 feet to cross the

15,000-foot-high peaks of the north-south Santsung Range that the American fliers had christened "the Rockpile." The burned-out hulks of airplanes on the rocks below were mute testimony to why the Hump pilots referred to this route as "the aluminum trail." Before the end of the war, some 600 planes would go down trying to tame the Hump with a loss of more than a thousand men including pilots, crews, and passengers. No pilot, Love included, wanted to dwell on what might have happened to anyone who survived the crashes. Desolate windswept crags or the insect and reptile-infested jungle, neither was a place a pilot would want his airplane to end up.

Sometimes Hump pilots had to dodge anvil-shaped thunderheads that, reaching well over 40,000 feet, towered over the rooftop-of-the-world Himalayas. Sometimes it was pea soup murk that required them to fly on instruments. If the Hump's stomach-churning downdrafts and gravity-defying updrafts were blowing, the airplane was tossed about at the will of those winds. If their C-54 encountered such capricious winds on the way to Myitkyina from Kunming, or from Myitkyina back to Calcutta, Love and her passengers would feel the pull of their momentarily weightless bodies against the webbed harness followed by the crushing weight of the counter trip back down. The crew chief on Hump flights invariably passed along advice to those aboard for the first time—be sure to buckle your seatbelt and harness extra tight.

If ice began to form on the wings, the de-icing equipment did its work and soon chunks of the stuff loosened and flew backwards, striking the fuselage of the airplane with resounding thumps. The general's C-54 might sport a few king-sized dents to show for their trouble.[19]

The trip, apparently, was uneventful. The Hump had blown itself out three days earlier—as least for the moment.

Though other American women had preceded her over the Hump as passengers in an airplane, Nancy Love does appear to be the first American woman to pilot an airplane—specifically a military aircraft—over one of the Hump routes. But she was *not* the first woman to fly the Himalayas. Germany's twenty-five-year-old adventuress, Elly Beinhorn, flew within a few miles of Mount Everest in 1932.

Beinhorn and a passenger flew her 125-horsepower sport airplane at 16,000 feet "above the sea of clouds towards the snow-covered mountains which lay directly in front of us. There lay the coveted Everest, of which I had been dreaming for the last two nights.... I felt as if I could stretch out my hand and touch the nearest crags of the great Himalayan tableland." She carried with her an oxygen "apparatus."[20]

Julia McWilliams and several other OSS women flew the Hump from Calcutta to Kunming as passengers on March 15, 1945. Fellow passenger Betty MacDonald describes that hair-raising journey over the southern part of the Hump—the same route Nancy Love had flown two months earlier.

> After three hours, Julia's plane suddenly began to plummet, the lights went out, pieces of ice ticked against the window, and one of the men got quietly sick into his handkerchief. According to Betty Mac-Donald, who would give the best description of flying the Hump, "the C-54 shuddered, leveled off with a roar," found a hole in the clouds, and eventually headed for the red clay runway just south of the city of Kunming. Julia sat confidently reading a book. Betty, who thought Julia was "so cool," still clutched [her] lucky charm.[21]

MacDonald was a fellow OSS employee and a journalist. She writes, "By war's end, thirty women had been stationed in this frontier country of western China."[22]

Such were the vagaries of wartime assignments on the Hump and women now shared in them. On August 3, seven months after Nancy Love's flight, General Stratemeyer flew his WAC contingent to his new headquarters in Chungking.[23]

Love didn't spend all her time in India working. Though not a shopper by inclination, she did take advantage of this rare opportunity. In Agra on January 25, 1945, she bought several bracelets, two necklaces, and four rings to take back to the States. On January 26, she bought three dolls. And she did visit the Taj Mahal.[24]

She also had a social life, meeting higher ups in the U.S., British, and Indian armies at dinner parties. But as a woman traveling without her husband, Nancy was fair game for the occasional romantically inclined, lonely male, military or civilian. In later years, she told her daughters that she had to parry occasional amorous advances as she made her way through the various cultures and social customs that flourished in India in 1945.[25]

Nancy left India on January 29 in the company of General Smith and his aide, Captain Wiseman. The trip from Calcutta to Hickam Field in Honolulu took fifty hours in the C-54. Love flew twenty of those hours as first pilot: four hours from Colombo, Ceylon to Exmouth Gulf on Australia's west coast; four and a half hours from Exmouth Gulf to Darwin, on Australia's north coast; three hours from Darwin to Hollandia in Dutch New Guinea; five hours from Biak, Indonesia, to the embattled island of Tarawa; and four hours and twenty minutes from Tarawa to Honolulu. Her logbook is her witness.[26]

The final paragraph of her trip report for General Nowland reads: "After several side trips to China and the Assam Valley stations, I left Calcutta on 29 January with Gen. C.R. Smith and his Aide, Captain Wiseman, and returned to Cincinnati via Australia, arriving here on 6 February."[27]

Back at Ferrying Division Headquarters at 309 Vine Street in downtown Cincinnati, Love completed her official Trip Report for General Nowland and dated it February 9, 1945. With that, the name of civilian Nancy Harkness Love faded forever from the duty rosters of the Ferrying Division, Air Transport Command, U.S. Army Air Forces.

Why was Love's flight over the Hump and halfway around the world never publicized? The mission was a fact-finding one, consequently hush hush, if not full-blown secrecy, was essential. Of major concern, as of December 20, 1944, on General Arnold's orders, women were no longer allowed in the cockpits of Army airplanes.

> It has been brought to my attention that there is talk in the Air Force of hiring certain women pilots after their discharge on 20 December you will notify all

concerned that there will be no repeat no women pilots in any capacity in the Air Force after December
twenty except Jacqueline Cochran I do not want any
misunderstanding about this.

No women will be employed by the AAF in any
flying capacity either as pilot, copilot, or member of
a flying crew after date of WASP inactivation on 20
December 1944.[28]

That directive remained in force until the 1970s. Love's work
in her former position of command and the trust and respect
accorded her by her superiors was what placed her in India and
in the cockpit of that C-54. Nevertheless, her flight could *not* be
official. She flew only because General Smith asked her to and he
was willing to be responsible for his—and her—actions. Quite a
compliment to her when all the ramifications are considered.

Love knew better than to go home and tell tales of such
flights. And to what end? The import of such a flight would be
lost on the average person. Nancy Love was not one to brag. She
downplayed her aviation accomplishments. After she arrived
back home, instead of writing about those significant flights,
how they came about, what happened, how she felt about it, or
what it could mean in the future for women pilots, she went on
with her life. And though unlikely, forces within the AAF could
have made trouble for General Smith. Totally in character, Love
chose not to betray her friend's trust.

She enjoyed the privilege of being allowed to fly such special flights. She enjoyed the company of men like Generals C.R.
Smith, George, and Tunner. She enjoyed being part of the power
structure—being on the inside. It was all part of her makeup—
what made her special to the men of the ATC.

Delphine Bohn writes in her memoir: "[Love] learned early
and followed well the long- and short-term wishes and plans of
the Ferrying Division.... Her ability as a broadly capable pilot
was highly respected by the best. She was a pathfinder but not
obnoxiously so."[29]

Besides, more newsworthy things were happening on the war
front. Dresden, Germany, was destroyed by a firestorm follow-

ing a night raid by the RAF Bomber Command on February 14, 1945. U.S. Marines raised the American flag on Iwo Jima's Mount Suribachi, February 23, and on March 7, American troops captured the one bridge still standing over the Rhine River—the bridge at Remagen—and the advance into the heart of Germany began.[30]

Why not write about the trip in later years? Love wasn't a writer and she sought neither praise nor publicity. Her logbooks, her memories imparted to her three daughters, her comment in her trip report, and brief comments like these in later years must suffice: "I also checked out in and ferried C-54s in the U.S. in addition to the one I flew overseas.... I managed to fly around the world, about half of the trip as pilot."[31] And, "Most of my wartime flying was done in the United States, but I managed to promote one flight around the world doing at least half of the flying during which I flew over the Hump."[32] Love's personal take on these flights is forever lost to us.

With her report filed, Love left behind, forever, a life she had never expected to lead. Technically a civilian, she served as a military pilot for two and a half years during wartime. Her every move had been dictated by the needs of the WAFS, the WASP, the Ferrying Division, the Air Transport Command, and the U.S. Army Air Forces.

Both C.R. Smith and William H. Tunner remained lifelong friends of both Nancy and Bob Love. Smith returned to American Airlines when the war was over. In 1946, he hired Nancy to make a series of fact-finding trips for the airline. She filed a report with him when her job was completed.[33]

All of the WASP released on December 20, 1944, felt that they had been dropped into a black hole and forgotten. Skilled in flight and various other aspects of wartime aviation, they wanted nothing more than to do the jobs for which they had been trained. Once they were home and the newness of seeing family and friends at holiday time wore off, they discovered that they couldn't share their experiences. No one understood; no one really wanted to hear their stories; some people thought they were bragging; a few thought they were outright making it up. It's no surprise that some of the women sought refuge living together in groups called WASP nests in places like Florida, Texas, Oklahoma, and California. Several found ferrying jobs with Reconstruction Finance Corporation, the organization Love had contacted back in November. Some found solace in the bottle. This affliction eventually contributed to the deaths of several WASP.

Love suffered the same sense of loss as did the other women; hers simply was delayed a few more weeks by her trip to India and China.

WASP Bee Falk Haydu (Class 44-7), as president of the WASP organization in October 1976, spoke with Love by telephone not long before her death. Haydu called to tell Nancy that the WASP planned to honor her at the reunion later that month. Bee relates—with some degree of doubt and wonder in her voice—that Nancy told her "the first thing I did when I got home after deactivation was burn my WASP uniform."[34]

What pain in Nancy's soul must have driven her to do that? She did *not* burn her WAFS uniform, though it was put away in a box. Her daughters remember playing dress-up in her flight jacket. Eventually that uniform, too, disappeared. All that she accomplished, to her, must have seemed lost, forgotten in that deep dark moment of despair. She, as much as any GI, was a soldier returning from war.

And though Nancy's war was over, Bob's was not.

Col. Robert M. Love's wartime assignments were cloaked in secrecy. He was out of the country a lot, as his letters to Nancy indicate. He was, say his daughters, the man the ATC sent when they needed something done. "Dad was a take-charge and get-it-done guy. He might not be right, but he'd do something." Bob told a reporter in 1975 that on his trip to CBI he carried secret orders for General Stilwell.[35]

On April 14, 1945. Bob was named commander of the West Coast Wing of the ATC, 152nd AAF Base Unit Headquarters,

San Francisco. When he headed west, Nancy went east to check on their home in Framingham, Massachusetts, where they hadn't lived since soon after the war began. She would join him in San Francisco. Bob Love had had enough of living alone and so had his wife. No sooner was he established in San Francisco when, on May 8, 1945—V-E Day—the war in Europe was over. All the attention then focused on the Pacific, the island hopping, the intensifying battle with the Japanese, and the impending invasion of Japan.

Nancy had not given up all ideas of ferrying airplanes. On May 4, she spoke by phone with a Mr. Lambert in New York about six women pilots ferrying three twin-engine C-53 transports to Madrid for Iberia Spanish Airlines. Five were Originals—Barbara Erickson London (B.J. recently had married Jack London, the head of Flight Operations for transition at Long Beach), Delphine Bohn, Helen Mary Clark, Barbara Donahue, and Nancy herself. The sixth was Helen Richey, Nancy's longtime friend from Airmarking days and one of her Wilmington ferry pilots.

"All of these pilots have made at least three deliveries of DC-3-type aircraft as First Pilots. They all have Army Instrument Cards and have had a minimum of 2½ years as Army pilots," she wrote to Lambert the same day the conversation was held.[36]

B.J. remembers the proposed ferrying trip. "It sounded really exciting. Nancy talked to me about it and I know Delphine was involved too. It happened right at V-E Day and then nothing ever came of it—probably because the war in Europe was over."[37]

Faced with a lonely coast-to-coast, cross-country trip in the family automobile, Nancy stopped first in Michigan to visit her parents. From there, she called Barbara Donahue and invited her to come along on the drive to California. Donahue said "yes," and flew out from New York to meet Nancy. The two took off and headed west. "We had a wonderful trip," Donahue recalls. "We met Bob in Nevada at the gaming tables. Then Nance had to put up with Bob and me. We both liked to gamble and she didn't."[38]

Nancy and Bob set up housekeeping in a San Francisco apartment in June, expecting to remain there for the duration—which turned out to be much shorter than anticipated.

On August 6, Col. Paul W. Tibbets piloted the *Enola Gay* over Hiroshima, Japan, and dropped the first atomic bomb. Three days later, August 9, another B-29 dropped a second atomic bomb on Nagasaki. On August 14, the Japanese surrendered and the war was over. No invasion, no grand scale bloodletting on the Japanese homeland, no more war.

When Colonel Tibbets and his crew successfully bombed Hiroshima, Nancy had to have felt a certain pride in the fact that two WASP had helped him convince the men who were destined to fly the B-29 that it was "flyable and safe." Early on, the engines in the B-29 had had a reputation for catching fire in the air. WASP Dora Dougherty (43-3) and Dorothea Johnson (43-4), handpicked by Tibbets and with his patient, exacting instruction, mastered the B-29 and flew it on several demonstration flights around the country. When pilots and crew on the ground saw the two young women climb down from the cockpit, they took notice. Though Hap Arnold and AAF Chief of Staff Gen. Barney Giles stopped the demonstration tour when they heard about it—much as Arnold had stopped Love and Gillies's B-17 flight to England in 1943—Tibbets had already proved his point. If the men saw a woman could fly the B-29, then they would fly it too![39]

Nancy and Bob wanted to stay on the West Coast. On September 12, 1945, she wrote to Fred M. Babcock, Deputy Administrator, Real Estate Division, Surplus Commodities Board in Washington, D.C. In the letter she expressed interest in the use, through sale or lease, of the Oxnard Flight Strip at Oxnard, California.[40]

She also sent a copy of the letter to Constance Bennett in Santa Monica. Constance Bennett, a movie star in the 1940s, was married to AAF pilot and flight instructor John Theron Couper. During the war, Couper served as executive officer to Jack London (B.J. Erickson's future husband) at Long Beach.

"After the war, the government was decommissioning airports and turning them back for civilian use," London says. "We were all part of it, Jack and me, Nancy and Bob, Connie and her husband. We were all going to work together. Nancy and Bob were trying to establish an airline. They were the ones who had the money, along with Connie. She was busy in Hollywood but was looking for a postwar job for her pilot husband. We all got to know each other well.

"The Oxnard training base had been well maintained and would have been a super place for a charter flight set up. But we lost out. The municipality got the airstrip instead of private enterprise."[41]

Constance replied to Nancy that she was "horribly disappointed about the sad news of our project....we'll just hold the thought that things will level off by spring or even later and go on from there as I do think it's an idea worth following up."[42]

As did so many attempts by WASP to utilize their training and skills in the postwar field of aviation, this idea withered on the vine. Besides, the fates were moving Nancy and Bob in another direction despite their interest in remaining in California.

✈ 20 ✈
Peace, Prosperity, and Parenthood

Nancy and Bob wanted to settle in San Francisco, but circumstances already were changing. Before the war, Bob and his friend Richard C. duPont had agreed that—if they made it back—they would take duPont's All American Aviation, a mail pouch pickup run, and turn it into a passenger airline.[1]

A champion glider pilot and Delaware businessman, duPont founded what, in 1937, became All American Aviation. DuPont's airline inaugurated a permanent mail delivery service on August 12, 1940, and continued to carry the mail for nine years. But duPont didn't come back. He died September 11, 1943, in a glider crash.[2]

Bob Love did survive the war. Even though the Army didn't discharge him officially until January 4, 1946, Bob was released from active duty on October 4, 1945. His commitment to his friend heavy on his mind, Bob and Nancy ended their brief postwar idyll in romantic San Francisco and returned east.

Charles Wendt, chief financial officer for All American and the one who had guided duPont in financial matters from the beginning, contacted Bob Love in the fall of 1945 about the presidency of All American Aviation. At the board meeting on December 18, Bob was elected president and a member of the board, to become effective January 7, 1946.[3]

The Loves sold their home in Massachusetts and moved to Wilmington, Delaware. On January 11, 1946, Nancy and Bob had been married for ten years, they were childless, she was about to turn thirty-two and he was thirty-seven. Was Nancy Love, at this point in her life, tempted to forego having children and pursue a career in aviation? If any woman had the credentials for such a postwar career, she did. She had demonstrated her strengths, skills, and capabilities to powerful Army brass and the political power structure. She had received a sterling commendation from General Tunner. She was well liked and well respected. And she had all the right contacts in the aviation world—not only the moneyed people and the technologically innovative, but also the business minds that made it happen, one of them being her husband.

As a schoolgirl, Nancy had set her cap for a career in aviation. Little did she realize quite what that would come to mean. For a time, she was the most powerful woman in aviation in the country—the leader of the women ferry pilots with Tunner, his staff, and the whole of the ATC staunchly behind her. Even when Cochran was named Director of Women Pilots, Nancy was secure in her job and continued to perform at the highest level.

To illustrate how extensive her influence on the women of the WASP had been, thirty years later, in August 1976, Dora Dougherty Strother (WASP 43-3), Chief, Human Factors Engineering, Bell Helicopter Textron wrote to Nancy and enclosed a copy of the speech she had given at the recent opening of the WASP exhibit at the U.S. Air Force Museum in Dayton, Ohio. Strother concludes her letter: "You have frequently been the subject of my writing and speaking and I almost feel I know you. I admire so many things about you—to name a few: your obvious skill as a pilot; your foresight and administrative skills in establishing the WAFS; and the ladylike way you have handled unladylike individuals and situations."[4] Dora Dougherty Strother was one of Colonel Tibbets's two female B-29 pilots in 1944.

But what now for Nancy? As 1946 dawned, it was all behind her: the WASP, the ATC-sponsored trip around the world, the plans to ferry airplanes to Spain and to start a California-based aviation business. She had just spent months climbing out of the black hole the dismissal of the WASP had created. Nancy Love had to take stock of herself, who she was, and what she wanted.

Nancy's "girls" were getting married—Helen Richards in December 1944; B.J. Erickson in April 1945; and Nancy Batson's wedding date was set for February 1, 1946. Soon there would be babies. She knew Bob's mother and father would like to have grandchildren. Margaret had not married and Bob was their only hope. Nancy knew her parents wanted more grandchildren. Her late brother's two boys were now adolescents. Most important, Bob wanted a family.

Nancy was ready to move on. The war was over and done with and the WASP consigned to history. Both she and Bob were fed up with the military. They wanted out. They wanted to live their own lives on their own terms. By fall 1945, they were free of the military but duty and Bob's career were calling them back east. When they embarked on a new life as 1946 dawned, Nancy never looked back.

Both Bob and Nancy missed the freedom of owning their own airplane and being able to fly as they pleased. After settling in Chester County, Pennsylvania, near Wilmington in early 1946, they bought two airplanes. One was a Vultee BT-13 with a 450-horsepower engine—the plane flown by so many of the WASP in training at Avenger Field. The BT-13 appears for the first time in Bob's logbook on March 20, 1946. Nancy's first flight in it is recorded two days later, on March 22. In April, she flew the BT-13 to Hastings to visit her parents.[5]

On May 8, 1946, the notation "Lockheed F56, P-38," appears for the first time in Bob's logbook. The Loves had bought an Army-surplus twin-engine Lightning pursuit. The price: $1500. Nancy's first flight shows up a month later on June 8.

"We had neither of us recovered from the fun of flying 'hot' airplanes, I guess," Nancy wrote in 1955. "We promptly bought a surplus P-38 *without* an extra seat because we are both inclined to back-seat drive! We had a wonderful time with it, taking turns and having spot landing contests between us—much to the dismay of the Cubs at DuPont Airport, which scattered hastily when they heard the Allisons firing up."[6]

Their toy was an expensive one. The Army had paid for the gas to power the machines they flew during the war, but those days were long gone. And so was the need for the speed the P-38 produced, if not the excitement. So in mid-July 1946, they sold the sleek pursuit. "But not without regret," Nancy said. That was when they bought their first four-seater, single-engine Bonanza, a family plane.

On July 15, 1946, in a ceremony in Washington, the U.S. Army Air Forces awarded medals to both Bob and Nancy Love

General Harold L. George pins on Nancy's Air Medal. Bob Love center.
Courtesy Love family; electronic image NAHF.

for their service to their country during World War II. They were the first husband and wife in Army history to be decorated simultaneously. Longtime friend and supporter, Lt. Gen. Harold L. George, chief of the Air Transport Command and under whose command both had worked throughout the war, made the presentation. Col. Robert M. Love (he was still in the Air Reserve) received the Distinguished Service Medal for "exceptionally meritorious" service as deputy commander of the European Ferrying Division of the ATC and later as commander of the ATC West Coast Wing. Nancy Harkness Love received the Air Medal along with a citation signed by President Harry S Truman noting her "operational leadership in the successful training and assignment of over 300 qualified women fliers in the flying of advanced military aircraft."[7]

As it turned out, the military wasn't finished with Nancy. Two years later, she received a letter from the Vice Chief of Staff of the *new* United States Air Force dated August 9, 1948, offering her a commission as a lieutenant colonel in its Reserves.[8] On September 18, 1947, the Air Force had become a separate service. The Air Force was offering non-flying Reserve commissions to the women who had served with the WASP, who had stayed until deactivation or had been officially released prior to December 20, 1944, and who desired and qualified for Reserve status.

Nancy replied: "It is most gratifying to me that the women pilots who served in the Air Forces are to receive the recognition, which they have long deserved.... I am personally most appreciative of the Reserve commission as lieutenant colonel offered me and will forward on to you personally the necessary forms as soon as I have had the physical examination."[9]

Jacqueline Cochran was offered, and also accepted, the rank of lieutenant colonel.[10] She wrote a general letter to the WASP dated January 4, 1949.

> Dear Ex-WASP:
> At long last, the United States Air Force has agreed to offer all Ex-WASP who meet the standards and qualifications a commission of 2nd Lieutenant in the United States Air Force Reserve on a non-flying

status. The rank of commission in the Reserve will
be predicated on the length of service you had in the
WASP, exclusive of training periods.... There is always a hope that at a later date you may be put on a
flying status.[11]

"Flying status," of course, did not happen for nearly thirty
years when the Navy opened pilot training to women in 1972,
followed quickly by the Army. The Air Force didn't decide to
offer women pilot training until 1976.[12]

Nancy's original WAFS who accepted Reserve non-flying commissions went in as captains or majors because they had the longest time of service. Also, many of them had served in squadron
leadership positions. Accepting commissions were Helen Mary
Clark, Sis Bernheim, Betty Gillies, Teresa James, Barbara Erickson, Betsy Ferguson, Lenore McElroy, Del Scharr, and Esther Nelson. The number of WASP who took commissions was 149.[13]

Contrary to Bob's wartime concern, Nancy never really had
given up the dream of a family. Like so many women of her
generation, the war had simply precluded a family. By 1941,
when Nancy and Bob began to think seriously about the children they had not yet had, the war was upon them. Bob moved
from Reserve status to active duty in May 1941. Consciously or
unconsciously, they put off "for the duration" any decision to
seek medical input.

Nancy, it turns out, had been trying for ten years to get pregnant. When her daughters were nearly grown, she told them she
and Bob had always wanted children. And she explained what,
eventually, they had to go through in order to have them. In
1946, the war over, her Ferrying Division responsibilities behind
her, and Bob settling into All American Airways, Nancy sought
out a Boston-area doctor who was known for his studies in the
field of hormones. She and Bob both underwent the battery of
tests available at that time. What the physician determined was

that the problem was Nancy's and it could be remedied not with hormones but with surgery. She had a blocked Fallopian tube, the result of what he called "a kitchen table appendectomy" in her youth.[14]

The surgery was successful. Hannah Lincoln Love (the sixth in the family genealogy) was born August 1, 1947, in Wilmington. Bob took Hannah for her first airplane ride on June 11, 1949: a twenty-minute jaunt in the family four-seater Bonanza.

All American Airways struggled throughout 1946 and 1947. Then "in February 1948 the Civil Aeronautics Board issued its long-awaited ruling on the question of which airline(s) would have the right to provide passenger, freight, and airmail service in the Middle Atlantic region." The CAB "gave All American Aviation a year to phase out its existing pickup service and become a conventional feeder-line carrier."[15]

Now it was up to Bob Love to move the fledgling airline through this major transformation. After ten years of airmail pickup service, All American became a passenger airline. For this purpose, Bob purchased eleven war-surplus DC-3s—more familiar to Nancy and Bob as the C-47, the plane that both of them had flown so often during the war. Now the All American fleet consisted of the reliable and popular DC-3s instead of its trademark red Stinsons. Later in 1948, All American Aviation became All American Airways and the airline moved its headquarters from Wilmington to Hangar 12 at National Airport in Washington, D.C.[16]

When All American Airways moved from Wilmington to Washington, D.C., in 1948, the Loves moved as well. Their second daughter, Margaret Campbell, called Marky, was born March 22, 1949, in Alexandria, Virginia, as was their third and youngest daughter, Alice Harkness, born November 1, 1951, and known as Allie.

Marky says that Allie is the true "Love" child as she was conceived while their parents were taking a long-awaited second honeymoon in Paris in early 1951. There was never any question in Nancy's mind what she wanted. She just had to find out how to make it happen. Until then, she did what she had always done—pursued other goals and made the best of what came her way. The Loves did what became the norm for the postwar generation—they had a family. It was all part of the fervent quest to return to normalcy, to a world built on core values and on shaping something positive, something that didn't involve death and destruction.

Bob gained further control of All American's company policy acquiring additional shares of All American common stock."[17] On March 7, 1949, Bob Love personally greeted passengers embarking on the seven a.m. inaugural flight from Washington National to Pittsburgh.[18] The name was changed again January 1, 1953, to Allegheny Airlines. Soon after, Bob Love was named the chairman of the board.

As it turned out, the Loves didn't give up on the rest of the dream—escaping the humdrum big city existence for a quiet place in the country. In 1952, six months after Allie was born, the family moved permanently to Martha's Vineyard. Bob's father had died not long after the war. Bob's sister, Margaret, and their widowed mother, whom the girls called Granny, had settled on Martha's Vineyard. Nancy and Bob—tired of the Washington rat race—decided that they didn't want to bring up their daughters in that contentious climate and joined Marge and Granny on the island.

By that time Nancy's parents had moved from Hastings to Kennett Square near Philadelphia to be nearer them. After Dr. Harkness died in the mid-1950s, Nancy's mother—known to the girls as Grinny—also moved to the Vineyard. One of Bob's greatest disappointments was that his father never got to see his grandchildren. However, the three Love girls did get to know their other three grandparents.

Martha's Vineyard would turn out to be a mixed blessing, but that was something they could not foresee in 1952. Bob was committed to commuting to Washington on Monday mornings, flying their Bonanza, and returning on Friday. He served as chairman of the board of Allegheny Airlines until 1954 when he became a director, the position he held until 1974. After that his designation was director emeritus.

✈ 21 ✈
Life on the Vineyard

When the Loves first moved to Martha's Vineyard, they bought a large piece of property—the Oak Bluffs House—on Sengekontacket Pond near Trade Winds Airport. There, they could hanger their single-engine, four-seater Beechcraft at the airstrip. Former WASP (Class 44-6) Carolyn Cullen ran Trade Winds Flying Service, managed the Fixed Base Operation at the small airport, and taught flying. She leased the airstrip from owners Gerould and Helen Mary Clark—the Love's summertime next-door neighbors. Helen Mary was one of Nancy's original WAFS and also one of her close friends. Carolyn taught Helen Mary's two sons, Gerry and Bill, and later Hannah and Allie, to fly.

Many of the WAFS and WASP who knew Nancy and Helen Mary dropped in during the lovely island summers—among them Teresa James, Betty Gillies, Sis Bernheim Fine, Barbara Donahue Ross, who is Allie's godmother, Esther Manning Shively, and Ann Hamilton Tunner, along with her husband, Bill (General Tunner). Lobster cookouts on a nearby beach were commonplace in the 1950s.

The Loves had lots of company and most arrived by air. One man "dropped in" via helicopter, which little Allie called "a hectocopter," because the girls weren't supposed to say "hell." Many a friend—when taking off or landing on the grass strip—buzzed the house and waggled his or her wings for the Loves and their children down below.

Throughout the 1950s, when the Loves needed to go to the mainland, they flew whether it was business, social, or to shop for school clothes for the girls.

"We have owned a Beechcraft Bonanza since 1946—the same faithful 3908N until last fall when hurricane 'Edna' brought the hangar down on top of it," Nancy wrote in a 1955 article for the Beechcraft company magazine, *Beechcrafter*. "We now have a recent model, of which we are equally fond. Bob and I put about three hundred hours a year on our Bonanza separately and together." Her article continues: "Living on an island, an airplane is a particularly useful possession…. It is hangared at a small grass airport within three minutes of our house. We find it equally good for flying the children to Boston for dental appointments or flying marine equipment in from New Bedford for our shipyard. We do a good deal of long-distance cruising on our auxiliary cutter, which necessitates changes of crew every few weeks. I find myself running a very complicated summer taxi business, flying friends to points in Maine and Canada to join the boat, and bringing back those who have to return home."

The three girls, Nancy wrote, were brought up in an airplane as the Love family used the Bonanza the way most people did a car, carrying children, dogs, furniture, spare sails, marine parts, and assorted cargo. "In my many trips 'off-island,' as we say up here, I have taken my car only once and then was scared to death by mainland traffic."

In 1955, Nancy still believed that an airplane for every family was the wave of the future. "People have been saying hopefully for years that the glamorous and hazardous angle must be removed from flying before it is really accepted. I think the time has at last arrived. I find on my trips with the children that we create no more curiosity arriving in our [airplane] than we

Nancy and her three girls: Marky, Hannah and Allie.

Courtesy Love family; electronic image NAHF.

would in a station wagon and that's as it should be. I believe that more and more women will take to private flying as they learn the practical utility of it."

And Nancy still enjoyed flying by herself, "exploring a mysterious road that might lead to a good picnic beach, or even just shooting landings, as I used to do so earnestly twenty-five years ago."[1]

Hannah and Marky recall one particular flight in the Bonanza with some amount of chagrin. "We were sitting in the back," says Hannah, "and Allie was in front with Mum. Marky and I started singing. Pretty soon we were swaying and bumping in time to whatever we were singing. Mum, of course, couldn't see us and because of the engine noise she couldn't hear us either."

The strange motion coming from the rear of the plane caused Nancy to think there was a malfunction. She began to look for a place to make an emergency "forced landing." Finally, when she had one lined up, she calmly told the girls to be sure their seatbelts were fastened, not to be afraid, but that she had to land. Hannah and Marky stopped singing and they also stopped bumping and swaying. Immediately, the flight smoothed out and Nancy realized what had happened.

The first two years the Loves lived on the island, Bob took the Bonanza on Monday mornings, flew off to Washington, and didn't return until Friday evening. The girls, of course, didn't like it when their Daddy flew away. One Monday, six-year-old Hannah hid the keys to the airplane so he wouldn't leave. After Bob and Nancy tore the house apart hunting the lost keys, Nancy noticed her eldest hanging back, strangely quiet. "Hannah?" she said. Hannah—Daddy's girl from the start—turned on her heel, ran out to a field and, miraculously, found the keys where she had thrown them in a vain attempt to keep her father home.

In 1954, Bob stepped down as chairman of the board at Allegheny. Though he remained active as a member of the board of directors and still flew to Washington for conferences, board meetings and other business, he no longer was gone every Monday through Friday.

After that, growing up on Martha's Vineyard was a family affair.

Bob Love loved three things: Nancy, flying, and sailing. He had learned to sail in the summers of his childhood at a family cottage on Walloon Lake in northern Michigan. That summer home was a legacy from his mother's Indiana family. To that list of three, beginning in 1947, he added Hannah and subsequently his other two daughters. Nancy and Bob began life together flying and, together, they segued into sailing. For Nancy, sailing was an acquired taste, but one she came to love. Sailing became a much larger part of their life than flying after the girls came along.

Every spring and fall through the 1950s, Nancy and Bob raced the family cutter against other sailing craft all over the East Coast. In the summer, they took a leisurely cruise during which "we explore obscure little ports looking for adventure and the good company of other yachtsmen," Nancy once told a reporter.[2]

When Nancy and Bob took these sailing excursions in the early days, they left the girls at home in the care of a babysitter/housekeeper. The girls quickly grew accustomed to this and took it in stride—in fact, liked most of their babysitters, finding them to be good companions. Besides, living on Martha's Vineyard in the summer *was* vacation! When one summer sitter thought it was terrible that Mr. and Mrs. Love would go off and leave their children—even though she took on the job—the girls couldn't figure out what all the fuss was about. To them, it was what they did.

With Bob home most of the time, the five Loves moved into a typical family routine. Every evening, Nancy and Bob sipped their ritual cocktails and watched the evening news on TV. Nancy employed a cook and the family ate dinner together, sitting at a set table in the dining room. The girls weren't allowed to watch TV during the day, but if their homework was done, they could watch after dinner. Nancy took care of cleaning up after dinner and would not sit down until everything was cleared and put away.

The three girls were supposed to help. "But we always wanted to go watch whatever was on TV, so she'd come out and watch with us for a few minutes and then go back to the kitchen on commercials. Pretty soon, we'd yell, 'Mum, come on, it's starting'."

Bob's mother and sister, Granny Love and Margaret, joined them for Sunday dinner. Marky was named for her Aunt Margaret, who also doubled as her godmother. "Dad and Aunt Margaret loved each other, were devoted to each other, but they could *argue*!" says Marky. "Dad was somewhere to the right and would get red in the face. Aunt Margaret was equally as far to the left and she would pound the table—she was a little powerhouse and ran on the same energy as Dad did. Mum didn't like politics and would leave the room when the political discussions became too heated. But she supported the underdog and leaned to the left."

Nancy never professed to be an ardent feminist, but the woman who paved the way for so many other women in aviation did support women's rights. She had no patience with prejudice. She didn't argue, she just went ahead and did what she wanted. "Remember, she laid the general out about not letting the WAFS fly when they had their periods," says Allie.

Nancy also taught her daughters to have the courage of their convictions. Her favorite saying was "Dare to be true," the Milton Academy school motto. And she added, "Stand up for what you believe is right."

Aunt Margaret also made life on the Vineyard interesting.

"She used to drive us all over the island at high speed in her big station wagon with the rear-facing third seat," says Marky. "She'd pile all the kids in to take us to Junior Choir practice or school activities. She always had a cigarette in her hand, gesturing. Scared us to death. Later on, she drove a VW station wagon with dozens of bumper stickers like 'Give so that others might live,' 'Save the whales!' and various local causes. She was a wild Indian!

"But Aunt Margaret also was a staunch Episcopalian—she was a bastion of the local church. Dad was too. He was a member of the vestry. Mum, however, never had much to do with church."

In spite of her lack of interest in organized religion, Nancy loved Christmas and the spirit of Christmas. When the girls were growing up, she got caught up in the decorating, hanging of stockings, wrapping presents, and preparing a festive Christmas dinner. The girls are convinced that her excitement stemmed from the war when, for four years, work always came first.

All three girls went to grade school on the island, and that was a happy time in the Love household. The needs of pre-teen girls back in the 1950s were not particularly trying. "Back then, 5,600 people lived on the Vineyard, September to May—us chickens and the fishermen," says Allie. "In the summer, there were 56,000! What a wonderful place to grow up."

Because the entire island was their backyard, the girls had space in which to spread their wings as well as collect all the animals they wanted—dogs, cats and, of course, horses. All three Love girls had inherited their mother's love for horses. Hannah's pony Tii, who joined the family April 1, 1957, was the first of many equine members of the Love clan on Martha's Vineyard.

Nancy and Bob may have taken their sailing vacations without the children, but they didn't deny their girls the opportunity to vacation. They also took a family winter vacation—"the children's vacation" they called it. One year they went to Florida and cruised the Everglades and Florida's West Coast in a borrowed power cruiser. Another year they flew a commercial airliner to Arizona and stayed at a dude ranch owned by WASP (Class 43-2) Ruth Dailey Helm and her husband "Slim." The girls all got cowgirl outfits complete with boots and hats. They went horseback riding every day, much to Hannah and Marky's delight.

As the girls moved into adolescence, horses became a way of life for the entire Love family. "You must understand what our parents did for us," says Marky. "They became totally immersed in this with us. Mum especially, because she understood our love of horses. She made it all possible. Her devotion to us and what we wanted to do with our riding and our horses was incredible."

Nancy, fastidious by nature, put up with the sweat, the horsy smell, the manure, the dust, and the dirt. None of that fazed her. She did all the organizing. The family loaded up the horses in the trailer every weekend, packed their gear, and hit the road for mainland Massachusetts or New Hampshire or wherever the shows were. They camped out at the horse shows. And then they drove home, dirty, smelly, tired, exhilarated. The more blue ribbons, the higher their spirits.

There was a Love horse on the Vineyard until Allie was nineteen and away at college.

The Loves also had a succession of sailboats: *Gay Gull I, II* and *III*. "I think gay had a different connotation then," says Allie. When Bob was no longer commuting every week to Washington, he and Nancy bought the Martha's Vineyard shipyard. "*Gay Gull I* and *II* were wooden boats and wooden boats are labor intensive. Dad always said he bought the boatyard so he could keep the *Gay Gull* from sinking."

The shipyard came equipped with marine fuel, ancient boat-hauling equipment, a lifetime supply of "bungs"—wooden stoppers for knotholes in wooden boats—and a motor launch, *Zsa Zsa,* the workboat for the yard. With the purchase of the boatyard, Bob acquired the duties of harbormaster. This entailed taking care of the public moorings. A 200-foot ferryboat came through the harbor four or five times a day. Bob was responsible for making sure the lane wasn't blocked.

"Dad had a dream about building boats," says Allie. "He was always looking for ideas, then on one trip he found this old hull—it had beautiful lines for a lobster boat. He had it cast, made a mold and used the design for a fiberglass boat. So Mum and Dad went into the shipbuilding business. Dad ran Vineyard Yachts Inc. and Mum was the vice president of the corporation. Dad didn't like running the day-to-day operation of a shipyard, so she did the office work and the paperwork.

"Mum worked like a dog. She wanted to help make it go."

In 1960, Nancy and Bob sold their first Vineyard property and bought what was known on the island as "the Wallace E. Tobin house on the Lagoon." They also sold the Bonanza, giving up flying in favor of sailing.

"They had watched several of their friends who kept flying beyond their abilities and made fatal mistakes," Hannah remembers. "They had every rating, but they decided that if they couldn't do it right, they weren't going to do it at all." Their life was moving away from airplanes and toward family activities and sailing. As Nancy told some of her WASP friends, "you can't go off living on a Bonanza for weeks at a time." But you could live off a sailboat.

For the girls, growing up on Martha's Vineyard was an idyllic existence what with the sun, the sand, salt water, sea air, the sailing and the horses, the laid-back lifestyle and vacation atmosphere. And it seemed to offer a laissez-faire way of looking at life, at least outwardly so. But as the girls hit junior high and puberty, life began to change.

Nancy had led a more urbane existence than most other mothers on the island—not just socially but professionally, what with her WAFS/WASP experience. She and Bob came from privileged backgrounds and money and he was a director of a commercial airline. On the Vineyard, they lived among shopkeepers, various maintenance and service people, and fishermen and their families. Making matters worse, Nancy's more liberated ideas—though far from radical—didn't always jibe with those of the island natives and permanent residents. This led to a sense of isolation.

"The island was an insular existence and we were trying to live with the people on the island. However, Mum did have a small but devoted group of women friends on the island who came from very different backgrounds," says Allie.

Nancy was, in fact, an enigma to many islanders. From an old Boston background, she nevertheless had her name removed from the Social Register. She did not want her daughters to go through the "coming out" debutant exercise, but was well acquainted with the behavior that was part of her social set. She knew how things should be done, and though she didn't always conform, she obeyed the instincts her manners-conscious mother had instilled in her. Nancy raised her daughters to know correct behavior, yet encouraged them to be independent.

Nancy had a knack for listening to young people. This came from her years at the helm of the women in the Ferrying Division. Then, her responsibility had been to keep 150 to 300 females—most, though not all, of them younger than herself—in line, happy, productive, and out of General Tunner's hair. She had performed this task with her characteristic low-key efficiency. Now, fifteen years later, she simply applied the same techniques, tempered and honed by maturity and several years of motherhood.

The island kids gravitated to her. Nancy was tolerant of differences—another lesson learned in the war. One of Allie's friends was dating a boy of foreign descent. In the mid-1960s, this wasn't looked upon favorably. Nancy allowed them to see each other in the confines of the Love home.

Nancy did *not* advocate teenage sex or promiscuity—far from it. She was, in fact, quite strait-laced. "She used the analogy, if you're easy, you've given up something precious for very little," says Allie. But she did advocate an open attitude about sex education. She believed in personal responsibility and knowing all the facts.

Nancy was dismayed that all the young people on the Vineyard had to do to amuse themselves was to drive, drink, and have sex. She talked to her girls about sex. And their friends sought her out to talk about periods and other concerns. "Mum told a good friend of mine about sex when her own mother wouldn't," says Marky. This was the result of Nancy's own traumatic experience in the far less enlightened 1920s. When she had her first period at the early age of ten, she thought she was dying. It was from her physician father, not her mother, that Nancy learned the facts of life. Dr. Harkness was very down-to-earth and, because she and her father had a good relationship, she could talk to him.

Though she could talk to her daughters and their friends about sex, Nancy—according to Marky and Allie—was ambivalent about sex, a holdover they think from her mother's Victorian reticence to discuss such matters with her. "She was a beautiful woman and she wanted to be physically attractive to men," says Allie. "But she wasn't a flirt. She could have used sex if she had wanted to. But she didn't. Dignity was too important to her. Besides, she knew she was competent, and that she didn't have to resort to such measures."

In spite of being a powerful woman, a woman who flew bombers, a woman in control, with Nancy there was always that niggling doubt—a latent lack of self-confidence. "She wouldn't go where she couldn't be confident," say her daughters.

In 1962, the Loves went into the charter boat business. Bob and Nancy scraped the bottoms of all the boats and then repainted them—an unceasing as well as backbreaking chore. "Mum got paint flakes in her hair and all over her face. She wore her hair tied back with a 'marlin'—jute treated with creosote. Of course her hair was totally gray by then," says Allie. The girls helped some, but by 1962 Hannah had gone off to boarding school and Marky would be on her way in a year. So help, other than in the summertime, was not so plentiful and most of the work fell to Nancy, including cleaning the decks, the galley, the head, the icebox. "If you didn't clean out the ice box regularly, you'd get moldy vegetable pieces on the bottom."

Surely the woman who had led the women flyers of the Ferrying Division and been on first-name basis with generals must

Carolyn Cullen hands Nancy a bouquet of flowers. Nancy's friend Ellen Manning in sunglasses.

Courtesy the Love family.

have—at least on the bad days—wondered to what depths she had sunk that her days consisted of scraping the bottoms of boats and cleaning toilets, sinks and ice boxes made dirty by someone else. But Nancy was a good sport and always support-ive of Bob in his endeavors.

When the girls got older, they learned to crew, so the summer sailing excursion to Maine became a family affair. Hannah, a natural sailor, recalls these with great relish. Marky, with her motion sickness, didn't weather the trips as well, and recalls them with some degree of chagrin.

"Hannah was the brave one," she says. "She did everything. Allie was the baby, she was too small to keep up. I was scared to death. I spent most of my time below decks in my bunk with a book. And Mum? She had an iron stomach. She could handle bad weather and not get seasick."

Bob was a daredevil—a cowboy in an airplane, as Nancy had discovered early on, and a cowboy on a sailboat as well. There was nothing he wouldn't try. They had many adventures and lived to tell about them, but two stand out in the girls' minds.

"We were 'gunk holing' up in Eastern Maine in *Gay Gull III* near the Bay of Fundy with its sixty-foot tides, getting the boat into tiny places," Allie relates. "We snuck into a good place for the night. *Gay Gull III* was a heavy fiberglass boat and we could barge through mud. We found a spar, a telephone-pole-like mooring for a fishing boat. It had a hole and a big metal ring.

"Hannah asked Dad, 'How much line should I give it?'

"'About six feet,' he told her.

"We had a nice dinner, then went to bed," says Allie. "Mum woke up at 2 a.m. to use the head. As she got out of her bunk, she almost fell." The boat was tilted decidedly uphill.

"Mum and Dad slept in the bow. We slept in the stern. We heard the commotion. Carefully, we all got out of bed and made our way to where we could see out. It was like climbing up the aisle in a DC-3. We were hanging by the mooring line, almost perpendicular to the water, stern down. A *log* was holding up this eleven-ton boat! Dad wanted to take a picture and send it out as that year's Christmas card with the message, 'We don't anchor our boats, we hang them up to dry.' But by the time it was light enough, we were afloat again."

But the scariest was the accident they had—also in the *Gay Gull III*—at Jonesport, Maine, again up near the Bay of Fundy. The boat survived the crash only because it was so heavy.

This time, the Loves were under power—moving through the water at six to seven knots. They were having lunch on deck—leftovers from a party held the night before. The fare included sardines, lobster, cold peas, sliced tomatoes, mayonnaise, and bread served on paper plates.

Nancy was steering when they hit an unmarked ledge and came to a dead stop. Everybody else was sitting down except Nancy, who fell forward into the aluminum boom crutch and split her face down the middle. She was bleeding badly, as only a head wound can bleed. Bob couldn't stand the sight of blood and nearly fainted. When Nancy asked for a cigarette, he tried to light it for her and promptly turned green. Bob didn't smoke.

"We radioed for help and went into the nearest dock at Jonesport," says Allie. "Because of the extraordinary tides, Mum had to climb thirty feet up a seaweed- and slime-covered ladder with family climbing above and below her to steady her. Eventually the ambulance, which doubled as a hearse, came to take her to the emergency room. The driver had come directly from a funeral and was dressed in black with white gloves. This was in the 1960s—before emergency medical squads—and we were out in the wilds of Eastern Maine. It was a long drive to the hospital. Dad went with Mum and we stayed to clean up."

The result was, Nancy had to have plastic surgery to repair the damage the boom crutch did to her face. The X-ray also found an old skull fracture. Nancy had actually fractured her skull when she fell out of the airplane when she was at Vassar, though they had thought she only had a concussion.

"Dad finally brought her back and we got her comfortable down below. Then we heard oars coming toward the boat. A voice called out in the darkness, 'Mr. Love, we're the people who drove you to the hospital. We have to charge you five dollars more. We only charged you the removal fee for a corpse.'

"Mum thought this was a hoot," says Allie. "When she heard the comment, she started chuckling. 'Bob, I'd have cost you less if I'd been dead.'"

Being the daughters of two famous pilots, the girls also grew up with airplanes. Eventually, they each had the opportunity to learn to fly.

Nancy told them early on, "I won't teach you." She thought it far better for someone else to do that. Instead, in 1966, she bought a Cessna 150—a small, two-seater high-wing trainer airplane—so that Carolyn Cullen could use it to teach the girls how to fly.

"Mum bought the Cessna when I went away to Milton," says Allie. "She called me at school and said, 'Guess what I did today. I bought an airplane.' I was excited. I already had done some flying with Carolyn. I soloed in the Cessna that summer when I was sixteen, before I got my learner's permit to drive a car. But when I went off to college at age seventeen, I still didn't have my private pilot's license."

And, as it turned out, that was the end of flying for Allie. She opted to attend college in southern California. The crowded airspace between LAX and its back-up airport, Ontario International, was not the place for a fledgling teenage pilot. When she came home from college that summer, she had other things going on—a fulltime job, a friend getting married. Then after Allie's freshman year, Bob and Nancy moved to Florida for the winters and sold the Cessna to Carolyn.

Hannah started flying at a later age than Allie. Nancy took her up for a tour of the island the summer she was eighteen. Hannah was promptly hooked and took instruction from Carolyn that summer, soloed, then continued to fly in college. She joined the East Hill Flying Club in Ithaca, New York, and got her license there when she was twenty-one. Marky tended to have motion sickness, had no interest in flying, and therefore took no advantage of either the Cessna or Carolyn's availability as a flight instructor.

Nancy did fly the Cessna, but after flying P-38s, B-17s, and C-54s, a 150 was a bit tame for her. In 1970, she did offer this bit of news for the WASP newsletter: "Hannah the oldest and Allie the youngest both learned to fly in my little Cessna 150, which I bought for the purpose, as it certainly wasn't my dish of tea. It has been fun flapping around the island in it, tracking down old fire trails and bridle paths, and checking up on beach characters. We've been loaded with hippies this year, and pot smoke rises to 500 feet, I swear." [3]

That Hannah got her license and Allie came close was a point of pride with Nancy.

Marky admits that she is the one who rebelled against her mother. That she looked like Nancy and was the most like her mother worked in reverse and she deliberately fled in the opposite direction. She was the one who did NOT learn to fly.

Though she had the grades to get in, she refused to go to Milton, the prep school outside Boston that her mother had attended, opting instead to follow her older sister Hannah to Oldfields in Maryland.

"Mum and I thought we knew what the other was thinking and we were both wrong."

But Marky also inherited her mother's artistic eye and creative ability. Nancy loved gardening and wild flowers and it was Marky who accompanied her on wildflower hunting expeditions around the island.

Marky sums it up. "She was a great mother."[4]

✈ 22 ✈
Empty Nest

Winters on the island got Nancy down. Most of the restaurants and stores closed for the winter, as did the movie theaters. Most of the friends Nancy and Bob enjoyed in the summer—the Boston and New York crowd—were long gone.

Late in 1959, Bob—who had turned fifty that year—had a cancer scare. He weathered it, but gave the family cause for concern. The year before, Nancy had lost her mother. Then in 1961, the girls began to go away to boarding school. Hannah, as the oldest, was the first to leave. But since Marky and Allie were still at home doing the things adolescent girls do, Hannah's departure for Oldfields School in Maryland that fall wasn't quite so hard on Nancy. The presence of the other two girls and their friends gave her a reason for "being." But then Marky followed Hannah to Oldfields in the fall of 1963.

"After Marky left, Mum felt life was getting stale," Allie says. "Her solution was to try to bring culture to Martha's Vineyard." Over the next few years, Nancy explored several such avenues. She tried to get an AFS (American Field Service) chapter started on the island. She thought a foreign student exchange program would give the local kids something to get involved with that would broaden their horizons. But she couldn't get enough families interested. "You have to understand the philosophy behind AFS," says Allie, "and not enough of the people did."

Nancy pursued setting up a girls' school on the island through the Ford Foundation, but that effort came to naught. She also tried to get Cape Cod Community College to offer courses on the island. "That didn't happen until later, after Mum and Dad had decided to spend their winters in Florida."

The conservation movement got Nancy's attention. She wrote to Marky in October 1968 that she was involved in the Conservation Society Membership Drive: "so unlike me to engage in good works." Never as far to the left as her sister-in-law, Margaret, Nancy now took notice of liberal causes.

Bob still traveled—to Washington D.C., New York, and other places, because of his board responsibilities with Allegheny and as part of the boat-building business, Vineyard Yachts Inc. Though Allie was home until the fall of 1965, she often was off with her friends. Nancy found herself alone a lot and the loneliness got to her.

In a moment of indulgence, Bob bought her a white Ford Sprint convertible with red leather seats and five on the floor. "Mum loved it. Driving it made her giggle," says Allie. When she drove that car around the island, the old Nancy was back—with all that *joie de vivre.* But the car didn't fill the growing void. Without something concrete and interesting to put her mind to, Nancy began to drink more than the two martinis with Bob before dinner.

The problem was, underneath, Nancy was dealing with a tendency to depression. The woman who, twenty years earlier, had shut down a highly successful ferrying operation while it was still needed, now faced a second dramatic shift in her life. And where other women had not borne the responsibilities of command like she had during World War II, all women could empathize with the crisis that was now upon her. Nancy, who didn't have children until she was well into her thirties and who had given her life over to them for seventeen years, was looking at age fifty and an empty nest.

Depression was not new to Nancy. She had suffered bouts in her school days at Milton and at Vassar as well as after the WASP deactivation. Now, her coping mechanisms were stretched to the limit as she no longer had responsibility—raising children or running a ferrying squadron to keep her busy—or the resiliency of youth on her side.

The questions that have stumped a couple of generations of women's aviation historians and Nancy Love followers are, "Why didn't Nancy take a more active stance in women's aviation in the 1950s, 1960s and 1970s? Why wasn't she active with the Ninety-Nines? (She let her membership lapse after 1956.) Why didn't she compete in the Powder Puff Derbies and other women's air races? Why did she virtually disappear from the aviation scene?"

The answers, of course, lie in Nancy's approach to life in general. She wasn't a joiner and she hadn't liked speed racing when she tried it in the late 1930s. Though the Powder Puff Derby was based not on speed but on the principles she had helped develop in the Ferrying Division to assure safe and economical delivery of an airplane from one point to another, she didn't enjoy competition of any kind. Nancy flew for pleasure. And, of course, that was not possible after they sold the Bonanza in 1960. It was six years before she bought the Cessna.

Beginning in 1947, Nancy was busy with her children and, until the mid-1960s, immersed in them and their activities. All indications are, this was her choice. Just keeping up with all of her daughters' horse shows was a fulltime commitment. She and Bob had purposely escaped first the military and then the Washington rat race and retreated to their quiet little island home. They had waited a long time for children and Nancy was intent on giving them as much of herself as she could.

And she had responsibility. From 1962 to 1965, when she might have gotten back into aviation as the girls went off to boarding school, she didn't have an airplane. And she and Bob were running the charter boat business. She was spending her time and energy keeping those boats "ship shape." None of this qualified as soul satisfying nor stretched her intellectually, but it did siphon off her energy.

Nancy had always enjoyed her cocktails. The rum and Coke cocktail hour of the WAFS years had evolved into the ritual martinis with Bob before dinner and they belonged to a social set that took great pleasure in cocktail parties.

She had witnessed the Roaring Twenties through the eyes of a rapidly maturing young girl. When Prohibition was repealed in 1933, she was nineteen. And she was an urbane young woman as the world—in spite of the Great Depression—was trying to live a Noel Coward existence. The songs of the 1930s—"Smoke Gets in Your Eyes," "Cocktails For Two," "Stardust," "I Get a Kick Out of You" and many more—bear this out. All cast a spell of romance and elegance, played out on the dance floors of New York's posh Art Deco nightclubs where the liquor flowed and curling cigarette smoke in the low sexy light made everyone into a member of the society of beautiful people. Hollywood of the 1930s offered similar escape cloaked in the magic and glamour of the silver screen.

Nancy belonged to the generation of women who reaped the fruits of the liberation brought about by World War I and practiced by their older sisters, the flappers of the 1920s. These younger girls, who became teenagers in the Twenties, also became the women who held up the home front in World War II or—as did Nancy—actually served in some capacity. They smoked and they drank. Smoking and drinking were sexy and Hollywood made it all quite glamorous.

"Mum smoked Chesterfields during the war and was featured in Chesterfield ads in all the glossy magazines," says Marky. "She later switched to filtered Trues. She thought they were the least damaging, but she never made an attempt to stop." Nancy also drank and enjoyed it. Cocktail hour was a ritual for the original WAFS back at Wilmington and it was still a ritual in the Love household, as in so many other households around the country. It was a cultural thing, definitely a sign of the times.

"Depression and alcohol go together," says Allie who, today, is a certified Emergency Medical Technician (EMT)-Cardiac Technician and chief of the local volunteer fire department rescue squad. The volatile mixture is something she understands.

That is what happened to Nancy. And Allie was the one who saw it unfolding during her last two years at home, alone, without her sisters. Nancy was drinking more than a couple of martinis before dinner. If Bob noticed, he said nothing. "Dad, for a long time, was in denial about Mum's drinking problem."

When Allie went off to boarding school in the fall of 1965, Nancy was left very much alone, with time on her hands and not much intellectual stimulation to fill that time and to burn some of that bottled-up creative energy. Out of boredom, she would seek out one or two of her island friends and begin drinking in the afternoon. That, combined with the depression that always lurked beneath the surface, began to take its toll. Nancy had, Marky points out, seen a therapist for depression off and on throughout her adult life.

When Marky refused to go to Milton, Allie realized that it was up to her to carry on the family tradition. She chose Milton. Since it was in nearby Boston, not far-off Maryland like Oldfields, she often came home weekends. Allie was the one close to her mother. "I was the compliant one. I did the right thing." Allie, still today the caregiver of the family, realized early on that her mother needed her.

Once Allie was away in school, Nancy's depression deepened and her dependency on alcohol increased. "That's when she bought the Cessna. I think she bought it in an effort to quit drinking. Mum did *not* mess with drinking and flying!

"Dad had his boatyard. Sailing was his passion, not Mum's— though she enjoyed it. She didn't really have anything of her own. She had nothing to compare with those war years, and even though she didn't talk about it as any great thing, she had to miss it.

"Dad was not a deep thinker, but Mum was, and she had such a tremendous untapped talent—for poetry, literature, art. But she was shut out of all that because, on the island, she was cut off from cultural resources. That's what those attempts to bring culture in were all about. At one point she started taking an anthropology course."

In 1968, while Allie was at Milton and the other two girls were already in college, Nancy made her one and only foray into politics. She became an avid supporter of, and campaigned for, Eugene McCarthy's candidacy for the presidency. She was quite upset over all the strife that year—the assassinations of Martin Luther King Jr. and Robert Kennedy and the rioting at the Democratic Convention in Chicago—but she was particularly unhappy about the results of the election. She also had a Civil Rights conscience, serving on the board at Oldfields working to get young African Americans admitted to the school.

Hannah chose Ithaca College in upper New York State and enrolled in the fall of 1965. Two years later, Marky opted for Colorado College in distant Colorado Springs. When it was Allie's turn to choose a college, again she had a dilemma. The head mistress at Milton recommended that she attend Lawrence College in Appleton, Wisconsin. Allie wanted to go to California to school. So Nancy and Allie went college hunting in 1967.

"Mum didn't openly side with me against the head mistress. 'You've never seen my part of the world,' she said. Wisconsin is much like upper Michigan where she grew up. So we did go to Appleton to look at Lawrence. Though the campus was lovely, I felt no connection."

Allie was adamant about California, so she and Nancy went from Wisconsin to California, and there, Allie found her college. She opted for the newly established Pitzer College, part of The Claremont Colleges that also includes Scripps, Harvey Mudd, and Pomona. "On that trip, we stayed in San Francisco and visited Mum and Dad's old haunts."

In the fall of 1969, Allie left for college in California. "The reason they could afford to send me to California to college—and Marky to Colorado for that matter—was Dad was entitled to airline passes through Allegheny."

In those days long before e-mail, Nancy faithfully wrote to the girls when they were away in boarding school and college. They talked on the phone every Sunday night as well. Often a letter followed close on the heels of an intense phone conversation prompted by one of the girls feeling the need to unburden some problem. She kept up a good correspondence with all three, but Marky saved her mother's letters. They span November 1964 to November 1975, offer an abbreviated commentary on Nancy and Bob's life without their girls, and give an indication of how Nancy coped with her empty nest. Her letters are overwhelmingly upbeat.

The close relationship her daughters had developed delighted Nancy, and she said so. "Pop and I are pleased you kids call each other up as you do—a worthy extravagance," she wrote on one occasion. On another, she called Marky at Oldfields only to find Hannah there, all the way from Ithaca, for the purpose of cheering up her sister after some crisis. The following day, Nancy wrote, "Pop and I are really pretty pleased about the relationship in our family. Not to get all sentimental, but I wish I'd had sisters who worried, and did something about low morale!" This was a clue that Nancy's formative years may have been somewhat lonely.

Nancy's letters were full of the travels she and Bob were planning or had taken together, as well as notes about him flying off to this meeting or that conference all over the eastern seaboard. Occasionally Nancy mentioned riding one of the horses or flying the Cessna. Letters in 1969 relate the sale of the *Gay Gull III*. "If the Loves ever did a 180, this is it." She and Bob bought a houseboat and Nancy named it, appropriately, *Switch*.

The houseboat was destined to take them to Florida. Nancy and Bob were tiring of the harsh winters on the Vineyard and had decided to escape for the worst months of the year. In the fall of 1969, they sailed the new houseboat down the inland waterway, moored it enroute while they returned home to the Vineyard for family Christmas, and then picked up where they left off to continue their journey south. They lived on the houseboat that winter.

In April 1970, Nancy and Bob moved ahead with plans for a house in Sarasota. Following that summer on the Vineyard, they once again became "Snow Birds"—northerners who "fly" south to winter in Florida—traveling via the houseboat down the inland waterway. This time, they took up permanent residence at 5235 Hidden Harbor Road, Siesta Key.

When they moved into the house, they sold the houseboat and bought a sailboat, which they named *C'est ça*. Nancy always named the boats and this time she chose "*C'est ça,*"which means, "that's it," because she said it was the last sailboat they would ever buy. In 1972, Bob and Nancy sold the house on the Vineyard. They retained an apartment on the island—the manager's quarters of the retirement community, Haven Side, that Bob and Margaret had established. The manager didn't need the apartment because he had a house next door. The Loves used the apartment as a staging point for sailboat trips in the summer.

Allie—who was nineteen when the move began—felt displaced, even though Nancy told her that when she went to the island, she could stay in the small apartment. In Florida, she could stay on the houseboat and, later, in the house with them. Bob and Nancy also sold their last airplane—the Cessna—to Carolyn.

Hannah graduated from college in 1969 and that fall took off to spend a postgraduate year abroad in Grenoble, France. At the same time, Marky opted to take her junior year abroad in Australia. So Bob and Nancy only had one "chick" in the continental United States for part of 1969 and 1970. When Marky returned, she resumed classes at Colorado College and graduated in 1972.

Allie developed severe back problems in 1971 and Nancy and Bob pulled her out of college for a semester. Her problem was a shredded disc. Nancy and Bob were ready to head back to the Vineyard, so instead of having the recommended surgery, Allie went north with them. But the problem didn't go away.

"I couldn't lie still. By July, I said, 'this isn't working.' The doctor said for me to come back to Sarasota. Mum went with me. I had surgery. When it was time for me to go back north, Dad got into the act. I rode from Sarasota to Martha's Vineyard in the back of the family station wagon lying on a mattress."

Spending several months with her parents after being away at boarding school and then college, Allie realized how bad Nancy's drinking had become. In 1971, the girls and Bob tried to intervene. "It came from all of us—even though Dad had been in denial about it—and she knew it came from the heart. She would not go through AA and she would not go for a God approach. She considered that Holy Roller. So we appealed to her academic side. She started writing. But we don't know what happened to what she wrote. She probably ripped it up because it wasn't perfect." Nancy was dealing with her demons in the way she knew how, the way she understood—intellectually.

Then early in 1974, life turned upside down for Nancy and her family. For the first time in her adult life, Nancy Love came up against serious illness. She was diagnosed with breast cancer.[1]

✈ 23 ✈
Fighting Spirit

The best description of her two-year battle with cancer is given by Nancy herself, in a letter written June 16, 1976, to her old friend, Jack Ray, her flight instructor in her Vassar days.

> June 16, 1976
> Dear Jack,
> Many thanks for the nostalgic photographs—could we possibly have been so young—ever?
> I'm sorry for the delay in thanking you, (they arrived early in April) but I have a very legitimate, if not very happy excuse. This old healthy Amazon came down with cancer in the spring of 1974. I joined the distinguished company of Mrs. Ford and Mrs. Rockefeller, and promptly decided to ignore the whole thing. However, the pesky thing popped up a year later in my neck, and after another operation I tried to ignore it again. Now it's in my throat and inoperable except for the wretched cobalt treatments, which I've had too many times already. I'm just out of the hospital at this point, and feeling very chipper, but have to go back to the cobalt horror, starting tomorrow.[1]

That's how Nancy began her letter to Jack, with whom she had corresponded off and on for nearly forty years.

Nancy had undergone a radical mastectomy in the spring of 1974. Her reference to Mrs. Ford and Mrs. Rockefeller in the 1976 letter is because both had been diagnosed with the disease and had had highly publicized surgeries. It was the first time that breast cancer had been that widely talked about in the press and in public. It took Mrs. Ford (wife of then President Gerald R. Ford) and Mrs. Rockefeller (wife of then Vice President Nelson A. Rockefeller) to bring the hush-hush topic out into the open.

Once on the mend, in typical Nancy fashion, she set her sights on the next project: getting ready to take an anticipated trip up the West Coast to Alaska with Allie who by then had graduated from Pitzer and was working at the Alaska Methodist University in Anchorage.

"When I moved to Alaska and saw how incredibly beautiful it was, I told Mum 'you've got to see this,'" Allie says. "She and Dad came to visit me in September 1974. We met in Seattle and took the Alaska Marine Highway part of the way, then the state ferry system, and finally drove the rest of the way to Anchorage on the Al-Can Highway. Then we took the train to visit Mt. McKinley. Mum was fragile, but she did well and enjoyed the trip."

Nancy and her youngest daughter shared some very personal moments during that trip—moments Allie has never forgotten, but moments she never expected because of her mother's attitudes toward outward displays of emotion and talking about personal things.

"She asked if I wanted to see the scar. That was out of character. I think she needed validation—that it was OK. It made me feel that she trusted me. It was personal, and Mum wasn't always personal. The mastectomy was a wake-up call."[2]

Nancy had written to Marky that she was gaining strength following the surgery, was looking forward to the trip to Alaska, that she had just seen the doctor and he had cleared her for "anything she felt like doing." Then she added that she regretted "my stubborn refusal to believe that I was not impervious to the evils of drink and the terrible times I put my long-suffering family through before I got the word."

In a series of letters to Marky during the summer and fall of 1974, as Nancy was dealing with the reality of the cancer and what had happened to her, she wrote about her beloved poodle, Sprite. She adored the little dog and took great comfort in her. "It's a bit lonely here, I must confess, but Sprite is my salvation. She's the most sympathetic, fun and altogether charming dog I've ever known.... Much as I adored Nugget and a few of the others in our long list of canines, they were all too big to cozy up on the sofa when they knew the old lady was low!"

In her letter of August 16, 1974, Nancy did something else she rarely did—she spoke of love—her love for her husband of thirty-eight years: "As you know, Daddy has been my salvation—sounds funny, but it's really true, as I'd have gone off in every possible wild direction—even more than I did—without his steady and understanding tolerance of my vagaries. Having respect for a man sounds mid-Victorian, but it's true, and is an important element in loving him. Mutual respect is a necessity."

Soon after they returned home from Alaska, Nancy and Bob headed to Norfolk to pick up *C'est ça* and bring her the rest of the way back to Sarasota. Bob and a friend had brought the sailboat from the Vineyard as far as Norfolk before the Alaskan trip.

In her letter to Marky dated September 30, written before they took off for Norfolk, Nancy already was planning Christmas, hoping all three girls would come to Florida for the holidays. "Hannah is coming," she wrote. "She hasn't told him yet, but wants Bron to come too." Nancy got her wish. The Love clan, more accustomed to a New England Christmas, gathered instead in sunny Florida on December 25, 1974.[3]

When Hannah and Robert Bron Robinson announced that they planned to be married the fall of 1975, Nancy knew she had her next project. The mother of three daughters, she had been waiting for this. Unfortunately, Nancy's cancer returned in the spring of 1975. The recurrence slowed her down, but she dealt with her illness and made the best of the situation. Nancy had a wedding to plan and nothing was going to prevent her from doing so.

The September 27 wedding was held on Martha's Vineyard. Marky and Allie were bridesmaids. Nancy carried it off, but it cost her dearly in energy and staying power. And it was painfully obvious to everyone there that she was, in fact, quite ill. From that point, the downhill slide was unstoppable.

When Marky and Allie first saw an archival copy of the letter their mother wrote to Jack Ray, they were amazed to find that their mother had written such a personal letter to anyone describing her illness. Again, they knew so well her lifelong quest for privacy and her tendency to downplay anything personal. But twice in two years, Nancy had heard from Jack and was tardy answering both times because of health reasons. Maybe it was a relief for her to unburden herself to someone she had known so long ago and whom she probably was never going to see again. Maybe she felt she owed him an explanation.

Nancy continued her June 16, 1976, letter to Jack Ray with a blow-by-blow description of the events of those weeks in May and June just past:

> My latest crisis was so bad that the docs gave up and the kids were called. Marky came from California, Hannah from Ithaca, and youngest daughter, Allie, who was driving down from Alaska, was intercepted by the Canadian Mounties, left her car with a friend to drive on, and chartered a Cessna 172 at Dawson Creek to fly to Edmonton to catch Air Canada. They had a hairy ride (Allie has soloed, so knew something about what was going on) through a front, hail, lightning and the works, finally coming through on the east side, only to find it was blowing 75-80 at Edmonton, so back through the front, to end up at Grand Prairie, only 40 miles from where they'd taken off from the gravel (Alcan Highway) in the first place. She finally got here after almost 48 hours of travel, waiting, and no sleep, only to find me out cold and not recognizing anyone.

"The doctor was realistic," says Marky, of that day in early June 1976 when they thought they had lost her. "She had been in a coma. We left the hospital that evening and figured that was it. The next morning, we hadn't heard anything. When we got to the hospital, she was sitting up in a chair! 'Did anybody bring my reading glasses?' was the first thing she said.

"I can't tell you what, emotionally, that does to you. Dad had a hard time. He didn't like medicos anyway.—There she was, as if nothing had happened."

"Mum had pulled a 'Lazarus,'" says Allie. "That's what she called it. In fact, she did this a couple of times. When Dad called me, he told me he didn't think she'd be alive when I got there. She was sitting in the chair. Two days later, she walked out of the hospital!"

In early May 1976, Bob and Nancy had taken *C'est ça* and started north for the Vineyard when Nancy's cancer symptoms resurfaced. They had gotten part way through the Okeechobee Waterway on their way east to the Atlantic side. Now, six weeks later with Nancy just out of the hospital and very weak, taking the sailboat north was impossible. At a family pow wow, the Loves resolved several dilemmas.

Nancy concluded her letter to Jack, written not long after her "Lazarus":

> So here I am, feeling fine in spite of 95 pounds (imagine old buxom me!) We've had a marvelous reunion with the girls, much giggling and reminiscing.
>
> They're scattering again now, Hannah to her new husband near Ithaca, Allie to Boise, Idaho, to collect her car, and Marky back to California where Allie will join her to drive back here, as we have to stay until at least August 1 for my treatments. House is air-conditioned, fortunately, as Florida in summer is hell to this old Lake Superior type!
>
> When I'm through with this latest siege, we are going to Maine, where we've rented a cottage near our islands in Penobscot Bay. Can't wait. We'd planned to take the boat up this year. Bob and Allie are going to bring her back here to store [in Sarasota] for the rest of the summer, while we drive north in convoy with Allie's Alaskan Fiat. So it's Bob and his harem again—two daughters, one wife, not to mention one female poodle puppy.

Allie flew back to pick up the car and belongings she had abandoned in her rush to get home. She had been in the process of moving from Alaska to Florida when Bob's emergency call came. She retrieved her car and took everything to California to store at Marky's house.

Marky flew back to California to put her life in order so that she could return to Florida and help her father care for her mother. In late June, Allie and Marky made the trip back across country from southern California to Sarasota in Allie's car. Then, Marky stayed with Nancy while Allie and Bob went to pick up *C'est ça* and bring her back.

That August trip to Maine was not to be. Nancy wasn't strong enough. The cancer had spread to her esophagus and larynx.

"When Mum was diagnosed as terminal, a lot of her friends just disappeared from sight," says Marky. "Nobody called—except C.R. Smith. He called at least once a month to talk to her." An unfortunate side effect many terminal cancer patients soon learn is that many of their friends will cease to call and come around. Whether they are afraid of "contracting" the disease, don't want to face someone so afflicted, or uncomfortable with the sudden realization of their own mortality in the face of a friend's—who knows. Nevertheless, it was something Nancy's family saw happening and dealt with.

Teresa James recalls the last time she saw Nancy in late summer 1976. Teresa and Kay Rawls Thompson, both from Florida's east coast, went to Sarasota to visit her. Nancy was thin as a rail, Teresa recalls. "I remember her standing in the door saying goodbye to us, still puffing on that infernal cigarette."

For some time, Allie had been planning to take an around-the-world backpacking trip. She was going to Scotland and England to look for ancestral gravestones, then on to a safari in east Africa and more touring in South Africa. She was to finish up by visiting friends in New Zealand and hoped to teach at the university there for six months.

"Mum insisted that I go." Allie departed for England in September.

Marky remained in Florida to help care for her mother.

The first of October, Marky received a phone call from WASP President Bee Falk Haydu. The WASP had named Nancy "1976 Woman of the Year." The award was to be presented at the reunion October 21–23. They hoped to give the award to Nancy in person.

Bee spoke briefly with Nancy. "She was sorry she couldn't attend, and she told me that she was dying of cancer. 'All my life,' she said, 'I thought I would go down in a blaze of glory in an airplane. Here I am hardly able to do anything at all.' She was so disappointed to be going the way she was."[4]

When Bee learned that Nancy might not live until the reunion, she contacted Ann Atkeison (Class 44-10), chairman of the awards committee. Ann immediately had the award engraved and sent to Nancy in Sarasota. On October 10, Marky wrote to the WASP: "The Award arrived last Thursday (7th) and Mum has asked me to convey her thanks and appreciation.... At this point we have almost begun to wish that Mum had less of a fighting spirit; although completely aware of it she continues to defy her impossible situation. It is at the same time awful and wonderful to be with a person who simply cannot or will not give up. Thank you for your understanding."[5]

Allie got as far as Scotland when, in mid-October, once again Bob had to call her home. She flew from London and, again, made it back in time. But when she saw her mother, she realized it wouldn't be long.

"Mum was mortified. She was so conscious of her dignity," says Allie. "By then she only weighed fifty-five pounds. She was heavily sedated, still, while they were giving her an IV, she was wisecracking—like she always did. She lasted another 36–48 hours, then pneumonia set in."

Nancy knew that the family line would continue. They learned of Hannah's pregnancy the second week of August, just before Nancy was declared terminal. Nancy and Bob were going to be grandparents.

Nancy died at 6:30 in the morning, October 22, 1976, as the WASP were gathering to honor her. Marky called Bee Haydu to tell her and Bee vividly recalls having to make that sad announcement to the gathering.

A memorial service was held Friday, October 29, 1976, at Grace Episcopal Church in Vineyard Haven with the Rev. Donald H. Lyons officiating. Nancy's ashes were interred next to her mother's at the cemetery on Martha's Vineyard.

The December 1976 WASP Newsletter Special Edition carried Marky's note of October 10, as well as the following: "In telephoning us at the reunion, Marky Love requested there be no flowers sent to the private family funeral at Martha's Vineyard. Instead would those who desire, send a contribution to The American Cancer Society.... We have lost a fine person who led well in time of great need."[6]

Betty Gillies wrote the following for the WASP a week before Nancy died.

> The full responsibility for WAFS/WASP activities within the Ferrying Division rested squarely on her shoulders. Throughout her years of service, she combined desk work with her first love, ferrying aircraft.
>
> The great success of the WASP program within the Ferrying Division was due largely to Nancy Love's ability to organize, to lead, and to cooperate with the "powers that be" within the Division. She had the respect of all with whom she worked smoothly and efficiently, from its start in September 1942 until deactivation in late December 1944.[7]

Epilogue

Bron and Hannah Love Robinson's first two children were boys: Brad MacLure and William Northrup Robinson. Then, on April 20, 1983, Nancy's namesake, Hannah Lincoln Robinson was born. She is the seventh Hannah Lincoln in Nancy's maternal line that begins with the wife of Gen. Benjamin Lincoln, the man who took Cornwallis's sword at Yorktown.

Bob Love lived to see all three of his grandchildren.

Deborah G. Douglas sums up Nancy's contribution:

> Love's plan for the WAFS, both in conception and execution, remains an important model for the integration of women into the military. One important factor was that the WAFS program was never a matter of ego. It was absolutely critical to her that both men and women believed that members of either sex had something to contribute.... That she convinced others ... of this idea represented her most profound and lasting legacy. The gender debate in the military has never been the same since. And that makes Nancy Love one of the more productive historical figures of the first half of the 20th century—a heroine with the "real stuff."[1]

Nancy Love has received many posthumous honors, but the greatest tribute was her induction on July 16, 2005, into the National Aviation Hall of Fame (NAHF), located in the Museum of the United States Air Force in Dayton, Ohio. Only the ninth woman so honored, she followed Amelia Earhart, Anne Morrow Lindbergh, Jacqueline Cochran, Olive Ann Beech, Louise Thaden, Ruth Nichols, Harriet Quimby, and Patti Wagstaff. Nancy Love has taken her well-deserved place among aviation's greats.[2]

Appendix: Biographical Overview of Nancy Harkness Love

- Earned Private Pilot Certificate # 17797 on November 7, 1930, at age sixteen; earned Limited Commercial License on April 25, 1932, at age eighteen; earned her Transport License on August 13, 1933, at age nineteen.
- Appointed one of three (two more were subsequently appointed) women pilots working for the National Air-marking Program through the Bureau of Air Commerce (1935, 1937).
- Charter pilot with Boston-based Inter City Aviation (1934–41).
- Demonstration pilot for the Bureau of Air Commerce experimental tricycle gear safety plane, the Hammond Y Plane (1937).
- Demonstration pilot for the Gwinn Aircar Co. Aircar where she tested the tricycle landing gear (1937-38).

- First proposed that the Army Air Corps consider using civilian women ferry pilots, May 21, 1940.
- Operations planner with Domestic Wing of the Ferrying Command, renamed the Ferrying Division, Air Transport Command (March-June 1942).
- Established, with Col. William H. Tunner, the Women's Auxiliary Ferrying Squadron (WAFS), Ferrying Division, ATC, U.S. Army Air Forces (Summer 1942).
- Appointed by Secretary of War Henry Stimson, Leader of the Women's Auxiliary Ferrying Squadron (WAFS) in the Ferrying Division, ATC, USAAF (September 10, 1942).
- First female pilot to fly many of the Army's airplanes: the P-51 Mustang, B-25 Mitchell, B-17 Flying Fortress, P-38 Lightning, C-47 Skytrain, and C-54 Skymaster, among others.
- Appointed WAFS Senior Squadron Leader (January 1943); WAFS Executive on staff of the commander of the Ferrying Division (July 1943); WASP Executive on staff of the commander of the Ferrying Division (August 1943). Exercised staff supervision over WASP ferrying squadrons in the ATC until deactivation, December 20, 1944.
- Conducted special air operations and flight safety assessment for ATC in India and China, January 1945, following termination of the WASP.
- Received Air Medal July 15, 1946, authorized by President Truman, in recognition of wartime performance as leader of 303 women ferry pilots.
- Commissioned a lieutenant colonel in the United States Air Force Reserve in 1948 for her role as a founder of the women pilot program that evolved within the wartime Army Air Forces.
- Designated Woman of the Year in 1976 by the WASP organization the Order of Fifenella, October 23, 1976.
- Inducted into the International Forest of Friendship, Atchison, Kansas—Amelia Earhart's birthplace—June 1979.

- The Houghton, Michigan, Chapter # 638 of the Experimental Aircraft Association (EAA) changed its name to the Nancy Harkness Love Memorial Chapter, May 1980.
- Inducted into the Michigan Aviation Hall of Fame, Kalamazoo, October 13, 1989. Presented by friend and fellow member of the Ninety-Nines Alice Hammond and accepted by Hannah Love Robinson.
- Inducted into the Airlift/Tanker Hall of Fame, November 1996.
- Inducted into the Michigan Women's Hall of Fame, Lansing, November 1, 1997. Accepted by Nancy Walters, Michigan Ninety-Nine.
- Named one of the 100 Most Influential Women in Aviation's first 100 years. The occasion was Women in Aviation International's "Celebration of the Centennial of Powered Flight," held March 22, 2003, to commemorate the Wright brothers' December 17, 1903, first successful flight at Kitty Hawk, NC. WAFS Betty Gillies and Cornelia Fort were included in that number as was Jackie Cochran.
- Inducted into the National Aviation Hall of Fame, The National Museum of the United States Air Force in Dayton, Ohio, July 16, 2005.[1]
- Nominated for the Pioneer Hall of Fame, Women In Aviation, 2008. Selection pending.

Endnotes

Preface

1. Leon Edel, "The Figure Under the Carpet," in *Telling Lives: The Biographer's Art*, edited by Marc Pachter (Washington D.C.: New Republic Books, 1979), 24–25.
2. Catherine Drinker Bowen, *Adventures of a Biographer* (Boston: Little, Brown and Company, 1959), 47.

Learning to Fly

1. http://history.cityofhoughton.com/
2. Information on Nancy Harkness (Love) and her family is from personal interviews by the author with her three daughters: Hannah Love Robinson, Margaret Campbell (Marky) Love and Alice Harkness (Allie) Love, June 2000, June 2002, and June 2003.
3. "A Penny a Pound, Up You Go Was Bug That Bit Nancy H. Love," *The Stephens Life* (Stephens College, Columbia Missouri), April 26, 1946.; clipping found in the Nancy Harkness Love (NHL) private collection held by her daughters Margaret and Alice Love. Hereafter known as NHL collection. Complete copies also are in the author's possession. Partial copies are held by the International Women's Air and Space Museum (IWASM) in Cleveland, Ohio.
4. Interviews with Marky Love.
5. The Nancy Harkness quotations and written passages telling of her earliest flights are taken from: a questionnaire that she answered in 1935; a letter she wrote to H. A. Bruno & Associates (public relations) in December 1937; an article she wrote in 1955 for the public relations department of Beechcraft that was subsequently printed in *The Beechcrafter* magazine in October 1955; and assorted newspapers and magazine articles describing her early flight experiences. All are found in the NHL collection.

6. N. H. Love's logbooks and the newspaper article (no name or date), all found in the NHL collection.
7. Letter, NHL collection.
8. 1935 questionnaire in NHL collection.
9. Stories of Nancy Harkness at Milton are from interviews with Allie Love.
10. Crocker Snow, *Logbook: A Pilot's Life* (Washington, D.C.: Brassey's, A Roger Warner Book, 1997), 77.
11. Milton stories, Allie Love.
12. "Society Girl Lands Safely As Plane Fails," unidentified newspaper, approximate date, April 17, 1931, clipping found in NHL collection.
13. Nancy's school records, Milton Academy, academic year 1930–1931 found in NHL collection.
14. "Miller Is Hurt in Plane Crash: Vassar Student Learning to Fly, Uninjured," unidentified Poughkeepsie, New York, newspaper, April 5, 1932, found in the Women Airforce Service Pilots (WASP) Archives, Texas Woman's University (TWU) Library, Denton, Texas. Hereafter, TWU.
15. Letters from Nancy Love to Jack Ray dated October 16, 1971, and March 14, 1974, TWU.
16. "Flying Freshman of Vassar College Obtains Limited Commercial License," news article from unidentified newspaper, April 26, 1932, clipping found in NHL collection.
17. Clipping pasted into a scrapbook, *Sportsman Pilot Magazine*, 1932, found in NHL collection.
18. N. H. Love's logbooks in NHL collection.
19. "No Time for Parties, They'd Rather Fly," *Detroit Times* photo and caption, circa February 1933 (date not shown), clipping found in NHL collection.
20. "More Vassar Girls Flying: Several Follow Lead Set by Nancy Harkness," unidentified newspaper, no date, clipping found in NHL collection.
21. Nancy Harkness Love's Ninety-Nines application dated January 3, 1934, NHL collection.

Learning to Live

1. Letter, undated, but thought to be early 1934, from Nancy to her uncle Thomas Chadbourne, NHL collection.
2. Margaret Thomas Warren, *Taking Off* (Worcestershire, England: Images Publishing, Malvern Ltd., 1993), 160–65.
3. Margaret Thomas Warren, "The Early Years," *Ninety-Nine News,* March 2002. From the files of Dr. Jacque Boyd, aviation historian.
4. Warren, *Taking Off,* 166–67.
5. Allie and Marky Love interviews.
6. Snow, *Logbook,* 77.
7. "Passengers Find Flier Is Hub Deb," unidentified Boston newspaper, April 28, 1934, clipping in NHL collection.
8. Robert C. Codman, "Woman Flier Given Praise ... To Demonstrate Waco Line," *N.E. Aviation,* May 1934, clipping found in NHL collection.

9. N. H. Love logbooks, NHL collection.
10. Warren, "The Early Years."
11. N. H. Love and Robert M. Love's (RML) logbooks. Both Nancy's and Bob's logbooks are in private collections in possession of their daughters.
12. Newspaper article, Houghton, Michigan, September 10, 1934, clipping found in NHL collection.
13. N. H. Love and R. M. Love logbooks in NHL and RML collections.
14. Information on Robert MacLure Love and his family is from personal interviews by the author with his three daughters.
15. John Haviland Love, unpublished memoir, in possession of his grand-daughters Marky and Allie Love.
16. Interviews with the Love daughters.
17. R. M. Love's logbooks in RML collection.
18. Article, *Aero Digest*, July 1934, clipping found in RML collection.

Stretching Her Wings

1. Letter from Eugene Vidal to Nancy Harkness dated February 2, 1935, in NHL collection.
2. Letter from Eugene Vidal to Nancy Harkness, no date, in NHL collection.
3. Louise Thaden, "Five Women Tackle the Nation," *N.A.A. Magazine* (National Aeronautic Association), August 1936, clipping found at IWASM.
4. Airmarking information is taken from several sources and covers several paragraphs: Thaden, "Five Women Tackle," *N.A.A. Magazine*; Nancy Love, "Pilots Believe In Signs," *Yankee Pilot: The Magazine of Eastern Aviation*, January 1939; "Three Women Mark the Airways," *The Democratic Digest*, November 1935; "Air Markers," *Time* magazine, August 24, 1936, all clippings found in NHL collection.
5. Louise Thaden, *High, Wide and Frightened* (New York: Air Facts Press, 1973), 163–64.
6. Thaden, *High, Wide,* 165.
7. Thaden, *High, Wide,* 167.
8. Travel Order, Department of Commerce, September 14, 1935, NHL collection.
9. Letter from Nancy to John Wynne re: her progress on her Airmarking assignments dated October 6, 1935, NHL collection.
10. "It's Go East, Not West, for Girls," *Boston Post,* October 21, 1935, clipping found in NHL collection.
11. Exchange of letters between John Wynne and Nancy, Nov. 22 and 29, 1935, NHL collection.
12. "Hannah Harkness, Hastings Woman Flyer, Is Wedded," datelined Hastings, Michigan, Jan. 11, 1936, probably taken from the Battle Creek, Michigan, newspaper, Jan. 12, 1936, clipping found in NHL collection.
13. N. H. Love and RML logbooks, their collections.
14. "Women's Ferry Commander Once Feted in City," *Wyoming Eagle,* Cheyenne Wyoming, October 3, 1942 (after Nancy was announced as the commander of the WAFS), Jacqueline Cochran Collection, Dwight

D. Eisenhower Presidential Library, Abilene, Kansas. Hereafter Cochran/
Eisenhower.

15. Deborah G. Douglas, "WASPs of War," *Aviation Heritage* magazine, January 1999, 48.
16. Joseph J. Corn, *The Winged Gospel: America's Romance with Aviation 1900–1950* (New York: Oxford University Press, 1983), 73.
17. Corn, 73–74.
18. Corn, 75.
19. Corn, 76–77.

Tricycle Gear Test Pilot

1. Telegrams from Bill Ong to Nancy, dated August 26 and 27, 1936, regarding her potential entry as Louise Thaden's copilot in the Bendix Race, NHL collection.
2. Thaden, *High, Wide*, 179–97.
3. The Harmon Trophy is a set of three international trophies, to be awarded annually to the world's outstanding aviator, aviatrix (female aviator), and aeronaut (balloon or dirigible pilot). A fourth trophy, the National Trophy, was awarded 1926-1938 to the most outstanding aviator in each of the twenty-one member countries and again from 1946-1948 to honor Americans who contributed to aviation. The award was established in 1926 by Clifford B. Harmon, a wealthy balloonist and aviator who died in 1945. http://en.wikipedia.org/wiki/Harmon_Trophy
4. Second Bill Ong telegram, NHL collection.
5. Douglas, "WASPs of War," 49.
6. Nancy's daughters.
7. Minutes, the Annual Meetings of the Ninety-Nines dated September 5, 1937, Cochran/Eisenhower.
8. Hammond Y Plane information comes from this source and several listed immediately below: "Nancy Love Spots Airways," *Boston Traveler*, March 1, 1937, clipping found in NHL collection.
9. A.D.H, "Learner Proves Air Safety of Flivver Plane," *Christian Science Monitor*, March 6, 1937, clipping found in NHL collection.
10. "Society Heiress Maps Sign Posts for Fliers From Air," *Boston Evening American*, date unknown, clipping found in NHL collection.
11. "Official Praises Airmarking Program of WPA in Maine," unidentified publication, April 2, 1937, clipping found in NHL collection.
12. Letter found in NHL collection.
13. "Binghamton Asked to Provide Proper Fliers' Airmarkings," Binghamton daily newspaper, no date, clipping found in NHL collection.
14. N. H. Love and RML logbooks, their collections.
15. Press Release, Bruno & Associates, 30 Rockefeller Plaza, New York City (no date), NHL collection.
16. "Silhouette," *The Sportsman Pilot* magazine, May 15, 1938, clipping found in NHL collection.
17. N. H. Love logbooks NHL collection.

18. Lemuel F. Parton, "Who's News Today: Vivacious Nancy Love Makes Career as Plane Expert," *New York Sun*, September 2, 1937, clipping found in NHL collection.

19. Letter from Harry Bruno to Joseph M. Gwinn, with copy to Nancy Love dated October 25, 1937, NHL collection.

20. Letter from Nancy Love to Harry Bruno dated December 14, 1937, NHL collection.

21. "This Week in Aviation," *Boston Transcript*, May 23, 1938, clipping found in NHL collection.

22. *Time* magazine, September 4, 1938, 19, clipping found in NHL collection.

23. *Boston Herald*, August 24, 1938, clipping found in NHL collection.

24. Dorothy G. Walker, "Society Fliers Are Getting Ready for Annual Cruise," *New York World Telegram*, July 8, 1939, clipping found in NHL collection.

War in Europe!

1. C. J. Wollheim, *Siesta Key Pelican*, April 17, 1975 (interview with Bob and Nancy Love), clipping found in NHL collection.

2. William H. Tunner and Booton Herndon, *Over the Hump: The Story of General William H. Tunner, the Man Who Moved Anything Anywhere, Anytime* (New York: Duell, Sloan and Pearce, 1964), 13–14.

3. Doris L. Rich, *Jackie Cochran: Pilot in the Fastest Lane* (Gainesville: University Press of Florida, 2007), 99–100. Her source is the *Los Angeles Times*, May 11, 1936.

4. Rich, 98–99.

5. Harmon Trophy, source: http://en.wikipedia.org/wiki/Harmon_Trophy

6. Jacqueline Cochran and Maryann Bucknum Brinley, *Jackie Cochran: The Autobiography of the Greatest Woman Pilot in Aviation History* (New York: Bantam Books, 1987), 150. Also Rich, *Jackie*, 78–79.

7. "Women Pilots in the AAF, 1941–1944," *Army Air Forces Historical Studies*, No. 55 (March 1946), 2-3. Copies held by TWU, Cochran/Eisenhower, and the author. Referred to hereafter as #55, "Women Pilots AAF."

8. For more about Russian women pilots in WWII, please see: Reina Pennington, *Wings, Women, and War, Soviet Airwomen in World War II Combat* (Lawrence: University Press of Kansas, 2002); and Anne Noggle, *A Dance with Death: Soviet Airwomen in World War II* (College Station: Texas A&M University Press, 1994).

9. Lettice Curtis, *The Forgotten Pilots: A Story of the Air Transport Auxiliary 1939–1945*. 4th ed. (Cheltenham, England: Westward Digital, 1998), 7–9.

10. Jeffrey P. Rhodes, compiler, "Chronology: The Army Air Corps to World War II, Air Force History Support Office." Material courtesy *Air Force* magazine, December 1993.

11. Letter from NHL to Col. Robert Olds, May 21, 1940, NHL collection.
12. *The Boston Record,* June 4, 1940, clipping found in NHL collection.
13. #55, "Women Pilots AAF," 3–4.
14. Jacqueline Cochran, *The Stars at Noon* (Boston: Little, Brown and Company, 1954), 97–98.
15. Rich, *Jackie,* 103; also Cochran and Brinley, *Autobiography,* 167.
16. Rich, 103–4.
17. Cochran and Brinley, *Autobiography,* 169-171.
18. Helena Page Schrader, *Sisters In Arms: British & American Women Pilots During World War II* (Great Britain: Pen & Sword Books, 2006), 265.
19. Deborah G. Douglas, *American Women and Flight since 1940* (Lexington: University Press of Kentucky, 2004), 60.
20. The Lend Lease Act of March 1941 empowered the U.S. president to sell, lend, lease, and transfer material such as food, machinery and services to its allies before the U.S. entered World War II. *The Concise Columbia Encyclopedia* (New York: Avon Books,/The Hearst Corporation, 1983), 474.
21. Wollheim, *Siesta Key Pelican.*
22. #55, "Women Pilots AAF," 4 (see note 7 above).
23. #55, "Women Pilots AAF," 5–8.
24. Douglas, *American Women and Flight,* 62–63.
25. #55, "Women Pilots AAF," 6.
26. AAF historian Lt. Col. Oliver La Farge, "Notes on Interview with Mrs. Nancy H. Love, October 3, 1945," TWU.
27. Jacqueline Cochran's report to Col. Robert Olds, dated July 21, 1941, page 4. Cochran/Eisenhower.
28. #55, "Women Pilots AAF," 6–7.
29. Rich, *Jackie,* 108.
30. #55, "Women Pilots AAF," 8–9.
31. Byrd Howell Granger (WASP Class 43-1), *On Final Approach: The Women Airforce Service Pilots of World War II* (Scottsdale, Arizona: Falconer Publishing Company, 1991), 12, F-2.
32. Letter from Jacqueline Cochran to General Arnold marked "Urgent and Important," January 18, 1942, Cochran/Eisenhower.
33. #55, "Women Pilots AAF," 11.

Wanted: Ferry Pilots

1. Col. Onas P. Matz USAFR (Ret.), *History of the 2nd Ferrying Group,* Sponsored by the Wilmington Warrior Association (Seattle, Washington: Modet Enterprises, 1993), 6–7.
2. Mardo Crane, "The Women With Silver Wings," Part One, *The 99 News,* Special Issue 1978, clipping found in NHL collection.
3. Lt. Col. Oliver LaFarge, "History of the Air Transport Command, Women Pilots in the Air Transport Command," prepared by the Historical Branch, Intelligence and Security Division, Headquarters, Air Transport Command in accordance with ATC Regulation 20-20, AAF Regulation 20-8, and AR 345-105, as amended, 12-14. Lt. Col. LaFarge is official

historian for the Air Transport Command. This is the accepted history on the women ferry pilots of the ATC. From the private collection of Mrs. Ann Hamilton Tunner, widow of General William H. Tunner. A copy also is in the hands of the author. Hereafter, LaFarge, "Women Pilots ATC." See note #7 below for additional explanation.

4. Robert Serling, *Eagle: The Story of American Airlines* (New York: St. Martin's/Marek, 1985), 46, 161–62; and James M. Mangan, *To The Four Winds: A History of the Flight Operations of American Airlines Personnel for the Air Transport Command, 1942–1945, including Project 7A* (Paducah, Kentucky: Turner Publishing Company, 1990), 7.

5. Cyrus Rowlett (C.R.) Smith resigned as president and director of American Airlines to enter the Army in April 1942. At General Arnold's personal request, Colonel Smith was made executive officer of the Air Transport Command (ATC), thereafter assuming the positions of chief of staff, and finally deputy commander. He rose to the rank of major general. Source: Airlift/Tanker Association Hall of Fame: www.atalink.org/hallfame/c.r.smith.html

6. Serling, *Eagle*, 162–63.

7. Capt. Walter J. Marx, "Women Pilots in the Ferrying Division, Air Transport Command," a history written in accordance with AAF Regulation No. 20-8 and AAF Letter 40-34. 15 (including footnote #16). (Captain Marx's manuscript was *not* accepted by the Air Transport Command due to Jacqueline Cochran's objections, but was the basis for the accepted history rewritten several months later by Lt. Col. Oliver LaFarge—see note #3 above.), NHL collection. A copy also is in the hands of the author. Hereafter, Marx, "Women Pilots Ferrying Division."

8. Tunner, *Over the Hump*, 19, 26, 28.

9. Tunner, 3, 6–7.

10. Tunner 34–35. This is General Tunner's written recollection of the conversation as quoted in his book.

11. #55, "Women Pilots AAF," 12–14.

12. #55, "Women Pilots AAF," 13 (including footnote #28); and LaFarge, "Women Pilots ATC," 14 (including footnote #21).

13. LaFarge, "Women Pilots ATC," 14–15, 18.

14. LaFarge, 15–16.

15. LaFarge, "Women Pilots ATC," 16-17; Marx, "Women Pilots Ferrying Division," 17–23.

16. Marx, "Women Pilots Ferrying Division," 26–27.

17. LaFarge, "Women Pilots ATC," 18.

18. LaFarge, 20–21.

19. Delphine Bohn, unpublished WAFS memoir "Catch a Shooting Star," Chapter 4, pages 16–17. Copies in hands of the author and at the WASP Archives, TWU.

20. LaFarge, "Women Pilots ATC," 19.

21. Eleanor Roosevelt, "My Day," syndicated newspaper column dated September 1, 1942, clipping at TWU.

22. LaFarge, "Women Pilots ATC," 22–23.

23. #55, "Women Pilots AAF," 16 (including footnote #35).
24. LaFarge, "Women Pilots ATC," 23, 29.
25. LaFarge, 23 (including footnote #35).
26. Marianne Verges, *On Silver Wings* (New York: Ballantine Books, 1991), 41.
27. Leisa D. Meyer, *Creating GI Jane: Sexuality and Power in the Women's Army Corps During World War II* (New York: Columbia University Press, 1996), 11.
28. Paul Whelton, "American Women Are in There Fighting," *Boston Sunday Advertiser* Pictorial Review, October 4, 1942.
29. Whelton, Oct. 4, 1942.

Two Women Pilot Groups

1. #55, "Women Pilots AAF," 17 (see his footnote 41).
2. LaFarge, "Women Pilots ATC," 23 (see his footnote 35).
3. Memo from Jacqueline Cochran to General Arnold, September 11, 1942, subject: Use of Women Pilots, Cochran/Eisenhower.
4. Cochran memo.
5. #55, "Women Pilots AAF", 17.
6. #55, "Women Pilots AAF," 17 (see his footnote 40).
7. Memo from Major General H. L. George to General Arnold (copy to General George E. Stratemeyer), September 12, 1942; subject: Training of Women Pilots; Cochran/Eisenhower. (Emphasis added).
8. Memo from Captain James I. Teague to Colonel William H. Tunner, September 22, 1942, NHL collection.
9. Teague memo.
10. #55, "Women Pilots AAF," 18.
11. LaFarge, "Women Pilots ATC," 57; also #55, "Women Pilots AAF," 21–22. (Emphasis added.)
12. Memo from General George to General Arnold, September 12, 1942, Cochran/Eisenhower.
13. Douglas, "WASPs of War," 52.
14. Granger, *On Final*, 476.
15. H.H. Arnold (General U.S. Army), *Global Mission* (Blue Ridge Summit, Pennsylvania: TAB Books/Harper & Row, 1950), 356–57.
16. LaFarge, "Women Pilots ATC," 58–60; also Marx, "Women Pilots Ferrying Division," Teague's memo, 42–44.
17. Douglas, "WASPs of War," 52.
18. Verges, *Silver Wings*, 63.
19. Marx, "Women Pilots Ferrying Division," 55.
20. Douglas, "WASPs of War," 52.
21. Maj. Gen. Jeanne Holm (USAF Ret), *Women in the Military: An Unfinished Revolution*. rev. ed. (Novato, California: Presidio Press, 1992), 35.
22. Douglas, "WASPs of War," 51.
23. Barbara Erickson London, phone conversation with author May 26, 2007.
24. Iris Cummings Critchell, e-mail to author dated May 25, 2007.

25. Thaden quoted in Corn, *Winged Gospel*, 85.
26. Rich, *Jackie*, vii, quoting from *Pictorial Review*, June 1930.
27. Letter from Bob Love to Nancy Love, September 12, 1943, NHL collection.
28. Letter from Gen. Robert Olds to Nancy Love dated Oct. 2, 1942, NHL collection.

The Originals Gather

1. Minutes, the Annual Meetings of the 99s dated September 5, 1937, and September 3, 1939, Cochran/Eisenhower.
2. Memo from Betty Gillies to Delphine Bohn dated November 20, 1983; subject: Answers to Your Questions of 10/18/83. Gillies is quoting from her diary. TWU.
3. Information documented in a series of letters dated August 7, 1939, to June 7, 1940, exchanged between Betty Gillies and Haven B. Page, the attorney for the Private Fliers Association, Inc., also acting on behalf of Betty Gillies, president of the Ninety-Nines, found in Cochran/Eisenhower.
4. Douglas, *Women and Flight*, 18.
5. Betty Gillies diary, as quoted in November 20 memo to Delphine Bohn.
6. Gillies diary, quoted in above memo.
7. Patricia Strickland, *The Putt-Putt Air Force: The Story of The Civilian Pilot Training Program and The War Training Service (1939-1944)*; Department of Transportation, Federal Aviation Administration, Aviation Education Staff, GA-20-84; Foreword, p. iii. The Civilian Pilot Training Program (it became the War Training Service after Pearl Harbor) originated in the mind of Robert H. Hinckley, a member of the newly created (1938) Civil Aeronautics Authority. It used facilities already in existence. The ground training was handed over to colleges and universities; the flight training to established flight operators. CPTP began with 13 colleges and 330 students. By the time it ended in 1944, 1,132 educational institutions had been involved and 1,460 contractors had qualified 435,165 trainees, including several hundred women. Information also online at www.centennialofflight.gov/essay/GENERAL_AVIATION/civilian_pilot_training/GA20.htm
8. "Flying Mothers: Hands That Rock the Cradle Now Wield WAF Control Sticks," *Wilmington Morning News* (Delaware), October 23, 1942, copy of clipping in author's possession.
9. "WAFS to Fly In Gray-Green Slacks, Jackets," September 16, 1942, article from *Times Herald*, clipping found in NHL collection.
10. La Farge, "Notes on Interview with Nancy Love," TWU.
11. Gertrude Meserve Tubbs LeValley, interview with author Dec. 2, 2004, Bradenton, Florida. Tapes and oral history on file at TWU.
12. Bohn, "Catch," Chapter 5, page 9.
13. Nancy Batson Crews interview with author, January 12, 1992, Centerville, Ohio.
14. Teresa James interviews with author, Lake Worth, Florida, March 2–5, 2000.

15. Holm, *Women in the Military*, 22.
16. Interviews with Love daughters.
17. Bohn, "Catch," Chapter 4, page 13.
18. Marx, "Women Pilots Ferrying Division," 94, 97.
19. Marx, "Women Pilots Ferrying Division," referencing a letter from the Ferrying Division to War Department Bureau of Public Relations, March 29, 1943, subject: "Ghost-writing on WAFS," 101–2.
20. Rich, *Jackie*, 115.

Growing Pains

1. #55, "Women Pilots AAF," 23.
2. #55, "Women Pilots AAF," 21 (see footnote 47).
3. #55, "Women Pilots AAF," 23.
4. Letter from Col. William H. Tunner to commanding officers, All Ferrying Groups, April 26, 1943, NHL collection.
5. #55, "Women Pilots AAF," 25.
6. Bohn, "Catch," Chapter 6, page 9.
7. N. H. Love logbooks, NHL collection.
8. Memo, TWU.
9. Bohn, "Catch," Chapter 10, page 2.
10. #55, "Women Pilots AAF," 26–27.
11. Betty Gillies, "The When-Why-Who-Where of the WAFS," a talk presented at the Southern California WASP Meeting, Laguna Hills, California, June 14, 1987, the Betty Huyler Gillies collection, IWASM.
12. Glenn Kerfoot, *Propeller Annie, The Story of Helen Richey* (Lexington, Kentucky: The Kentucky Aviation History Roundtable, 1988), 84–95.
13. Barbara Jane (B.J.) Erickson London, interviews with author, Birmingham, Alabama, June 1999; January 15–18, 2003 and March 17–20, 2004, Long Beach, California.
14. See Airplane Glossary.
15. Bohn, "Catch," Chapter 10, page 13.
16. Ibid.
17. N. H. Love's logbooks, NHL collection. Nancy flew a total of three hours and fifteen minutes in the P-51 over a three-day period, February 27 and March 1 and 2.
18. Letter from Bob Love to Nancy Love, NHL collection.
19. James C. Fahey, ed., *U.S. Army Aircraft 1908–1946* (New York: Ships and Aircraft, 1946), 21.
20. Betty Gillies, taped interview with Dawn Letson of Texas Woman's University, October 6, 1996, Rancho Santa Fe, CA, TWU.

Killed in Service of Her Country

1. Rob Simbeck, *Daughter of the Air: The Brief Soaring Life of Cornelia Fort* (New York: Atlantic Monthly Press, 1999), 226–30.
2. Report of Aircraft Accident, U.S. Army Air Forces, 6th Ferrying Group, Long Beach, California, March 21, 1943. U.S. Air Force Academy Archives, Academy Library. Copy also held at TWU.

3. B.J. London, interview with author, June 21, 1999.
4. Cornelia Fort, "At Twilight's Last Gleaming," *Woman's Home Companion*, June 1943 (published posthumously).
5. Nancy Batson Crews, interviews with author, May 24, 1999, Fairborn, Ohio; June 11–15, August 14–17, November 13–16, December 19–23, 2000, Odenville, Alabama.
6. Letter from B.J. Erickson (London) to her parents dated March 27, 1943, from B.J. London's private collection.
7. Simbeck, *Daughter*, 234.
8. Simbeck, 235.
9. B.J. London, interview with author, January 15–18, 2003.
10. Iris Critchell, interview with author, January 16, 2003, Long Beach, California.

Transport and Transition

1. #55, "Women Pilots AAF," 37–38.
2. www.pbs.org/wgbh/amex/flygirls/peopleevents/pandeAMEX03.html People & Events, Nancy Harkness Love (1914–1976), The American Experience. *Fly Girls*, a documentary film written, produced and directed by Laurel Ladevich, *2000* PBS, WGBH Educational Foundation.
3. #55, "Women Pilots AAF," 40.
4. LaFarge, "Women Pilots ATC," 85.
5. #55, "Women Pilots AAF," 40–41.
6. LaFarge, "Women Pilots ATC," 82–83.
7. Rickman, *The Originals*, 166.
8. #55, "Women Pilots AAF," 41; also Marx, "Women Pilots Ferrying Division," 114–15.
9. Marx, "Women Pilots Ferrying Division,"114–15.
10. Schrader, *Sisters in Arms*, 42.
11. LaFarge, "Women Pilots ATC," 83; also Marx, "Women Pilots Ferrying Division," 111.
12. Tunner letter of April 26, 1943, NHL collection.
13. Bob Love letter to Nancy dated April 25, 1943, NHL collection.
14. Conversations with Manning's daughter, Julie Shively, May 2002. Also Rickman, *The Originals*, 368, 388.
15. Tunner, *Over the Hump*, 28–29.
16. Tunner, 27.
17. Ibid.
18. Tunner, 27–28.
19. Marx, "Women Pilots Ferrying Division," 118.
20. Author's note: The earthier military translation was "fucked up."
21. Bohn, "Catch," Chapter 6, pages 11–12.
22. LaFarge, "Women Pilots ATC," 87.
23. N. H. Love logbooks, NHL collection.
24. #55, "Women Pilots AAF," 25.
25. Rough draft of letter from Jacqueline Cochran to General Arnold, Cochran/Eisenhower; also, Granger, *On Final Approach* (Granger places the

date of the letter as May 3, 1943), 119; and Rich, who alludes to the letter in *Jackie Cochran*, 127–28.

26. #55, "Women Pilots AAF," 44–45.
27. #55, "Women Pilots AAF," 46.
28. LaFarge, "Women Pilots ATC," 40.
29. "Coup for Cochran," *Newsweek*, July 19, 1943.
30. Adela Riek Scharr, *Sisters in the Sky*, Volume I, *The WAFS* (St. Louis: Patrice Press, 1986), 495–96.
31. Verges, *On Silver Wings*, 103.
32. Marx, "Women Pilots Ferrying Division," 130.
33. Gillies, "The When, Why, Who, Where of the WAFS," IWASM.
34. LaFarge, "Women Pilots ATC," 101–7. This was known as the Camp Davis affair.
35. "WASP Nest—Cross Country News," *Ninety-Nines* newsletter, date unknown, TWU and NHL collection.
36. "New Wasp Uniforms Give Women Fliers Swank and Lift Them Nearer Rank of Army Officers," unidentified newspaper article dated November 16, 1943, and datelined Washington, clipping found in NHL collection.

A B-17 Bound for England

1. Tunner, *Over the Hump*, 37–38.
2. Tunner, 38.
3. Makanna and Ethell, *Ghosts: Vintage Aircraft*, 111.
4. Marion Stegeman Hodgson, *Winning My Wings* (Albany, Texas: Bright Sky Press, 2005), 114.
5. Betty Gillies diary, information read by B.J. London at Gillies's request. The diary is in the possession of Betty Gillies's heirs.
6. N. H. Love logbooks, NHL collection.
7. Tunner, *Over the Hump*, 14, 43, 66.
8. Two articles: "Presentation of Army-Navy 'E' Is Viewed by Hundreds at Aeronca" also "Huge B-17 Bomber Lands at Local Airport for First Time in History," *Aeronca Wing Tips*, Vol. 3, No. 8, Middletown, Ohio, September 1943. Clippings found in the W.O. Baldwin private collection. Copies in author's hands.
9. Interview with W. O. "Wally" Baldwin, June 13, 2002. He had been flying with Aeronca's test pilot Lou Wehrung since 1940, later enlisted in the AAF October 18, 1944, and in 1945–1946 served as a crew chief on a B-17. Baldwin, now deceased, lived in nearby Franklin, Ohio. He had been working on a book about the Middletown Airport and Aeronca history.
10. Baldwin interview, June 13, 2002, with input from Marcia Greenham, corporate pilot with Martco, Inc., Middletown Airport.
11. Betty Gillies diary, as read by B.J. London.
12. Bohn, "Catch," Chapter 14, page 2.
13. Ibid.
14. Lt. Commander Leon Eugene "Tony" Barnum (USN Ret.), interview with author July 25, 2007, Oshkosh, Wisconsin. Barnum was a Navy pilot

stationed at Traverse City during WWII and part of the Navy's program to develop and build guided missiles.

15. Letter from Colonel George D. Campbell, Director of Operations and Training, Ferrying Division, to the Commanding General re: qualification of Nancy and Betty as B-17 crew, August 16, 1943, NHL collection.

16. N. H. Love logbooks, NHL collection.

17. Letter from Bob Love to Major Roy Atwood, executive officer of the ATC European Wing in London, September 1, 1943, NHL collection.

18. Telex dated September 4, 1943, from Gen. C.R. Smith to General Paul Burrows and Major Roy Atwood, TWU.

19. Betty Gillies, taped interview with Dawn Letson, TWU.

20. Cable from General Arnold in London to Presque Isle Air Base, September 5, 1943, TWU.

21. Letter from Nancy Love to Marty Wyall, June 9, 1975, responding to Wyall's request for photographs of the WAFS to show at the upcoming reunion in Reno, TWU.

22. Letter from Bob Love to Oliver La Farge, November 10, 1945, RML collection.

23. La Farge, "Notes on Interview with Nancy Love, Oct. 3, 1945, TWU.

24. "Noted Aviatrix Flies 'Aerial Taxi' From Island Home Near Boston," *The Beechcrafter* (Beechcraft company magazine), Wichita, Kansas, October 27, 1955, 10. Reprinted with permission, Raytheon (formerly Beechcraft). The article was sent by Nancy Love, May 24, 1955, to J. C. Bradford, Public Relations Department, Beechcraft, in which she describes her aviation career, NHL collection.

Change in the Air

1. Memo from Brig. Gen. C.R. Smith to Maj. Gen. Barney M. Giles, Chief of the Air Staff, dated September 7, 1943, TWU.

2. Verges, *Silver Wings*, 140–41.

3. Author interviews with two WASP Class 43-6 graduates who were sent to B-17 school: Pat Bowser Gibson (May 20, 2005, in Tacoma, Washington) and Virginia Broome Waterer (June 30, 2005, in Griffin, Georgia). Both on file in the WASP Archives, TWU. Bowser and Broome graduated from B-17 school, Lockbourne Army Air Base, Columbus, Ohio, as qualified B-17 pilots; also, Verges, *Silver Wings*, 142.

4. #55, "Women Pilots AAF," 73–74.

5. Gibson and Waterer interviews.

6. Yvonne C. "Pat" Pateman, WASP Class 43-5, *Aviation Quarterly*, "WASPs and WAFS in A Fortress," Spring 1985, 121,124. Pateman quotes WASP B-17 pilot Julie Ledbetter (Class 43-5).

7. Barbara Erickson London, logbooks, her private collection.

8. Barbara Erickson London, as told to Sarah Byrn Rickman, "The Lady Flew the B-17," *Aloft*, The Museum of Flight Foundation Magazine, Seattle, September/October 2005, 11.

9. Verges, *Silver Wings*, 143–44.

10. Letter from 1st Lt. R.O. (Pappy) Fraser to Nancy Love, October 16, 1943, NHL collection.
11. Verges, *Silver Wings,* 137; author interviews with Barbara London.
12. "Nancy Love Visits Avenger Field," *The Avenger* (base newspaper), unknown date. Copy from Margaret H. (Reeves) Riviere (WASP Class 43-4), private collection. Interview with Riviere conducted March 31, 2006, in Barnesville, Georgia, on file in WASP Archives, TWU.
13. N. H. Love logbooks, NHL collection.
14. #55, "Women Pilots AAF," 53-55; also La Farge, "Notes on interview with Nancy Love, October 3, 1945"; and Marx, "Women Pilots Ferrying Division," 164–74.
15. #55, "Women Pilots AAF," 56.
16. La Farge, "Notes on interview with Nancy Love," TWU.
17. #55, "Women Pilots AAF," 57.
18. Oliver La Farge, *The Eagle in the Egg* (Boston: Houghton Mifflin Company, Riverside Press Cambridge, 1949), 133–34.
19. Marx, "Women Pilots Ferrying Division," 290–91.
20. Letter, Walter J. Marx to Nancy Love. February 28, 1946, TWU.
21. Letter, Marx to Nancy Love, April 5, 1946, NHL collection.
22. Letter, Oliver La Farge to Bob Love, October 29, 1945, RML.

Pursuit School

1. Marx, "Women Pilots Ferrying Division," 207.
2. Marx, 198–200.
3. Marx, 194.
4. Marx, 198.
5. Marx, 202–3.
6. Official WASP Roster, compiled by WASP Treasurer Catherine Murphy (44-1) and published biannually by TWU.
7. Marx, "Women Pilots Ferrying Division," 207; also #55, "Women Pilots AAF," 63.
8. Bohn, "Catch," Chapter 9, pages 11–12.
9. Bohn, Chapter 13, page 1.
10. Marx, "Women Pilots Ferrying Division," 211.
11. LaFarge, "Women Pilots ATC," 138.
12. LaFarge, "Women Pilots ATC," 140; Marx, "Women Pilots Ferrying Division," 233.
13. Marx, "Women Pilots Ferrying Division," 234.
14. Letter from WAFS Dorothy Scott to Nancy Love dated November 26, 1943, NHL collection.
15. Scott letter continued.
16. LaFarge, "Women Pilots ATC," 141.
17. Bohn, "Catch," Chapter 13, pages 3–4.
18. Author's taped interview with Florene Miller Watson, June 24, 1999, in Odenville, Alabama; also, Rickman, *The Originals,* 223–25.

19. "WASP Leader KO's Love Field Lights, Lands Big Fighter by Emergency Beams," *Dallas Morning News*, November 29, 1943, clipping found at TWU.
20. Miller Watson interview.
21. Diane Ruth Armour Bartels, *Sharpie: The Life Story of Evelyn Sharp* (Lincoln, Nebraska: Dageforde Publishing, 1996), 217. Bartels is the recognized authority on Evelyn Sharp.
22. Copies of the Individual Flight Records and Pilot Qualifications Records of Barbara Jane Erickson, U.S. Air Force Academy Library Archives.
23. Kay Gott, *Women In Pursuit* (Self Published, 1993), 77 (photo of the first class of student pursuit pilots to report to Palm Springs). Number of men taken from Dorothy Scott's letter, see note 28 below.
24. Orders: Nancy Batson and Helen McGilvery in the author's possession.
25. N. H. Love Logbooks, NHL collection.
26. Ibid.
27. Critchell, e-mail, May 25, 2007.
28. Dorothy Scott letters home, collection donated to the WASP Archives at TWU by her brother, Edward Scott.
29. Conversation with Florene Miller Watson at the WASP 64th Reunion, Portland, Oregon, September 6, 2006.
30. Photocopy of the aircraft accident and description of accident, TWU.
31. Marx, "Women Pilots Ferrying Division," 243.
32. Aircraft accident report photocopy, TWU.
33. Watson taped interview.
34. Marx, "Women Pilots Ferrying Division," 235–36.
35. Granger, *On Final*, 270.
36. Marx, "Women Pilots Ferrying Division," 236–37.
37. Marx, 237.
38. Marx, 238.
39. Marx, 240–41.
40. Gott, *Women In Pursuit*, 75–93. These pages contain photographs of pursuit school graduates 1943–1944.
41. The P-38 National Association and Museum, I-215 at Van Buren Boulevard, Riverside CA, adjacent to March Air Reserve Base: http://p38assn.org/museum.htm; names of women P-38 ferry pilots from the museum exhibit furnished by Iris Critchell.
42. Dorothy Scott collection, TWU.
43. Letter from Edward Scott to Nancy Love dated February 10, 1944, NHL collection.
44. Letter from Dr. Robert B. Harkness, Hastings, Michigan, to daughter Nancy dated February 12, 1944, NHL collection.

The Quest for Militarization

1. LaFarge, "Women Pilots ATC," 161–64.
2. Cochran and Brinley, *Autobiography*, 198.
3. Marx, "Women Pilots Ferrying Division," 295–96.

4. Edward Bunting, senior editor, et al., *World War II Day by Day* (London: Dorling Kindersley, 2001), 474.
5. Bunting, 479–87.
6. #55, "Women Pilots AAF," 91–93; Marx, "Women Pilots Ferrying Division," 298–99.
7. Betty Gillies's memo to Delphine Bohn dated February 8, 1984, TWU.
8. #55, "Women Pilots AAF," 89–90.
9. Bohn, "Catch," Chapter 15, pages 5–7.
10. London, phone interview, July 7, 2004.
11. Verges, *On Silver*, 188.
12. Merryman, *Clipped Wings*, 63.
13. Merryman, 51–52.
14. Jean Bethke Elshtain, *Women and War* (New York: Basic Books, 1987), 7.
15. Doris Kearns Goodwin, *No Ordinary Time, Franklin and Eleanor Roosevelt: The Home Front in World War II* (New York: Simon & Schuster, 1994), 555–56.
16. Goodwin, 555.
17. Goodwin, 557,
18. Nancy Harkness Love deposition, Pat Pateman Collection, TWU.
19. Marx, "Women Pilots Ferrying Division,"313–14.
20. Marx, 315–17.
21. Marx, 317.

In Pursuit, Coast to Coast

1. Kay Gott, *Women In Pursuit*, 96, 120, 140. 168, 198.
2. Gillies's February 8, 1984 memo to Bohn.
3. LaFarge, "Women Pilots ATC," 146.
4. Marx, "Women Pilots Ferrying Division," 238.
5. Marx, "Women Pilots Ferrying Division," 238–41.
6. Four WASPs (Dawn Seymour 43-5, Clarice I. Bergemann 44-2, Jeannette J. Jenkins 44-1, and Mary Ellen Keil 44-2) researched and wrote the brochure, "In Memoriam, Thirty-eight American Women Pilots" (Denton, Texas: Texas Woman's University Press, nd), 18, 20, 25, 33, 37, 40.
7. Bartels, *Sharpie*, 5, 238–44.
8. Aircraft accident report, witness statement, TWU.
9. Bartels, 5–10.
10. Nancy Batson Crews interviews.
11. Granger, *On Final*, 317–18.
12. Author interview with Mary Lou Colbert Neale, by telephone, April 7, 2007.
13. Marx, "Women Pilots Ferrying Division," 293; also photograph on page 191 showing other Originals and Training School graduates at Orlando.
14. N. H. Love's OTC notebook, NHL collection.
15. Bohn, "Catch," Chapter 16, pages 7–8.
16. Bohn, "Catch," Chapter 16, page 9.
17. United States Air Force Museum, Aircraft Brochure: A-20, 71.

18. Postcard addressed to Nancy Love dated May 14, 1944, TWU.
19. Crews interviews.
20. #55, "Women Pilots AAF," 66.
21. Granger, *On Final*, 368–69, 396–97.
22. Marx, "Women Pilots Ferrying Division," 221–22.
23. Transcript of phone call from Jacqueline Cochran to Nancy Love, July 3, 1944, Cochran/Eisenhower.
24. "Nancy H. Love Visits Field, Sees Largest Class of Pilots Graduate," Ferrying Division/Air Transport Command base newspaper, June 10, 1944, clipping found in NHL collection.
25. Critchell interview, September 3, 2006.
26. Granger, *On Final*, 397.
27. London, interview October 1, 2006.
28. LaFarge, "Women Pilots ATC," 147–48.

Militarization Denied

1. #55, "Women Pilots AAF," 94.
2. #55, "Women Pilots AAF," 98.
3. LaFarge, "Women Pilots ATC," 165–66.
4. Marx, "Women Pilots Ferrying Division," 350–52.
5. #55, "Women Pilots AAF," 100.
6. Marx, "Women Pilots Ferrying Division," 352, as printed in the *Cincinnati Enquirer*, Oct. 3, 1944.
7. Marx, "Women Pilots Ferrying Division," 354. Release of the War Department Bureau of Public Relations, Oct. 3, 1944.
8. Sally VanWagenen Keil, *Those Wonderful Women In Their Flying Machines* (New York: Four Directions Press, 1979), 318–19.
9. #55, "Women Pilots AAF," 101.
10. Arnold, *Global Mission*, 358–59.
11. Arnold, Speech at the graduation of WASP Class 44-10, Avenger Field, Dec. 7, 1944.
12. Marx, "Women Pilots Ferrying Division," 358–62.
13. Merryman, *Clipped Wings*, 121–22.
14. Douglas, *Women and Flight*, Chapter 8, "Women with the 'Right Stuff'—the 1970s," 172–96. This source gives a comprehensive explanation of what happened.
15. Merryman, *Clipped Wings*, 44.
16. Merryman, 2.
17. Merryman, 3.
18. Leila J. Rupp, *Mobilizing Women for War, German and American Propaganda, 1939-1945* (Princeton, New Jersey: Princeton University Press, 1978), 137, 142.
19. Cynthia Enloe, *Does Khaki Become You? The Militarization of Women's Lives* (Boston: South End Press, 1983), 176, 193–94.
20. London, interview October 1, 2006.
21. Critchell, interview September 3, 2006.
22. Marx, "Women Pilots Ferrying Division," 440.

23. Jean Hascall Cole, *Women Pilots of World War II* (Salt Lake City: University of Utah Press, 1992), 155.
24. Mattie E. Treadwell, *The Women's Army Corps* (Washington, D.C.: Office of the Chief of Military History, Dept. of the Army), xii. Lt. Col Treadwell served as assistant to the Director WAC (Col. Oveta Culp Hobby), assistant to the Air WAC Officer, and assistant to the Commandant, School of WAC Personnel Administration—WWII. She was a member of the first class of women sent to the Command and General Staff School. From 1947 to 1952, she was an historian in the Office of the Chief of Military History.

Denouement of the WASP

1. Tunner commendation, July 31, 1944, NHL collection.
2. Letter from Bob to Nancy Love, undated, but from the content assumed to be August 1943, NHL collection.
3. Letter from Bob Love to Nancy Love, dated April 11, 1944, NHL collection.
4. Article for *Beechcrafter*, NHL collection.
5. N. H. Love logbooks, NHL collection.
6. *Cross Country News*, "WASP Nest," an article on Nancy Love, unknown date, but probably 1962 or 1963, TWU.
7. Bohn, "Catch," Chapter 17, page 5.
8. Ibid.
9. Phone interview with B.J. London, October 1, 2006.
10. Phone interview with Iris Critchell, September 2, 2006.
11. Genevieve Report, NHL collection.
12. Article for *Beechcrafter*, clipping found in NHL collection.
13. Mardo Crane, "The Women With Silver Wings," Part One, *Ninety-Nines News*, Special Issue 1978.
14. N. H. Love logbooks, NHL collection.
15. Letter from Nancy Love to Mr. Traylor, Reconstruction Finance Corporation, November 17, 1944, NHL collection.
16. Marx, "Women Pilots Ferrying Division," 372–73.
17. News clipping and photo, unidentified newspaper (probably Chicago), TWU; also Nancy Love's individual flight records (military), TWU.
18. London and Critchell, phone interviews Oct. 1 and Sept. 2, respectively, 2006.
19. London interviews.
20. #55, "Women Pilots AAF," 66–67; LaFarge, "Women Pilots ATC,"148.
21. Betty H. Gillies, "The WAFS: Women's Auxiliary Ferrying Squadron," presented at The Ninety-Nines Inc. International Convention Banquet, Baltimore, Maryland, July 27, 1985, Gillies Collection, IWASM.
22. Katherine (Kaddy) Landry Steele (WASP Class 43-7) interview with author, June 1996, Springfield, Ohio.
23. Source, Nancy Batson Crews interviews. Also Rickman, *The Originals*, 327–29.

Flying the Hump

1. Gen. C.R. Smith's Letters, NHL collection.

2. C.R. Smith: Colonel (his initial rank) Smith was largely responsible for ATC's considerable expansion in operations, especially strategic airlift. He proposed that the ATC be given that mission and left alone to do its job. After that, strategic air transport functioned under centralized control, without interference from theater commanders except in emergencies. Brigadier General Smith activated the India-China Division in October 1942 to provide airlift support to the American and Chinese forces fighting in China. The Crescent route had been in operation since spring 1944. The airlift was conducted from bases in India and designated the "Hump" because of its air route over the Himalayan Mountains. It was the greatest sustained and intensive use of air transport up to that time. Airlift/Tanker Association Hall of Fame: www.atalink.org/hallfame/c.r.smith.html.

3. Special Orders Number 267 dated 26 December 1944, Headquarters Ferrying Division, ATC Cincinnati, Ohio, NHL collection.

4. Barbara W. Tuchman, *Stilwell and the American Experience in China 1911–1945* (New York: The Macmillan Company, 1970–1971), 392; also Holm, *Women in the Military:* "As early as October 1943, members of the WAC served with [Britain's] Adm. Louis Mountbatten's Southeast Asia Command, first in New Delhi and later in Ceylon.... The WACs were initially on trial in India because many Army officials, including General Stilwell believed that American women would not be able to withstand for long the climate and diseases found in Asian countries," 207–8.

5. Noël Riley Fitch, *Appetite for Life, The Biography of Julia Child* (New York: Doubleday, 1997), 92–93.

6. Elizabeth P. McIntosh, *Sisterhood of Spies, The Women of the OSS* (Annapolis, Maryland: Naval Institute Press, 1998), 226.

7. Treadwell, *The WAC,* 464–65; also Holm, *Women Military,* 207.

8. Col. Mary T. Sarnecky (U.S. Army retired), *A History of the U.S. Army Nurse Corps* (Philadelphia: University of Pennsylvania Press, 1999), 205–6.

9. Sarnecky, 257, 260.

10. N. H. Love Trip Report to General Nowland, February 9, 1945, TWU and NHL collection.

11. Logbooks, NHL collection.

12. The following sources were used to construct the Hump flight story: N. H. Love logbooks; "Once National Celebrity Has Post-War Project," *The Vineyard Gazette,* April 6, 1956; Obituary, Nancy Love, *The Vineyard Gazette,* October 26, 1976; Obituary, WASP Newsletter, Special Edition, December 1976; *The Beechcrafter* (see note 31 below); "WASP Nest," Cross Country News, circa 1962, TWU; personal interviews with Nancy's three daughters. Other more specific sources are noted throughout the paragraphs.

13. Otha C. Spencer, *Flying the Hump: Memories of an Air War* (College Station: Texas A&M University Press, 1992), Prologue, 7.

14. Moser, et al., *CBI*, 80, 82.
15. Tunner, *Over the Hump*, 49.
16. Spencer, *Flying the Hump*, 156–58.
17. Tunner, 47.
18. Moser, et al., *CBI*, 133.
19. Descriptions in these several paragraphs of flying The Hump are gathered from: *Flying the Hump: The China Airlift*, video, Commemorative Edition, Volume 2 (Seattle, Memory Maker Productions, 1990); Carl Frey Constein, *Born to Fly the Hump, A WWII Memoir* (Shawnee Mission, Kansas: Johnson County Library, 2000); Spencer, *Flying the Hump: Memories of an Air War*; Tunner and Herndon, *Over the Hump;* and Moser, et al., editors, *China-Burma-India*.
20. Elly Beinhorn, *Flying Girl* (New York: Henry Holt and Company, nd), 129–31, 241. Also Elly Beinhorn, Solo Flights Around the World, http://soloflights.org.elly_text_e.html.
21. Fitch, *Appetite for Life*, 106. Fitch is quoting Betty MacDonald (Elizabeth P. McIntosh) and her book, *Sisterhood of Spies*. MacDonald remarried after the war, thus the name change.
22. McIntosh, *Sisterhood*, 230.
23. Holm, *Women Military*, 207–8; and Treadwell, *The WAC*, 471.
24. Sales slips from shops in India, NHL collection.
25. Love daughters.
26. N. H. Love logbooks, NHL collection.
27. N. H. Love Trip Report, NHL collection.
28. LaFarge, "Women Pilots ATC," 167. Memo from General Arnold to General Giles dated October 5, 1944.
29. Bohn, "Catch," Chapter 16, page 10.
30. Bunting, *WWII Day By Day*, 606, 608, 611.
31. "Noted Aviatrix Flies 'Aerial Taxi,'" *The Beechcrafter*, 10.
32. "Once National Celebrity Has Post-War Project," *The Vineyard Gazette*, April 6, 1956.
33. Letters from C.R. Smith to Nancy Love, on American Airlines stationery, dated Oct. 16 and Dec. 23, 1946, NHL collection.
34. Phone interview by author with Bee Falk Haydu, WASP Class 44-7, June 6, 2006.
35. Wollheim, *Siesta Key Pelican*.
36. Letter from Nancy Love to M. B. Lambert in New York, re: ferrying three C-53s to Madrid for Iberia Spanish Airlines, dated May 4, 1945, NHL collection.
37. Interview, B.J. London, phone, fall 2003.
38. Taped oral history with Barbara Donahue Ross, Warrenton, Virginia, May 17, 2006, on file at TWU.
39. Keil, *Those Wonderful Women*, 281–82.
40. Letter from Nancy Love to Fred M. Babcock, Deputy Administrator Real Estate Division, Surplus Commodities Board, Washington D.C., dated September 12, 1945, NHL collection.
41. Interview, B.J. London, phone, fall 2003.

42. Handwritten letter from Constance Bennett to Nancy Love, not dated, NHL collection.

Peace, Prosperity, and Parenthood

1. Interview with Allie Love.
2. *USAir* magazine, May 1989: History of the various airlines that became USAir. The story of Richard duPont and Bob Love and All American Aviation/Airways/Allegheny Airlines, as told in this chapter, is excerpted from this article and other sources listed here.
3. W. David Lewis and William F. Trimble, *The Airway to Everywhere: A History of All American Aviation, 1937–1953* (Pittsburgh: University of Pittsburgh Press, 1988), 133–34.
4. Letter from Dora Dougherty Strother McKeown to Nancy Harkness Love dated August 27, 1976, NHL collection. Used with Mrs. McKeown's permission.
5. N. H. Love logbook, NHL collection.
6. "Noted Aviatrix," *The Beechcrafter.*
7. "Col. R. M. Love, Wife Given Medals at Joint Ceremony," *Wilmington Morning News* (Delaware), July 16, 1946.
8. Letter signed by General Muir S. Fairchild, United States Air Force, Vice Chief of Staff, dated August 9, 1948, TWU.
9. Letter from Nancy Love to General Muir S. Fairchild dated August 20, 1948, TWU.
10. Rich, *Jackie*, 158.
11. Letter from Jacqueline Cochran, U.S. Air Force Academy Archives, Yvonne (Pat) Pateman (Lt. Col. Retired) Collection.
12. Douglas, *Women and Flight*, 187, 189, 212–13.
13. WASP Military Service Listing dated February 1989, U.S.A.F. Academy, Pateman Collection.
14. Love daughters.
15. *USAir* magazine, May 1989.
16. National Postal Museum Web site: www.postalmuseum.si.edu/resources/6a2w_airpickup.html, December 14, 2003. In 1953 All American Airways became Allegheny Airlines. Fifteen years later, it merged with Lake Central, and in 1972 with Mohawk. On October 28, 1979, Allegheny Airlines became US Air. In 1989 it acquired Piedmont. Finally, on February 27, 1999, US Air became US Airways.
17. Lewis and Trimble, *Airway to Everywhere*, 163.
18. *USAir* magazine, May 1989, photo, clipping found in NHL collection.

Life on the Vineyard

1. "Noted Aviatrix," *The Beechcrafter,* clipping found in NHL collection.
2. *Vineyard Gazette*, April 6, 1956, clipping found in NHL collection.
3. WASP newsletter, Volume 6, December 1970, NHL collection.
4. The story of the Love family on Martha's Vineyard in this and subsequent chapters is taken from interviews with the Love daughters.

Empty Nest

1. Information in this chapter comes from interviews with the Love daughters.

Fighting Spirit

1. Letter from Nancy Love to Jack Ray dated June 16, 1976, TWU. Excerpts used throughout the chapter.
2. Interviews with Allie and Marky Love.
3. Series of letters from Nancy Love to Marky Love dated summer and fall 1974, in Margaret Love's possession.
4. Phone interview with Bee Falk Haydu, WASP Class 44-7, June 6, 2006.
5. Letter from Marky Love to the WASPs dated October 10, 1976, and printed in the WASP Newsletter, Special edition, Vol. 13, December 1976, NHL collection.
6. WASP Newsletter, December 1976, clipping found in NHL collection.
7. Betty Gillies, October 14, 1976, short biography of Nancy Love, TWU.

Epilogue

1. Douglas, "WASPs of War."
2. Female National Aviation Hall of Fame enshrinees since Nancy Love: Betty Skelton Frankman, also 2005; Bessie Coleman, 2006; and Sally Ride and Evelyn Bryan Johnson, 2007.

Appendix

1. Original list courtesy Dr. H. O. Malone, aviation historian. I have added to it.

Glossary of Military and Airplane Terms

AAB: Army Air Base

AAC: Army Air Corps

AAF: Army Air Forces

AF: Air Force

Alert Room: Where pilots await flight orders

AT: Advanced training aircraft, flown in the third of three-stage flight instruction

ATA: Air Transport Auxiliary (to the British Royal Air Force—see RAF)

ATC: Air Transport Command

AUS: Army of the United States

B-4 Bag: Canvas luggage that converts into a hanging bag.

Base Leg: Part of the landing pattern—the short leg lying at right angles to, and downwind from, the landing strip. The base leg follows the downwind leg and precedes the final approach in the landing sequence.

Beam: The sound made up of the combined Morse Code sound for A (dot-dash) and N (dash-dot), making a solid hum. This led a pilot to the airport. The signals became increasingly strong when flying to the broadcasting point and diminished when flying away from the station. It narrowed to a "cone of silence" directly over the emitting station. The sound of the beam is loudest immediately prior to that point.

Biplane: An airplane with double wings, one above the other

BOQ: Bachelor Officer Quarters

BT: Basic training aircraft flown in the second of three-stage flight instruction

Buddy Ride: Two pilots: one practices instrument flying "under the hood" while the other serves as the safety pilot and keeps an eye out for other aircraft.

CAA: Civil Aeronautics Authority (1938-1940); Administration (1940-1958)

CAP: Civil Air Patrol

Ceiling: Vertical distance from ground to cloud cover.

Class 26: Airplanes destined for the graveyard.

CO: Commanding Officer

Commercial License: A federal certificate that allowed a pilot to carry passengers for hire or to haul freight.

Control Tower: Tower at an airfield with air traffic controllers who stay in radio contact with pilots in the area, giving them orders until the plane leaves the area or turns off onto the taxiway and is under ground control via radioed orders.

CPT Program: Civilian Pilot Training Program, a federal program that subsidized individuals learning to fly 1939–1941.

Downwind Leg: The first leg of the flight path of the landing pattern. It parallels the runway opposite the direction in which you plan to land.

FERD: Ferrying Division

FG: Ferrying Group

Final Approach: The last or third leg of the flight pattern where the pilot descends from pattern altitude to the runway, normally into the wind.

Gosport: A tube with earphones at one end and a voice cone at the other, used in planes with no interphone system (no radio) to enable instructor to give orders to student.

Ground Loop: A high-speed skidding turn by an aircraft on the ground after landing. It is usually caused by loss of control.

HQ: Headquarters

IFR: Instrument Flight Rules or flying without visual reference to the ground.

Instrument Conditions: When there is no visible horizon or when the ceiling is lower than allowable for visual flying.

Link Trainer: A simulator with actual aircraft instruments and controls that allows a pilot to practice instrument flying without leaving the ground.

P: Designation for pursuit or fighter aircraft, as in P-47.

Pitch: The up-and-down motion of the nose of the airplane over its lateral axis.

Private License: A federal license earned by a pilot who has demonstrated sufficient skills to be allowed to carry passengers, but not for hire.

PT: Primary trainer, the first stage of three-stage flight instruction of military flight training in WWII.

RAF: Royal Air Force

Roll: An airplane's motion around its longitudinal axis (one wing is lowered to begin the roll).

RON: Remain Over Night

SNAFU: Situation normal, all fouled up: Ferrying Division's airline

SPARs: Women's Coast Guard Auxiliary: Semper Paratus Always Ready

Stick: A control device usually found in single-engine aircraft, which operates the ailerons and the elevators.

TDY: Temporary duty away from home base.

Transition: Instructing a pilot on how to fly an aircraft in which the pilot lacks experience.

VFR: Visual Flight Rules or clear weather where you can see the ground and the ceiling is high enough to allow the pilot to maintain cruising altitude without flying into clouds.

Under the Hood: practicing instrument flying while in the air with the aid of an instructor or a lookout or buddy pilot. Instrument trainer airplanes were equipped with a black fabric cover that the student pilot pulled over his/her part of the cockpit to eliminate all visual contact with the ground.

WAAC: Women's Auxiliary Army Corps

WAC: Women's Army Corps

WAFS: Women's Auxiliary Ferrying Squadron

WASP: Women Airforce Service Pilots. WASP followed by 43 or 44 and the number 1-10 designates the year and class that year in which a WASP graduated from training and received her wings. Example: 43-5—graduation year 1943; class number 5.

WAVES: Women Accepted for Volunteer Emergency Service

WFTD: Women's Flying Training Detachment

WTS: War Training Service (followed CPT, 1941–1944)

Yaw: An airplane's motion from side to side around its vertical axis (the wings stay level and the nose moves from side to side).

Glossary of Airplane Types

Primary Trainers

Designation	Manufacturer	Engine(s)	Horsepower	Maximum speed	Cruising speed	Range	Service Ceiling	Nickname	Style
PT-17	Stearman	1 Continental	220	124 mph	104 mph	450 miles	14,000		Bi-wing, open cockpit
PT-19	Fairchild	1 Ranger	175	124 mph	106 mph	480 miles	16,000 feet		Low wing, open cockpit
PT-23	Fairchild	1 Continental	220	130					
PT-26	Fairchild	1 Continental	175	124 mph	106 mph	480 miles	16,000 feet		Low wing, with cockpit canopy

Liaison Planes

Designation	Manufacturer	Engine(s)	Horsepower	Maximum speed	Cruising speed	Range	Service Ceiling	Nickname	Style
L-2	Taylorcraft	1 Continental	65	93 mph					
L-4	Piper	1 Continental	65	85 mph	75 mph	190 miles	9,300 feet	Grasshopper	Hi-wing
L-5	Stinson	1 Lycoming	190	130 mph	90 mph	360 miles	15,600 feet	Sentinel	Hi-wing

Basic Trainers

Designation	Manufacturer	Engine(s)	Horsepower	Maximum speed	Cruising speed	Range	Service Ceiling	Nickname	Style
BT-13	Vultee	1 Pratt-Whitney	450	155 mph	130 mph	880 miles	19,400 feet	Valiant or Vibrator	Low-wing with cockpit canopy
BT-15	Vultee	1 Wright	450	167					Low-wing with cockpit canopy

Advanced Trainers

Designation	Manufacturer	Engine(s)	Horsepower	Maximum speed	Cruising speed	Range	Service Ceiling	Nickname	Style
AT-6	North American	1 Pratt-Whitney	600	206 mph	145 mph	1,000 w/drop tank	23,200 feet	Texan	Low-wing with cockpit canopy
AT-9	Curtiss	2 Lycoming	295 each	197 mph	173 mph	750 miles	19,000 feet	Fledgling	Low-wing, enclosed cockpit
AT-10	Beech	2 Lycoming	295 each	190 mph		660 miles	20,000 feet	Wichita	Low-wing, enclosed cockpit
AT-17	Cessna	2 Jacobs	245 each	175 mph	150 mph	750 miles	15,000 feet	Bobcat	Low-wing, enclosed cockpit

Advanced Trainers

Designation	Manufacturer	Engine(s)	Horsepower	Maximum speed	Cruising speed	Range	Service Ceiling	Nickname	Style
AT-19	Vultee	1 Lycoming	280	135 mph					
UC-78	Cessna	2 Jacobs	245 each	175 mph	150 mph	750 miles	15,000 feet	Bobcat / Bamboo Bomber	Low-wing, enclosed cockpit

Cargo/Transport

Designation	Manufacturer	Engine(s)	Horsepower	Maximum speed	Cruising speed	Range	Service Ceiling	Nickname	Style
C-36	Lockheed	2 Pratt-Whitney	450 each	205 mph					
C-46	Curtiss	2 Pratt-Whitney	2,000 each	245 mph	175 mph	1,200 miles	27,600 feet	Commando / Ol' Dumbo	
C-47	Douglas	2 Pratt-Whitney	1,200 each	232 mph	175 mph	1,513 miles	24,450 feet	Skytrain	
C-52	Douglas	2 Pratt-Whitney	1,200 each	212 mph					
C-53	Douglas	2 Pratt-Whitney	1,200 each	210 mph					
C-54	Douglas	4 Pratt-Whitney	1,450 each	300 mph	245 mph	3,900 miles	30,000 feet	Skymaster	
C-60	Lockheed	2 Wright	1,200 each	257 mph	232 mph	1,700 miles	25,000 feet	Lodestar	

Attack Planes

Designation	Manufacturer	Engine(s)	Horsepower	Maximum speed	Cruising speed	Range	Service Ceiling	Nickname	Style
A-20	Douglas	2 Wright	1,600 each	317 mph	230 mph	1,025 miles	25,000 feet	Havoc	
A-24	Douglas	1 Wright	1,000	254 mph		1,100 miles	24,300 feet	Dauntless	
A-25	Curtiss	1 Wright	1,700	275 mph				Helldiver	

Bombers

Designation	Manufacturer	Engine(s)	Horsepower	Maximum speed	Cruising speed	Range	Service Ceiling	Nickname	Style
B-17	Boeing	4 Wright Cyclone	1,200 each	300 mph	170 mph	1,850 miles	35,000 feet	Flying Fortress	6,000 pound bomb load
B-24 (D-model)	Built by Consolidated, also Ford, Convair, Douglas & North American	4 Pratt-Whitney	1,200 each	303 mph	175 mph	3,200 miles	28,000	Liberator	8,000 pound bomb load
B-25 (B-Model)	North American	2 Wright	1,700 each	275 mph	230 mph	1,200 miles	25,000 feet	Mitchell	5,000 pound bomb load

Bombers

Designation	Manufacturer	Engine(s)	Horsepower	Maximum speed	Cruising speed	Range	Service Ceiling	Nickname	Style
B-26 (G-Model)	Martin	2 Pratt-Whitney	2,000 each	285 mph	190 mph	1,100 miles	19,800 feet	Marauder	4,000 pound bomb load
B-29	Boeing	4 Wright	2,200 each	357 mph	220 mph	3,700 miles	33,600	Superfortress	20,000 pound bomb load

Pursuits

Designation	Manufacturer	Engine(s)	Horsepower	Maximum speed	Cruising speed	Range	Service Ceiling	Nickname	Style
P-38 (L-model)	Lockheed	2 Allison	1,475 each	414 mph	275 mph	2,260 miles	40,000 feet	Lightning	Tricycle gear
P-39 (Q-model)	Bell	1 Allison	1,200	376 mph	250 mph	1,100 miles	35,000 feet	Airacobra	Tricycle gear
P-40 (E-model)	Curtiss	1 Allison	1,150	362 mph	235 mph	1,400 miles	30,000	Warhawk	Taildragger
P-47 (D-model)	Republic	1 Pratt-Whitney	2,430	433 mph	350 mph	1,800 miles	42,000	Thunderbolt or Jug	Taildragger
P-51 (D-model)	North American	1 Packard-built Rolls-Royce "Merlin"	1,695	437 mph	275 mph	2,300 miles	41,900 feet	Mustang	Traildragger

Pursuits

Designation	Manufacturer	Engine(s)	Horsepower	Maximum speed	Cruising speed	Range	Service Ceiling	Nickname	Style
P-61 (C-model)	Northrop	2 Pratt-Whitney	2,100 each	425 mph	275mph	1,200 miles	46,200 feet	Black Widow	Tricycle gear
P-63	Bell	1 Allison	1,325	410 mph		2,100 miles	38,600 feet	Kingcobra	Tricycle

Other

Designation	Manufacturer	Engine(s)	Horsepower	Maximum speed	Cruising speed	Range	Service Ceiling	Nickname	Style
OA-10	Consolidated	2 Pratt-Whitney	1,200 each	184 mph	120 mph	2,325 miles	22,400	Catalina	Army version of Navy PBY series—seaplanes and amphibians

Airplane descriptions taken from: *United States Air Force Museum, Aircraft Brochure*, newly revised edition, 2003; from, *Ghosts: Vintage Aircraft of World War II* by Philip Makanna (Charlottesville, Virginia: Thomasson-Grant, Inc., 1987); and from *U.S. Army Aircraft (Heavier Than Air) 1908–1946* (New York: Ships and Aircraft, 1946), James C. Fahey, author and editor.

Bibliography

Published Sources

Arnold, H.H. *Global Mission*. Blue Ridge Summit, Pennsylvania: Military Classics Series, TAB Books Inc., Harper & Row Publishers, 1949.

Ayers, Billie Pittman and Beth Dee. *SUPERWOMAN Jacqueline Cochran: Family Memories About the Famous Pilot, Patriot, Wife & Businesswoman*. Rev. ed. 1st Books Library (online publisher), 2001.

Bartels, Diane Ruth Armour. *Sharpie: The Life Story of Evelyn Sharp*. Lincoln, Nebraska: Dageforde Publishing, 1996.

Beinhorn, Elly. *Flying Girl*. New York: Henry Holt and Company, nd. circa 1933–34.

Bender, Richard R. *Maximum Effort in the Air War Over Germany*. Lake Alfred, Florida: Eagles Landing Publishers, 2004.

Bowen, Catherine Drinker. *Adventures of a Biographer*. Boston: Little, Brown, 1959.

——. *Biography: The Craft and the Calling*. Boston: Little, Brown, An Atlantic Monthly Press Book, 1968.

Bunting, Edward, et al., editors. *World War II Day by Day*. London: Dorling Kindersley, 2001.

Churchill, Jan. *On Wings to War: Teresa James, Aviator*. Manhattan, Kansas: Sunflower University Press, 1992.

311

Cochran, Jacqueline and Maryann Bucknum Brinley. *Jackie Cochran: The Autobiography of the Greatest Woman Pilot in Aviation History.* New York: Bantam Books, 1987.

Cochran, Jacqueline, *The Stars at Noon.* Boston: Little, Brown and Company, Atlantic Monthly Press, 1954.

Cole, Jean Hascall. *Women Pilots of World War II.* Salt Lake City: University of Utah Press, 1992.

The Concise Columbia Encyclopedia. New York: Avon Books/ Hearst Corporation, 1983.

Constein, Carl Frey. *Born to Fly the Hump, A WWII Memoir.* Shawnee Mission, Kansas: Johnson County Library, 2000.

Corn, Joseph J. *The Winged Gospel: America's Romance with Aviation, 1900-1950.* New York: Oxford University Press, 1983.

Curtis, Lettice. *The Forgotten Pilots: A Story of the Air Transport Auxiliary 1939-1945.* 4th ed. Cheltenham, England: Westward Digital Limited, 1998.

Douglas, Deborah G. *American Women and Flight since 1940.* Lexington: University Press of Kentucky, 2004.

Edel, Leon. "The Figure Under the Carpet." In *Telling Lives.* Pachter, Marc, editor. Washington D.C.: New Republic Books, 1979.

Elshtain, Jean Bethke. *Women and War.* New York: Basic Books, 1987.

Enloe, Cynthia. *Does Khaki Become You? The Militarisation [sic] of Women's Lives.* Boston: South End Press, 1983.

Fahey, James C. author and editor. *U.S. Army Aircraft (Heavier Than Air) 1908–1946.* New York: Ships and Aircraft, 1946.

Fitch, Noël Riley. *Appetite for Life, The Biography of Julia Child.* New York: Doubleday, 1997.

Goodwin, Doris Kearns. *No Ordinary Time, Franklin and Eleanor Roosevelt: The Home Front in World War II.* New York: Simon & Schuster, 1994.

Gott, Kay. *Women In Pursuit.* Self Published, 1993.

Granger, Byrd Howell. *On Final Approach: The Women Airforce Service Pilots of W.W.II.* Scottsdale, Arizona: Falconer Publishing Company, 1991.

Hodgson, Marion Stegeman. *Winning My Wings.* Albany, Texas: Bright Sky Press, 2005.

Holm, Jeanne. *Women in the Military: An Unfinished Revolution.* rev. ed. Novato, California: Presidio Press, 1992.

Keil, Sally Van Wagenen. *Those Wonderful Women In Their Flying Machines: The Unknown Heroines of World War II.* rev. ed. New York: Four Directions Press, 1990.

Kerfoot, Glenn. *Propeller Annie, The Story of Helen Richey.* Lexington, Kentucky: The Kentucky Aviation History Roundtable, 1988.

La Farge, Oliver. *The Eagle in the Egg.* Boston: Houghton Mifflin, Riverside Press Cambridge, 1949.

Lewis, W. David, and William F. Trimble. *The Airway to Everywhere: A History of All American Aviation, 1937–1953.* Pittsburgh: University of Pittsburgh Press, 1988.

Makanna, Philip and Jeffrey Ethell. *Ghosts: Vintage Aircraft of World War II.* Charlottesville, Virginia: Thomasson-Grant, 1987.

Mangan, James M. *To the Four Winds: A History of the Flight Operations of American Airlines Personnel for the Air Transport Command, 1942–1945, including Project 7 A.* Paducah, Kentucky: Turner Publishing Company, 1990.

Matz, Onas P. *History of the 2nd Ferrying Group, Ferrying Division, Air Transport Command.* Seattle, Washington: Modet Enterprises, Inc., 1993. Sponsored by the Wilmington Warrior Association.

McIntosh, Elizabeth P. *Sisterhood of Spies, The Women of the OSS.* Annapolis, Maryland: Naval Institute Press, 1998.

Merryman, Molly, *Clipped Wings, The Rise and Fall of the Women Airforce Service Pilots (WASPs) of World War II.* New York: New York University Press, 1998.

Meyer, Leisa D. *Creating GI Jane: Sexuality and Power in the Women's Army Corps During World War II.* New York: Columbia University Press, 1996.

Moser, Don, et al., eds. *China-Burma-India*. Alexandria, Virginia: World War II—Time-Life Books, 1978.

Noggle, Anne. *A Dance with Death: Soviet Airwomen in World War II*. College Station: Texas A&M University Press, 1994.

Perret, Geoffrey. *Winged Victory, The Army Air Forces in World War II*. New York: Random House, 1993.

Prefer, Nathan N. *Vinegar Joe's War, Stilwell's Campaigns for Burma*. Novato, California: Presidio Press, 2000.

Rich, Doris L. *Jackie Cochran: Pilot in the Fastest Lane*. Gainesville, Florida: University Press of Florida, 2007.

Rickman, Sarah Byrn. *The Originals: The Women's Auxiliary Ferrying Squadron of World War II*. Sarasota, Florida: Disc-Us Books, 2001.

Rupp, Leila J. *Mobilizing Women for War, German and American Propaganda, 1939-1945*. Princeton, New Jersey: Princeton University Press, 1978.

Sarnecky, Mary T. *A History of the U.S. Army Nurse Corps*. Philadelphia: University of Pennsylvania Press, 1999.

Scharr, Adela Riek. *Sisters in the Sky*, Volumes I and II. St. Louis: Patrice Press, 1986.

Schrader, Helena Page. *Sisters In Arms: British & American Women Pilots During World War II*. Great Britain: Pen & Sword Books, 2006.

Serling, Robert. *Eagle: The Story of American Airlines*. New York: St. Martin's/ Marek, 1985.

Seymour, Dawn, Clarice I. Bergemann, Jeannette J. Jenkins, and Mary Ellen Keil. *In Memoriam Thirty-eight American Women Pilots*. Denton, Texas: Texas Woman's University Press, nd.

Simbeck, Rob. *Daughter of the Air: The Brief Soaring Life of Cornelia Fort*. New York: Atlantic Monthly Press, 1999.

Snow, Crocker. *Logbook: A Pilot's Life*. Washington, D.C.: Brassey's, A Roger Warner Book, 1997.

Spencer, Otha C. *Flying The Hump: Memories of an Air War*. College Station: Texas A&M University Press, 1992.

Strickland, Patricia, *The Putt-Putt Air Force: The Story of The Civilian Pilot Training Program and The War Training Service (1939-1944)*. Department of Transportation, Federal Aviation Administration, Aviation Education Staff, GA-20-84.

Thaden, Louise. *High, Wide and Frightened*. New York: Air Facts Press, 1973.

Treadwell, Mattie E. *The Women's Army Corps*. Washington, D.C.: Office of the Chief of Military History, Department of the Army, 1954.

Tuchman, Barbara W. *Stilwell and the American Experience in China 1911–45*. New York: The Macmillan Company, 1970.

Tunner, William H. and Booton Herndon. *Over the Hump: The Story of General William H. Tunner, the Man Who Moved Anything, Anywhere, Anytime*. New York: Duell, Sloan and Pearce, 1964.

United States Air Force Museum, Aircraft Brochure featuring more than 175 aircraft of the U.S. Aircraft Museum, with aircraft photos, text, and specifications. Newly Revised Edition, 2003.

Verges, Marianne. *On Silver Wings*. New York: Ballantine Books, 1991.

Ware, Susan, ed. *Notable American Women, A Biographical Dictionary Completing the Twentieth Century*. Cambridge, Massachusetts: Harvard University Press, The Belknap Press, 2004.

Warren, Margaret Thomas. *Taking Off*. Worcestershire, England: Images Publishing, Malvern Ltd., 1993.

Government Historical Studies, WWII

"History of the Air Transport Command, Women Pilots in the Air Transport Command," prepared by the Historical Branch, Intelligence and Security Division, Headquarters, Air Transport Command in accordance with ATC Regulation 20-20, AAF Regulation 20-8, and AR 345-105, as amended. Author is Lt. Col. Oliver LaFarge, official historian for the Air Transport Command. This is the accepted history on the women ferry pilots of the ATC. Referred to in Endnotes as LaFarge, "Women Pilots ATC."

"History of the Air Transport Command: Women Pilots in the Air Transport Command." Historical data prepared by the Historical Branch, Intelligence and Security Division, Headquarters, Air Transport Command in accordance with ATC Regulation 20-20, AAF Regulation 20-8, and AR 345-105, as amended. WASP Archival Collection, Texas Woman's University Library, Denton, Texas. (An abstracted version of the volume listed immediately above). Referred to in Endnotes as "History of the Air Transport Command."

Rhodes, Jeffrey P. Chronology: The Army Air Corps to World War II, Air Force History Support Office. Material courtesy *Air Force* magazine, December 1993.

"Women Pilots in the Ferrying Division, Air Transport Command." A history written in accordance with AAF Regulation No. 20-8 and AAF Letter 40-34; unpublished. Capt. Walter J. Marx. The Nancy Harkness Love private collection. A copy is also in the author's files. Referred to in Endnotes as Marx, "Women Pilots Ferrying Division."

"Women Pilots AAF, 1941-1944." Army Air Forces Historical Studies: No. 55. March 1946.—This document is part of the WASP Archival Collection, Texas Woman's University Library, Denton, Texas. It also is part of the Jacqueline Cochran Collection, Dwight D. Eisenhower Presidential Library, Abilene, Kansas. Referred to in Endnotes as #55, "Women Pilots AAF."

Unpublished Sources

Memoirs

Delphine Bohn. "Catch a Shooting Star," copies in hands of the author and the WASP Archives, Texas Woman's University.

John Haviland Love. Untitled, in the hands of his granddaughter, Margaret C. Love.

Personal Papers
Eisenhower Library
Jacqueline Cochran Collection

International Women's Air and Space Museum
Collections:
Betty Huyler Gillies
Nancy Harkness Love
Helen MacCloskey Rough

U.S. Air Force Museum Library
Yvonne "Pat" Pateman Collection

WASP Archives, Texas Woman's University
WAFS Collection
Specific Collections:
Dorothy Scott Letters
Pat Pateman Collection

Video

Fly Girls. A Silverlining Productions Film for *The American Experience*, PBS, Boston: WGBH Educational Foundation, 2000. Written, produced and directed by Laurel Ladevich.

Flying the Hump: The China Airlift. Commemorative Edition, Volume 2. Seattle, Memory Maker Productions Inc., 1990.

Personal Interviews

Sherrill Arnet—daughter of WAFS Lenore McElroy
Bernice Batten—WAFS
W. Gerould and William Clark— sons of WAFS Helen Mary Clark

Nancy Batson Crews—WAFS

Iris Cummings Critchell—WASP 43-2

Jeannette Currier—niece of WAFS Betsy Ferguson

Eduardo Escallon—nephew of WAFS Helen Schmidt McGilvery

Phyllis Burchfield Fulton—WAFS

Betty Huyler Gillies—WAFS—oral history, Dawn Letson, Texas Woman's University

Teresa James—WAFS

Gertrude Meserve Tubbs LeValley—WAFS

Barbara Jane (B.J.) Erickson London—WAFS

Alice Harkness and Margaret Campbell Love and Hannah Love Robinson—daughters of WAFS Nancy Harkness Love

Mary Lou Colbert Neale—WASP 43-1

Honey Fulton Parker—sister of WAFS Dorothy Fulton

Don Prosser—husband of WAFS Helen Richards Prosser

Barbara Donahue Ross—WAFS

Tracy Scott—nephew of WAFS Dorothy Scott

Julie Shively—daughter of WAFS Esther Manning Shively

Barbara Poole Shoemaker—WAFS

Katherine (Kaddy) Landry Steele—WASP 43-7

Ann Hamilton Tunner—WASP 43-2

Florene Miller Watson—WAFS

The author has conducted personal interviews with approximately 40 more WASP (number continues to increase) as part of the WASP Archives Oral History project, Texas Woman's University.

Internet

Airlift/Tanker Association Hall of Fame: www.atalink.org/ hallfame/c.r.smith.html.

Civilian Pilot Training Program; www.centennialofflight.gov/ essay/GENERAL_AVIATION/civilian_pilot_training/ GA20.htm

Harmon Trophy, source: http://en.wikipedia.org/wiki/
Harmon_Trophy

Houghton, Michigan, http://history.cityofhoughton.com/

National Postal Museum Web site: www.postalmuseum.si.edu/
resources/6a2w_airpickup.html

North American Aviation, history (P-51), www.boeing.com/
company/offices/history/bna/p51,

Solo Flights Around the World, Elly Beinhorn, http://solof-
lights.org.elly_text_e.html.

The P-38 National Association and Museum—http://p38assn.
org/museum.htm

Index